Margaret Edgington (formerly known as Margaret Lally) is a freelance early years consultant who leads, or contributes to, in-service courses for early years staff in many parts of the UK. She also works as a consultant helping senior management teams and early years practitioners to evaluate and develop their practice. She trained as an early years teacher, and has taught in infant as well as nursery classes. However, she is a specialist in work with 3–6-year-olds. Her experience has included educational home visiting; lecturing on an NNEB course; work as an early years co-ordinator in two ILEA divisions; headship of a new nursery school in inner London; and work as a development officer at the National Children's Bureau, Under Fives Unit. She contributed as a writer to *Curriculum Guidance for the Foundation Stage* (QCA/DfES, 2000). She is the author of the booklet *The Great Outdoors* (Early Education, 2002), has written many articles for journals, is co-editor of *Working With Children: Developing a Curriculum for the Early Years* (NCB/Nottingham Educational Supplies, 1989), co-author of two chapters in *Assessment in Early Childhood Education* (Paul Chapman Publishing, 1992), and author of chapters in *Supporting Children in the Early Years* (Trentham Books, 1995) and *The Foundations of Learning* (Open University Press, 2002). She is an active member of the Early Years Curriculum Group and was one of the authors of *Early Childhood Education: The Early Years Curriculum and the National Curriculum* (Trentham Books, 1989), *Four Year Olds in School: Myths and Realities* (Madeleine Lindley, 1995), *Interpreting the National Curriculum* (Open University Press, 1998) and *Onwards and Upwards* (2000). She is a Vice President of the National Campaign for Real Nursery Education and of Early Education.

THE FOUNDATION STAGE TEACHER IN ACTION
TEACHING 3, 4 AND 5-YEAR-OLDS

Third Edition

Margaret Edgington

P·C·P

Paul Chapman
Publishing

First published 2004

Reprinted 2005

The Nursery Teacher in Action, 2nd edition, published 1998
The Nursery Teacher in Action, published 1991

 Paul Chapman Publishing
A SAGE Publications Company
1 Oliver's Yard
London EC1Y 1SP

SAGE Publications Inc
2455 Teller Road
Thousand Oaks, California 91320

SAGE Publications India Pvt Ltd
B-42, Panchsheel Enclave
Post Box 4109
New Delhi 110 017

Library of Congress Control Number: 2004104026

A catalogue record for this book is available from the British
Library

ISBN 0 7619 4418 4
ISBN 0 7619 4419 2 (pbk)

Typeset by by GCS, Leighton Buzzard, Bedfordshire
Printed in Great Britain by T.J. International, Padstow

Contents

Acknowledgements   *viii*
Preface to the Third Edition   *x*
Introduction   *xiii*

1   The specialist early years teacher: some key characteristics   **1**
Why do we need specialists?   1
Some essential characteristics of the early years specialist   3
Developing early years specialists   8
Some possible questions for interview   9

2   Leading the Foundation Stage team   **11**
Support for leadership   11
Who makes up the Foundation Stage team?   12
Aspects of leadership   14
Leadership challenges   27

3   Co-ordinating early years practice   **37**
What is the role of the early years co-ordinator?   37
Developing policies for the early years   .   41
Managing change in the early years   53
Supporting staff development   64
Monitoring and evaluating Foundation Stage practice   67
Co-ordination in action: case studies   71

4   Helping children feel 'at home'   **79**
The care and education debate   79
What do young children need?   82
The need for equality of opportunity   84
The need for security   88

The need for physical security and safety 89
The need for emotional security 97

5 Helping children to 'branch out' **108**
The need to develop social strategies 108
The need for an appropriate curriculum 123
Organizing for children's learning 130

6 Keeping records: planning and assessment **147**
A developmental approach 147
Why keep records? 149
What information should records contain? 151
Who should contribute to the records? 151
How can assessment information be recorded? 153
The importance of observation 154
The record-keeping process 157
Record-keeping in action 158
Planning the early years curriculum 162
Implementing plans and monitoring and evaluating what
actually happens 183
Identifying achievements and reviewing progress 185
Sharing perceptions with others and identifying needs 191
Making more plans 192

7 Learning with children **195**
The teacher's aims for children's learning 195
Responsive teaching – what is involved? 196
Enabling children to learn 201
Playing with children 217
Understanding children 225

8 Managing complexity: looking outwards, looking inwards **227**
Teaching as personal development: looking outwards, looking
inwards 227
Teaching in a developing society 229
Training opportunities 238
Teachers as agents of change 240
Raising the status of early years teaching 241

9 Supporting other practitioners **244**
Building relationships with other practitioners 245
Encouraging practitioners to develop their practice 247
The role of training in practice development 249
Providing resources to support practice development 254
Advisory team networks and support systems 255

10 Developing the Foundation Stage: some issues and priorities   **256**

Implementing the Foundation Stage Curriculum   256

Transition to Key Stage 1   257

Protecting nursery schools   257

Re-establishing real nursery education   258

Protecting the Foundation Stage teacher   259

References   *261*

Author Index   *269*

Subject Index   *271*

Acknowledgements

I still owe a huge debt of thanks to those who encouraged and supported me to write the first and second editions of this book – the late Vicky Hurst (who was a wonderfully enthusiastic companion as we both struggled with the process), Wendy Scott (whose support and encouragement I have valued for many years), Gill Hickman (photos in second edition), Ann Robinson (references), Richard Lally (index first edition), Pamela May (who inspired me with her commitment to the development of high-quality initial training for early years teachers), Paddy Chambers and Linda Walton (computer support and training), the staff, children and parents of all the schools I have worked in (inspiration), and Malachai Hickman and Chloe and Nicole Larson (for sharing their early childhood).

Additionally, I want to thank:

The many Foundation Stage teachers, headteachers and advisers I have met in the course of my in-service work and consultancy, for their willingness to share ideas and concerns, and for inspiring me to tackle the difficult issues with them.
The following teachers who have contributed case studies: Paddy Beels and Becky Wood, Wingate Nursery School, Co. Durham; Dimity Dawson, John Ball Primary School, Lewisham; Ben Hassan, The Portman Early Childhood Centre, Westminster; Jan Robinson and Joy Potter, Legh Vale Early Years and Childcare Centre, St Helens; Sarah Davies, Millennium Primary School, Greenwich; Sylvie Gambell, Mary Paterson Nursery School, Westminster; Lynn Hand, Adamsrill Primary School, Lewisham; Joan Thurgar and Rachel Curtin, Lee Manor Primary School, Lewisham; Tess Robson and Pauline Trudell for professional friendship and for acting as critical readers.
Colleagues in the National Campaign for Real Nursery Education (NCRNE), in Early Education and in the Early Years Curriculum Group (EYCG) for their professional inspiration, friendship and challenge.

Everyone at Paul Chapman Publishing for their encouragement, patience and advice.

Last but not least, my love and thanks to: Nick Foster for his encouragement and support and his expert help with editing; and Irmgard and Ewart Edgington for giving me the kind of start in life, which enabled me to believe I could achieve something (in spite of what some teachers told me!) and for always being there for me.

Preface to the Third Edition

Writing a third edition of this book has presented me with a number of challenges. First I had to decide who the book was about. I wrote the first edition to celebrate the work, and raise the status, of the specialist nursery teacher working with 3–5-year-olds in nursery schools and classes. Since 1991 (when the first edition was published) the concept of nursery education has been undermined by nursery vouchers and grants for 3 and 4-year-olds, the increased admission of 4-year-olds to reception classes, closure of some nursery schools and the shortage of early years trained teachers. The view of nursery education which I, and others, had in 1991 is no longer widely understood. This is why the National Campaign for Nursery Education, which has campaigned since the 1960s for high-quality state-funded provision, added the word 'real' to its title in 2003. Whilst the government may assert that all 3 and 4-year-olds now have a funded nursery education place, the National Campaign for Real Nursery Education argues that many of these places do not meet their quality criteria (see Introduction).

I welcomed the introduction of the Foundation Stage, believing it would re-establish the distinctive curriculum for young children, which has been developed over many years in the best nursery schools and classes. I also believed that the inclusion of the entire reception year in this statutory key stage would empower teachers to resist the top-down pressures they were experiencing and develop more appropriate approaches. However, I have been disappointed that the Foundation Stage curriculum has been difficult to implement fully in some schools. This is partly due to the history of reception classes. They have been perceived to be different from nursery classes and have been seen as a training ground for Year 1. It is also due to the shortage of specialist teachers and to the inadequacy of Foundation Stage training for practitioners and the wider school community.

I decided to retitle this book because I believe it is now unhelpful to talk about nursery and reception teachers. In England they are all Foundation

Stage teachers. This led to the second challenge. Increasingly, England has become isolated in the UK in terms of its approach to education. Scotland, Wales and Northern Ireland are all developing services somewhat differently. In Wales for example the Foundation Stage is for children aged 3–7 years. I have always believed that the term 'early years education' should be used to describe the education of children from birth to 7 or 8 and that the years from 3 to the end of the reception year should be referred to as the nursery education years. Because this book is still about teaching 3–5-year-olds and, because I am keen for nursery education approaches to permeate reception classes, I made the decision to use the English concept of a Foundation Stage teacher. I have added a subtitle to indicate that I intend the content to be relevant to all teachers working with 3, 4 and 5-year-olds wherever they are being educated. Although, inevitably some of the initiatives described are particular to the English context, I hope that colleagues working in other parts of the world will be able to apply most of the book's content to their own context.

My continued focus on 3–5-year-olds should not lead readers to believe that I do not acknowledge the importance of the education and care of children from birth to 3 years. I would love to see a *massive* network of *high-quality* centres of excellence designed to meet the needs of children from birth to 5 and their families. Neither should readers assume that I am happy about what is happening to children in Key Stage 1 in England. In June 2001 I launched a petition, primarily aimed at protecting the Foundation Stage, but also asking for a removal of pressure on Key Stage 1 children. The petition, containing over 2500 signatures from a wide variety of people including parents, was presented by my Member of Parliament to the House of Commons in December 2001. I would love to see a Foundation Stage which extends to the end of Key Stage 1. I am therefore heartened that some schools, excited by the opportunities offered by the government's Primary Strategy document *Excellence and Enjoyment* (DfES, 2003b), are beginning to extend Foundation Stage approaches into Key Stages 1 and 2.

However, I believe it is helpful to recognize that 3–5-year-olds have quite distinctive needs, which cannot be met if we skimp on resources (both human and physical). I believe we will never achieve high-quality care and education for children from birth to 3, or for children in Key Stage 1, unless we reverse current trends and recapture the concept of nursery education for 3, 4 and 5-year-olds.

I hope this book will clarify the educational needs of 3–5-year-olds and how they should be met by well-qualified adults. I hope it will raise the status of qualified teachers of young children and give them the confidence to argue against proposals and approaches which are not in the best interests of children. I hope that, for English teachers, it will expand on *Curriculum Guidance for the Foundation Stage* (QCA/DfES, 2000) and demonstrate how it can be achieved. Teachers working in other parts of the world should be aware that the approach promoted in this curriculum guidance document is supported by research evidence on effective early learning (Siraj-Blatchford et al., 2002).

The following strong beliefs, which have always informed my thinking and practice, continue to provide the rationale for this book:

- young children have a right to an enjoyable childhood which is free from pressure and stress;
- personal, social and emotional development and communication skills are the key priorities for children younger than six;
- the younger the children, the more highly trained and skilled their practitioners need to be;
- adults working with, and on behalf of, young children have a responsibility to challenge developmentally inappropriate initiatives and practices. They also have the right to professional support which boosts their confidence in this demanding role.

Because of these beliefs, readers will not find anything in this book, which helps them run a literacy hour! Instead I have focused on practice led by teachers who have refused to be intimidated by inappropriate initiatives.

In this edition, I have been privileged to be able to include some case study material from practising teachers. I am indebted to these teachers for their willingness to share examples of developments they have led. I hope readers will find their contributions as inspiring as I did.

I have also included two new chapters. Chapter 1 re-establishes the concept, and highlights some essential characteristics, of the early years specialist, while Chapter 9 explores some aspects of the work of teachers taking on an advisory role.

Moyles et al. (2002, p. 130) conclude that 'Early years pedagogy is an extremely complex phenomenon comprising a wide variety of practices ...'. Since first writing this book, we have learnt a great deal more about how young children learn and what best supports their development. Teaching 3–5-year-olds has therefore become more complex and demanding. I hope this book will convince all who read it that only the best teachers will be up to the job!

Margaret Edgington
February 2004

Introduction

This book was originally written to raise awareness, and to celebrate the work, of the qualified nursery teacher. The intention was to offer a detailed discussion of her responsibilities and achievements, and to dispel the myth 'that anyone can work with the little ones'. Anyone who has ever worked as a nursery teacher will know that, although their training is at the same level as all other teachers, they have often been regarded by the general public, and even by their colleagues, as little more than baby minders. The importance of, and complexity involved in, the education of young children is not widely understood.

The Conservative government's introduction of the nursery education voucher scheme in 1996 led to a redefinition of the term nursery education. It enabled all forms of provision for under-5s to be included in the scheme regardless of the quality of premises, resources, adult:child ratios and staff qualifications. In 1997 the new Labour government abolished the voucher scheme and made its own plans for the development of early years services. There is, however, little evidence that these plans have led, or will lead, to a re-establishment of the essential characteristics of high-quality nursery education, which the National Campaign for Real Nursery Education (NCRNE, 1997, p. 4) list as:

1. specialist staff
2. premises and resources (inside and outside) geared to the learning needs of young children
3. a distinctive early childhood curriculum
4. a system of assessment based on individual needs
5. partnership with parents
6. balance of three and four-year-olds.

(The term 'specialist staff' is defined as meaning 'a qualified nursery teacher and a qualified nursery nurse' and NCRNE assert that 'staffing ratios must be as good or better than the Department for Education and Employment (DfEE) guidelines i.e. 1 adult to 13 children under five years of age' – ibid., p. 2).

The Foundation Stage, which was introduced in 2000, should have made the concept of nursery and reception classes redundant. The *Curriculum Guidance for the Foundation Stage* (QCA/DfES, 2000), which was made statutory in 2002, requires all settings, including reception classes, to offer the kind of high-quality education which is entirely consistent with the best practice pioneered by, and developed over many years, in nursery schools. The challenge has been to embed the principles and guidance on learning and teaching, set out in this document, in thinking and practice across the whole sector.

In 2004 there are still far too few places which have all of the characteristics set out above. Voluntary pre-schools and playgroups often meet in premises which are not for the sole use of the children, and which may not include a safe outdoor area. In common with social services day nurseries and private nurseries, they rarely employ qualified teachers. A proportion of the staff employed in most voluntary and private provision will be inexperienced and/or have no relevant qualifications, and there may be a high staff turnover. Of the local authority nursery schools and classes, which cater for fewer than a third of 3–5-year-olds, very few now have a balance of 3 and 4-year-olds. A large majority of 4-year-olds has been admitted to reception classes. Additionally, due to the shortage of specialist teachers, a substantial number of nursery and reception classes are being led by teachers who have not been adequately trained to work with 3–5-year-olds. Some nursery classes have no teacher at all. They are being run by nursery nurses and overseen by the reception teacher.

As more and more 4-year-olds were admitted to reception classes, concern about their suitability for such young children increased. Classes which are too large, have insufficient and inadequately trained staff, unsuitable premises and resources (including a lack of outdoor learning opportunities) and an inappropriate curriculum are amongst the concerns which have been expressed within research and Office for Standards in Education (OFSTED) inspection reports. This is why many practitioners working in reception classes have found it difficult to implement the Foundation Stage curriculum.

With diverse forms of provision being funded to offer Foundation Stage education, it is not surprising that there is confusion. Politicians have used the phrase 'nursery education' loosely to hide the fact that what a lot of young children are being offered is a cheap substitute, which bears no comparison with the real thing. Research has confirmed that quality varies between different types of provision. The Effective Provision of Pre-school Education Project (a longitudinal national research study that followed the developmental progress of more than 3000 children across England), found that nursery schools, integrated centres developed from the nursery-school model and nursery classes were more likely to provide an excellent education than other services. 'Few local authority day care centres and playgroups were found in the "excellent range of provision"' (Siraj-Blatchford et al., 2003, p. 6). This research found that teachers make a difference. Good outcomes for children are linked to settings that 'provide a strong educational focus with trained teachers working alongside and supporting less qualified staff' (ibid., p. i).

The Early Excellence Centres (EECs) proposed and developed by the government (DfEE, 1997a) offered a way forward, which acknowledged the different but complementary contributions of the statutory, voluntary and private sectors. There are now over 100 centres but the programme has been abandoned in favour of Children's Centres in the most disadvantaged areas. Although many of the Early Excellence Centres will become Children's Centres, the high standard set by the first EECs to be designated (which included such well-established integrated centres as Hillfields in Coventry and Pen Green in Corby) is unlikely to be maintained. Newer centres may not be led by qualified teachers, and the involvement of teachers with the children may be minimal. Guidance from Sure Start (2003a, p. 10) states: 'Local authorities should ensure that proposed children's centres will have in place strong support for the teaching and learning offered. This should be secured through either the employment of qualified teachers or significant input from teachers in an advisory role.'

The government proposal that 'a qualified teacher should be involved in all settings providing early years education within an early years development plan' (DfEE, 1997a, Annex A) has in practice meant a peripatetic approach, where the teacher visits or oversees settings, rather than works directly with the children. On a more positive note, this initiative indicates an awareness of the role of the teacher in early learning. However, the shortage of early years trained teachers, has made it difficult for local authorities to achieve their targets (see Chapter 9).

It is clear from talking to some of the inadequately trained teachers working in nursery and reception classes that they are unaware of their responsibilities in relation to this age group. Some express frustration because the children do not respond as expected, while others show an alarming lack of sensitivity to emotional needs. Some teachers blame their own inadequacies on the children – they must have extreme behaviour problems or 'poor homes', or some other difficulty. These children are labelled before they reach statutory school age and this may be one of the reasons for the increase in exclusions from school of infant-age children. No one can be expected to understand what a job involves unless they have been trained to do it. However, while an untrained computer operator will at worst damage a machine, the inadequately trained early years teacher is placed in a position where she could harm the child's development.

To their credit, many teachers quickly realize their inadequacies and seek out training courses at the earliest opportunity. However, it is debatable whether a short in-service course can meet their needs. It is certainly no substitute for the kind of child development-based initial training early years teachers have traditionally received. The reintroduction of early years as a specialism on teacher training courses is therefore to be welcomed. It is essential that this phase is seen once more as a specialist area of work.

The knowledge and skills of the Foundation Stage teacher are not well understood. Even her nursery nurse colleagues do not always appreciate the breadth and depth of her concerns – except perhaps when they have trained to be a teacher themselves. A nursery nurse who had just completed her teacher training after years of nursery nursing commented, 'I never realized there was so much involved in teaching'.

This book focuses on the skills, knowledge and attitudes which are at the heart of effective Foundation Stage teaching. The teacher is referred to as 'she' in recognition of the fact that early years is still a predominantly female profession, and to acknowledge that women must be given most of the credit for achievements in the field. I believe the growing number of similarly skilled men now involved would want the women who supported them in the early stages of their career to be given this recognition. In no way does the use of 'she' imply that Foundation Stage teaching is, or can only be, a female profession. I have drawn on the work of experienced teachers (including men) in many parts of Britain, and all the practice referred to reflects developments currently taking place. It is not based on an impractical ideal. However, it is important to stress that this is a book about the most highly principled and innovative Foundation Stage teachers. They will recognize themselves and I am grateful to them all for the inspiration they have given me.

Those who do not recognize themselves and their practice must ask themselves why. It is certainly not the intention to imply that any of the practices referred to are the only ways of approaching an issue. The practical suggestions in the book highlight some of the ways effective teachers are translating principles into practice.

There is widespread agreement that Foundation Stage teaching involves:

- leadership responsibilities;
- understanding the developmental needs of young children and the role of families in that development;
- record-keeping;
- enabling all children to reach their full potential through a curriculum based on individual needs; and
- evaluation – of the provision made, of the children's experience and of oneself.

These are complex responsibilities and it is vital that they are better understood and articulated both within and outside the profession. This book makes a contribution to this understanding.

Although it is intended primarily for use by those involved in teaching 3, 4 and 5-year-olds and by those planning (or training) to work with this age group, this book should also be of interest to everyone else concerned with the education of young children. Parents, headteachers, governors and national and local policy-makers would all benefit from heightening their awareness of the professional skills involved in Foundation Stage teaching.

This book should also be of interest to other early years workers, in particular the nursery nurses who work so effectively alongside teachers in the Foundation Stage. I chose to focus on the teacher, but I hope that their nursery nurse colleagues will not feel that their skills are unacknowledged. Foundation Stage education gains its strength and quality from the *two* professionals involved. An effective specialist teacher plus an effective nursery nurse equals a very powerful combination of expertise. Nursery nurses were involved in developing all the initiatives described in this book. However, teachers carry ultimate responsibility for what happens. It was the intention in this book to focus narrowly on these responsibilities, and to provide a positive view of the teacher as a team leader, who regards the nursery nurse as a highly valued colleague.

This has been a difficult book to write. Effective teachers make their work look easy. Much of what they do they appear to do intuitively, but considerably more than intuition is required to enable them to operate on a range of different levels with children and adults, adapting their knowledge and skills and varying their approach in response to the individuals they are interacting with. They are only able to work in this way because of their training and because of their willingness to reflect upon, evaluate and revise their practice.

It may seem artificial, to separate the many strands involved in the Foundation Stage teacher's work, since they all overlap and link with each other, and yet, unless we do try to separate them, it is not possible to understand fully the complexity of the work. Any attempt at separation is bound to be inadequate in some ways. It is my hope that the book will make a strong contribution to the debate on quality education for young children, and that it will persuade parents and policy-makers that specialist teachers must be involved. It should also remind the teachers themselves that they still need to convince others of the value of their expertise. The overall impression should be one of Foundation Stage teaching as a dynamic profession. It is a book describing the current state of the art, but always with a view to future concerns and developments. The points for discussion included in many chapters are intended to support teachers as they evaluate their work either alone, with their team or on training courses. They may also help visitors to Foundation Stage classes to understand what they are seeing.

1

The specialist early years teacher: some key characteristics

This book is based on a strong view that young children need *specialist* teachers. In later chapters it sets out in considerable detail what being an early years specialist involves. This chapter highlights briefly some of the essential characteristics, which are consistently displayed by the most effective and inspiring early years teachers. Some of these can be learnt or acquired, but some need to be within the individual. During the many years I have been privileged to work with early years practitioners, I have become increasingly convinced that some people are simply not suited to working with young children, and that others could be, if they received some further training. It is intended that this chapter will help prospective early years teachers to decide whether this is the field they want/are suited to enter, and existing early years specialists to evaluate their own strengths and areas for development. It should also help those employing teachers to work with 3–5-year-olds to think carefully about whether prospective candidates have at least some of the essential characteristics – particularly those which are not easily learnt.

Why do we need specialists?

In most European countries the curriculum and approach to learning and teaching are different for 3–6 or 7-year-olds than for older children. In England, where most children now start primary school at 4 years of age, there has, for some years, been an ongoing campaign to retain the distinctive character of early years education. The introduction of the Foundation Stage and its *Curriculum Guidance* (QCA/DfES, 2000) in September 2000 was welcomed because it was seen to be reclaiming important pedagogical principles and highlighting the implications of these for practice. In 2002, when the Foundation Stage became a statutory key stage in its own right, teachers working in nursery and reception classes were actually required by the government to work in ways which were fundamentally different from the approach then being promoted for Key Stages 1 and 2. Teachers who had previously only worked with older children, and had been moved into nursery or reception classes following the introduction of the Foundation Stage, found they were on unfamiliar territory. Strategies which had worked with Year 2 or 3 children, were completely ineffective with younger learners. Some of these teachers have been able to adapt their teaching style, but others have not. Those who have not been able to adapt have found the Foundation Stage a miserable place to be – and so, inevitably, have their colleagues and the children. Pamela Hope, a former OFSTED inspector, sums this situation up very well when she asserts:

> It is not unusual for a teacher who has always worked with say, eight- or nine-year olds to be drafted in by the head teacher to teach four- and five-year olds. An untrained, unqualified classroom assistant, working alongside a teacher who is inexperienced in working with young children, can also pick up what can only be regarded as impatient, inappropriate and often bullying teaching methods. (*Nursery World*, 2001, p. 11)

Headteachers, particularly Key Stage 2 specialists, have found during the last few years that they have been less confident when monitoring practice in their nursery and reception classes. Some admit that they feel uncomfortable with the Foundation Stage because they do not understand it and are not sure whether what is happening in their school is actually of a high quality. The introduction of the Foundation Stage in England has therefore been instrumental in raising awareness of the need for specialist expertise. In Wales the Foundation Stage has been extended into Key Stage 1 in recognition of the very similar needs of 5–7-year-olds.

Young children are vulnerable and need adults who are sensitive to their needs and concerns. They need adults who can combine their knowledge of child development and how young children learn most effectively, with their knowledge of the curriculum content to be covered (Siraj-Blatchford et al., 2002). This involves:

- identifying each child as an individual with unique needs, life experience, personality, interests and learning styles;
- identifying the learning approaches and contexts which are most likely to motivate the child and promote positive dispositions; and
- identifying the appropriately challenging yet achievable curriculum content for each learner.

According to the Qualifications and Curriculum Authority (QCA/DfES, 2000), teaching in the Foundation Stage is 'a complex process', which 'has many aspects, including planning and creating a learning environment, organising time and material resources, interacting, questioning, responding to questions, working with and observing children, assessing and recording children's progress and sharing knowledge gained with other practitioners and parents' (p. 22). It is certainly not simply about delivering curriculum content. Few would now disagree that all teachers working with 3, 4 and 5-year-olds require at least some specialist training.

Some essential characteristics of the early years specialist

In the rest of this chapter some core characteristics and skills are briefly highlighted. These must be developed by early years teachers if they are to become specialists in their field.

Some of the characteristics probably need to be within the person to begin with (at least to some extent), although it is also possible that they can be developed and/or strengthened as a result of ongoing training and experience. For example, when practitioners understand how and what children learn through play they become less afraid of its somewhat random, unpredictable nature. Other characteristics can only be acquired through professional development opportunities and experience. These characteristics permeate and are developed further throughout the rest of this book.

Essential characteristics include all of the following:

Warmth and empathy

It is an inadequate cliché to suggest that early years specialists need to 'like children'. In Chapter 2 the wide range of people who make up the early years team is described. Early years specialists need to be able to respond in a consistently friendly and genuine manner to a wide range of colleagues, parents and children from all sections of the community. This demands high-level, professionally developed communication skills. It is essential that they are able to adopt an inclusive and non-judgemental approach (especially with those people who are not instantly likeable) and are able to see the best in all children and adults. Early years specialists must build strong partnerships with parents, including those with cultures and languages different from their own, (QCA/DfES, 2000). This requires an ability to see the world through the eyes of others and to develop a range of strategies to cater for different needs. There is no place for the teacher who dismisses some parents as being ones 'who don't care about their children'. The specialist knows that all parents care about their children in their own way and recognizes that it is up to her to develop a range of strategies that enables all parents to engage with their child's development and learning. She also knows that it is essential that she is seen to be treating all parents, children and colleagues fairly, and not seeming to favour some over others. Because she looks for the abilities of others rather than their faults or lack of competence, she is able to be a supportive, respectful enabler of others, empowering them to try new things and develop new skills. Interviews with parents, using the services of integrated centres, show genuine transformation of the lives of both adults and children (Bertram and Pascal, 1999).

Spontaneity and flexibility

Work with young children is unpredictable and the best laid plans have a habit of going entirely awry! This is because young children are busy making their own sense of their world and are not always able to see things in the way that adults do (Holt, 1989). They therefore interact with experiences, materials and people in ways which are not always expected. One deputy headteacher (experienced in working in Key Stage 1), when explaining why she hated covering for the nursery teacher said, 'It's the anarchy I can't stand'! To an early years specialist it is the apparent anarchy that makes the job such a joy and a challenge. But, if control and predictability are what make a person feel comfortable, it is likely that they will find working in the early years threatening. The specialist is able to be flexible and abandon plans when they are not working, to follow the children's lead. She is able to respond enthusiastically to spontaneous events or interests and see these as offering some of the most powerful learning opportunities. In other words, she thrives on uncertainty because she is not afraid of it. She knows that she can account for the spontaneous decisions she has made.

Skills of reflection and analysis

Early years teaching is not just concerned with practice or what has to be done. It is also concerned with thinking about, and continuing to learn about, its complexity. It requires teachers to raise questions, gather evidence, draw some tentative conclusions and plan for development. Teachers educated to degree level should be able to reflect on and analyse their practice, but not all can, or want to, go on learning in this way. For some teachers, teaching needs to be simple and clear cut and appear to be under their control. Some of the most recently trained teachers have been disadvantaged by their training, because they have been given the impression that there must be a rigid plan or strategy to follow. These teachers are not comfortable with 'why' questions, preferring to talk about what they do rather than why they do it. However, early years specialists are required to talk about their practice with a wide range of people. They must be able to explain and provide strong justifications for their practice. They are only able to do this if they are reflective and analytical, and can understand what lies behind opposing views.

Clear principles underpinning practice

The most effective early years teachers are highly principled individuals who are unwilling to compromise on certain strongly held beliefs. This is why they gain the respect of those who come into contact with them. They have almost certainly been strongly influenced by professional development opportunities, and many acknowledge that highly principled college tutors, course leaders or authors have inspired them. However, there also seems to be a personality trait which gives some early years teachers the courage to stand up for their convictions, whilst others, who appear to be similarly principled when working with like-minded colleagues, buckle at the first sign of external pressure. As mentioned above and in Chapter 3, early years specialists have to be articulate advocates and protectors of Foundation Stage practice – often in a hostile climate. They cannot do this if they are afraid to stand their ground. Many early years teachers feel passionate about their profession and their practice. They passionately defend and hold onto their practice because they know it works for children and their families. To these teachers it is actually upsetting to be asked or told to do things which they know are not appropriate for very young children, and strong emotions are not always easy to control. However, if they are to avoid being dismissed as being 'too emotional', they also need to be able to rationalize these feelings. Principles without reasons are vulnerable to pressure and this is why many practitioners pay lip service to the principles in Curriculum Guidance for the Foundation Stage (QCA/DfES, 2000, pp. 11–12). They have read them and say they believe them, but they do not understand why they believe them so they cannot defend them against opposing views.

Ability to communicate with a wide range of people

It is clear that the characteristics described above depend on the early years specialist having well-developed communication skills. These involve non-verbal and verbal communication skills, and include the ability to speak and write clearly as well as to listen to and hear what others are saying. Thompson (1996, pp. 84–5) emphasizes that listening is an active process and involves:

- acknowledging feelings
- appropriate use of body language
- resisting the temptation to interrupt
- paying careful attention to what is being said, to avoid misunderstanding

- avoiding jumping to conclusions or relying on stereotypes
- reflecting back key points of what has been said, to confirm understanding.

An ability to take the lead

Teachers have to lead their teams and take overall responsibility. They are required to maintain an overview of everything that happens during the day and oversee the work of other team members. They need to motivate and direct less experienced members of staff when necessary. When teachers are not employed, or are ineffective, it is usually this overview and sense of direction that is lost – no one takes overall responsibility and practice deteriorates over time. Teachers have to be able to lead the evaluation process and engage their team in action planning. Aspects of the leadership role are developed further in the next two chapters.

An ability to be playful and make learning fun

Early years specialists are expected to offer children access to the curriculum through play and through motivating first-hand experiences 'which are mostly based on real life situations' (QCA/DfES, 2000, p. 15). This involves them in setting up high-quality play contexts and planning exciting and relevant practical experiences indoors and outside. If they are to support children's learning within play-based contexts, they need to be able to join in as a play partner and to resist the urge to direct the play. Some adults have simply forgotten how to play and are therefore unable to participate in ways which children welcome. 'Children do not make a distinction between play and work' (QCA/DfES, 2000, p. 11) and it is vital that early years specialists are able to maintain an ethos and approach which ensures that all children 'continue to be interested, excited and motivated to learn' (QCA/DfES, 2000, p. 32). Teachers need to be able to put aside any inhibitions they may have. They need to be child-like and get involved as an equal participant in play – for example, taking on the role of the customer in shop play or the patient in hospital play. This aspect of the teacher's role is explained further in Chapter 7.

Imagination and creativity

The best early years specialists do not allow lack of money or resources to become an excuse for inaction or poor quality provision. They beg, borrow, fund-raise and scavenge skips and scrap projects to find the human and material resources they need to enrich the children's experience. Resources are important of course, but inventive and resourceful adults can provide high-quality experiences on a shoestring – at least in the short term. Some of the case studies which appear later in this book are written by teachers who were working in underresourced settings. They show that, with vision, ingenuity and persistence, anything can be made to happen. Early years teachers in England have demonstrated all kinds of creativity and imagination in finding ways of working with the pressures of the Literacy and Numeracy Strategies. They have not allowed rigid strategies to have a negative impact on the children's experience. Imagination and creativity of this kind derive from a highly principled approach to practice development.

In-depth understanding of child development and effective learning

This characteristic can obviously only be gained from training, reading and observation. In highlighting these elements and omitting subject knowledge, I am acknowledging that this is what is absent when a teacher is not a specialist. Non-specialists focus on curriculum content and learning objectives, but are unable to see which content is relevant to the stage of development or how to introduce the content in ways likely to engage the children. In other words, they deliver curriculum content with little regard for the learner. Specialists use observation to get to know children, and act on this information to plan a relevant curriculum. Both Department of Education and Skills (DfES)-funded Effective Pedagogy projects highlight the importance of practitioners having knowledge of child development and how children learn, as well as knowledge of the relevant areas of learning (Moyles, Adams and Musgrove, 2002; Siraj-Blatchford et al., 2002).

Conscientious record-keeping

In recent years many early years specialists inspired, at least in part, by the work of colleagues in Reggio Emilia (Abbott and Nutbrown, 2001) and New Zealand (Carr, 2001) have developed high levels of skill in documenting their practice. This takes many forms and may include observational records, learning stories, illustrated records of particular experiences, photo displays, booklets, handbooks and video material. This documentation serves two purposes. First, it focuses the practitioners on how children learn as well as on what they learn. As they write about children's learning, practitioners find they are also empowered to talk more articulately about it. Second, it makes early years practice accessible to others, including the children and their parents, and promotes dialogue and participation. Documentation generalizes knowledge and understanding within teams in a non-threatening and non-patronizing way. It provides a useful tool for continuing professional development in teams where members have different levels of experience. Many parents have been empowered to record their children's learning at home and share this with staff at the early years setting.

An optimistic disposition and 'can do' approach

Early years teachers provide a role model for their team members (see Chapter 2). If they are negative or unenthusiastic, even for a day, they sap the energy of everyone else. Specialists are aware that they set the mood for their team and make a point of being positive and optimistic even at times of great challenge. As Sir Winston Churchill put it: 'A pessimist sees the difficulty in every opportunity; an optimist sees the opportunity in every difficulty.' There is no place for pessimists or negativity in the early years field. Young children deserve to be surrounded by optimism and enthusiasm. This is particularly the case when they are learning outdoors. In Chapter 5, the importance of the outdoor curriculum to the young learner is described. Although the UK has a long tradition of high-quality outdoor environments for young children (particularly in nursery schools), many practitioners do not have a good understanding of how to develop a quality curriculum outside. Additionally, not all adults enjoy being outdoors all year round, particularly when the weather is cold or wet. Early years specialists have to be prepared to spend a substantial amount of time outside, working with the children. Those who do not (or cannot learn to) enjoy working outdoors are therefore not suited to teaching in the early years.

Developing early years specialists

It should be clear when considering the characteristics and skills outlined above, that teaching in the early years is both intellectually demanding and personally challenging. When recruiting, it is important to look for potential in candidates and then to ensure that ongoing personal and professional development opportunities are offered. Teachers new to early years teaching will inevitably find some aspects of their role challenging and may lose confidence if they are not effectively supported. They need to have regular access to mentoring from more experienced specialists. Unfortunately, because of the shortage of such specialists, many teachers working in primary schools find there is no one to turn to for this guidance. If this is the case, support should be accessed from a member of the local authority advisory team. All teachers need to have opportunities to discuss their challenges with someone who understands and can suggest ways forward.

Too many teachers have become disheartened in recent years because their specialist knowledge and skills have not been recognized or valued. In a climate where easily measured outcomes are valued above all else, the real impact of early education is inevitably marginalized, and teachers find they are being pressured to pursue targets often irrelevant to the children they are working with. The introduction of the Foundation Stage has offered an opportunity to reflect on what is most important for children at this crucial stage in their development, and on the kind of teacher most likely to provide it.

Some possible questions for interview

The following questions should draw out at interview some of the qualities and characteristics highlighted above. They are suggested to support those interviewing prospective Foundation Stage teachers. They have taken account of the view of an experienced nursery headteacher who felt that it was most important to find out about candidates' passions and motivations. She felt they could be taught other things.

- Can you tell us about an educational writer, piece of research or speaker that has inspired you over the last two or three years and explain how this has influenced your practice? Alternatively candidates could be given in advance a key message from research or an article from a journal. They could be asked to talk at interview about how they would develop their practice in response to this.
- Can you tell us how you have enabled/could enable a 'hard to reach' family to become involved and interested in their children's early learning?
- What are the main principles on which you base your teaching approach? Candidates could be asked to explain the implications for practice of one of their principles.
- Can you give us an example of how you adapted your planning to take account of something spontaneous, which happened?
- Ask the candidate to look at the indoor and outdoor environment in the Foundation Stage. At interview ask: can you identify the strengths and weaknesses of the environment and can you tell us how you would develop it?
- Can you give us some examples of how you have enabled children to learn in play-based contexts?
- How would you develop literacy and numeracy in the Foundation Stage?
- How do you envisage keeping a record of your work with the children?
- Can you give us an example of a situation where you did not have the resources you needed, or the commitment of other team members? Can you tell us how you worked through this to reach a positive outcome?

- Offer a scenario involving conflict in the team e.g. team members disagree about the length of time children should spend out of doors. Ask: How would you work with the team to resolve this conflict?

2

Leading the Foundation Stage team

Any newly qualified Foundation Stage teacher is likely to be most apprehensive about 'leading a team'. If she is not, her training has not prepared her adequately for the complexity of her future role. No other teacher is expected to take on this role, which can involve leading older more experienced adults, from the very first day of her career.

Support for leadership

The support offered to teachers to help them tackle this role varies and depends on whether they work in a class attached to a primary school or in a separate nursery school or centre, and on the ability of tutors and colleagues to understand the challenges involved in managing adults as well as children. This understanding may only come from actual experience of early years teaching. Given the shortage of teacher trainers and primary teachers with this experience, it is not surprising that many Foundation Stage teachers feel they are left to cope alone!

It is ironic that teachers have received so little help with what is undoubtedly the most important aspect of their job. Everything they do is affected directly or indirectly by their approach to the leadership role. However, since the introduction of the Foundation Stage, funding for training of early years workers has increased significantly and courses to support team leaders/co-ordinators are now more likely to be offered. This is still dependent on local authorities recognizing the need. Additionally some of the Early Excellence Centres now offer high-level courses on leadership and management in the early years. This DfES initiative recognizes that many early years practitioners will, in the future, find themselves working within complex multidisciplinary contexts where high level professional and interpersonal skills are required. In spite of these developments, many teachers attending courses feel they are not well enough supported in their role as team leader. It is therefore not surprising that informal discussions regularly focus on the challenging aspects of leadership. In this chapter, these challenges and some strategies for coping with them are explored.

Who makes up the Foundation Stage team?

The simple answer to this question is: everyone who comes into contact with the children during a typical day in the setting! However, it is worth identifying who these people might be in the interests of demonstrating the daunting nature of the leadership task. It will of course depend on the nature of the setting and the teacher's role within it.

The basic team

As an absolute minimum, the team in a nursery class will consist of the teacher and the NNEB or BTEC (or increasingly National Vocational Qualifications (NVQ Level 3) trained nursery nurse – the basic team recommended by the DfES to work with a group of 25 or 26 3–5-year-old children. In larger units, one (usually experienced) nursery teacher may be expected to lead a team consisting of up to two other teachers and up to four nursery nurses. In reception classes the team may consist of the teacher and a nursery nurse or a teaching assistant with or without specific training. In private settings the teacher may lead a team of qualified (at NNEB, BTEC or NVQ Level 2 or 3) and unqualified staff, some of whom may be very young and inexperienced. In some schools where headteachers have not understood the importance of the teacher working directly with the children, a reception class teacher may be expected to oversee the work of the nursery nurses running a nursery class.

Nursery nurses complete a modular training course, which is primarily a practical training in all aspects of the care and education of children from birth to 7 years of age. Those following the NVQ Level 3 route complete much of their training as they work building up a portfolio for assessment. Inevitably, the nature of their work placement will have an impact on the quality of their training and, for this reason, NVQs may still be mistrusted. Early years teachers must be educated to degree level and receive further training in the theory and practice of education, with specialist training and practical experience in their chosen age range. Recently there has been some concern that teacher training courses have not focused sufficiently on the specialist knowledge and skills required to work with young children. However, the increasing number of people approaching teacher training via the early childhood studies degree route should in the future ensure a good supply of teachers with the required levels of understanding. These two types of training should be complementary and, when both team members understand the contribution they can make jointly to the children's total experience, the result is the highest possible quality of care and education for 3–5-year-old children.

It is essential that teachers know what is involved in nursery nurse training so that they can encourage full use of their colleagues' skills – particularly their understanding of child development and their observation skills (see Professional Association of Teachers (PAT), 2003).

Other staff in the team

In addition to this basic team, settings where full-time places are offered will also employ supervisors to work with the children during the lunchtime period. Meal times are considered to offer tremendous potential for conversation with, and learning for, young children. The role of these supervisors is therefore crucial, and guidance and support have to be offered to these usually untrained staff.

Settings which admit children with special educational needs may employ staff to support individual children to attend mainstream provision, once a statement of needs has been produced. Similarly, schools with a high proportion of bilingual children often employ staff to offer home language support.

These support staff may be part-time or full-time, and can be trained or untrained. In either case, they will work as a part of the Foundation Stage team and need to be included in the teacher's management responsibilities. Support and guidance also need to be offered to relief staff who replace absent nursery nurses, meal supervisors and support staff.

Although not a regular part of the Foundation Stage team, there are a number of other members of staff who regularly come into contact with the children and therefore have an influence on them. These staff may include the school secretary, the caretaker, the cleaners and other teachers (including the headteacher). Although the Foundation Stage teacher is not directly responsible for managing these staff, she is responsible in her role as leader for ensuring that they are all aware of, and act consistently with, her aims for the children's learning.

Additions to the team

Basic staffing ratios recommended by the DfES are not generous. Most settings therefore offer opportunities for a range of other adults to involve themselves in work with the children. These other adults include students (on a range of secondary school and college courses including teaching, nursery nursing, NVQ, nursing and other community work courses), parents, members of the local community and other professionals, such as the school nurse, speech therapist and health visitor. In integrated early years centres a range of professionals from the education, health and social services sectors may be regularly employed. The contribution of these adults enriches the children's experience, but makes additional demands on the teacher. She has to ensure that they understand the ethos of the setting and the nature of their involvement, as well as offering them the support they need to become involved. Many teams have discovered that the addition of an immature secondary school pupil, who overexcites the children, is more of a hindrance than a help!

Parents as team members

Foundation Stage staff usually provide children with their first experience of being in a group setting. They are expected to make the transition from home a positive one. This requires them to work closely with parents before and during the child's attendance at the setting (QCA/DFES, 2000, Fabian 2002). Parents need to feel they are part of the team and can continue the contribution they have already made to the education of their children. Many primary headteachers acknowledge the vital work their Foundation Stage staff undertake to encourage the parents' confidence in, and commitment to, the school.

Acknowledgement does not necessarily mean that the skills or time involved in this undertaking are fully recognized. How many teachers of older children regularly fit home visiting, daily informal chats and sharing of concerns, discussions of children's progress and support of parents working in the class into their daily routine, alongside all the curriculum development work – without any additional time or resources? Foundation Stage teachers communicate and work with parents in these ways because they know that they cannot provide a high-quality education for the children unless they do (see Chapters 4, 5 and 6).

Aspects of leadership

Being a leader makes many demands on the Foundation Stage teacher. Leadership does not just involve telling people what to do or leading from the front. For the Foundation Stage teacher it also involves gaining trust, explaining, supporting, respecting, valuing, enabling, partnering, listening, including, co-ordinating, co-operating and sharing. No wonder the role seems so daunting!

Foundation Stage leaders – born or made?

The inadequacy of the support currently offered to Foundation Stage teachers to help them take on the leadership role seems to indicate, either

---

Assessing leadership skills: some points for discussion

Think about all the people you come into contact with in the course of your work and make a list of all those people who lead you (or offer you support) and all those you are expected to lead (offer support to).

What is an effective leader? Think of some of the situations where you have been well led/supported and make a list of the leadership qualities you think are most important or effective. Ask yourself:

- When and by whom was I led well? Why was this person's leadership effective?
- How did I feel about my work when I was led well?
- Could I have done anything to help the person leading me to lead more effectively? (Think about any times when you did not feel you were led well and try to identify anything you could have done to make the leader's role easier.)

Answering these questions should give you some insight into what it feels like to be led, which you can relate to feelings of the people you lead.

---

that the skills involved are not recognized, or that leadership is believed to be an intuitive process.

The Industrial Society (1969, p. 3) points out that managers need to understand what actions they need to take to be effective, and provides a useful 'working model for the leader'. This model emphasizes three areas of functioning for a team leader: 'achieving the task', 'building the team' and 'developing individuals'. These three areas act on each other, with effective leaders needing to pay attention to all three areas, often simultaneously. This is offered primarily as a model of industrial or business leadership but, when translated into the language of education, can also help the Foundation Stage teacher understand her responsibilities.

Although the three areas are considered separately below from the point of view of the team leader, it is important to stress that in reality they overlap and that responsibility for ensuring they are covered is often shared between members of the team. This will be clarified through the examples given.

Achieving the task

Before the team leader or the team can think about achieving anything, it is necessary for them to define the tasks which they need to accomplish. Foundation Stage teams have one main overall task, which can be summarized as follows: to offer a high quality, responsive experience to all the families in their setting. In order to achieve this the leader must keep the overall task in mind whilst identifying and breaking down the sub-tasks.

Clarifying principles

The Foundation Stage teacher has overall responsibility for ensuring that the children in her group are offered an education appropriate to their needs. She also has to ensure her approach is consistent with national policy and with current thinking in relation to the theory and practice of early childhood education. This responsibility requires her (with the help of national policy documents, local authority guidelines, in-service courses and reading) to make herself aware of current developments, and to clarify the principles on which she will base her work.

As we saw in Chapter 1, only if she understands these principles will she be able to identify ways of translating them into practice. For example, the literature has highlighted for some years the importance of early years staff working in partnership with parents. (Tizard and Hughes, 1984; Wells, 1986, Ball, 1994, QCA/DFES, 2000, Whalley and the Penn Green Centre Team , 2001). An awareness and understanding of why this is necessary leads to the formation of a principle, i.e. that parents have an important complementary role to play in their child's education, and to a commitment to developing that principle in practice, e.g. by providing them with opportunities to share their knowledge of their child in the home situation.

Teachers whose work is not underpinned by principles which they can back up with research evidence are less likely to be able to see a clear direction for the development of their practice. They are also less likely to be able to provide a strong lead for the other adults they work with. These other adults may not have had opportunities to learn about current developments in early childhood education, and may need sensitive support from the Foundation Stage teacher to enable them to develop their understanding of the issues at their own pace.

Teachers have found it useful to refer to and adapt for their own use, sets of principles which have been offered by others e.g. in the literature (Bruce, 1997, EYCG 1992) or in local authority curriculum documents. Teachers working in England have been supported greatly by the principles set out in *Curriculum Guidance for the Foundation Stage*. These are all principles, which early years staff have long subscribed to. Because they are part of a statutory document, it has been possible for teachers to refer to them when arguing against inappropriate ideas suggested by others (inside or outside the team). This moves the debate away from a situation where one personal opinion is being set against another, and takes at least some of the emotion away from the discussion.

Additionally, the section in the document on putting the Principles into Practice (QCA/DfES, 2000, pp. 12–17) sets out 'the common features of good practice that will result from these principles' (p.12). Team leaders need to look at these common features with their team and to highlight the evidence they could provide in their policies and practice that their setting displays these features. Inevitably, in the process of doing this, teams also highlight areas which need development and these can be prioritized and turned into action plans (see Chapter 3).

It is the Foundation Stage teacher's responsibility to set the overall standard for her team. This involves defining the ground rules and reaching some shared understandings. It is explored further in the section on team-building below.

Defining the tasks

The Foundation Stage team's tasks incorporate all aspects of early years education such as the organization of the learning environment and the daily routine; admissions procedures; the development of policy and practice statements and of planning and record-keeping systems; the promotion of equal opportunities policies and practices; the involvement of parents and the wider community; and the development of links with other settings and Key Stage 1 staff. It is the teacher's responsibility to ensure that team members understand what the tasks are and that they are prioritized and tackled. The details of these tasks will have been clarified at least partly by whole-school or setting development plans. For example, a particular school may wish to develop a whole-school policy on planning the curriculum. Teachers in the Foundation Stage would be expected to work out, in consultation with their teams and with their specialist knowledge of the needs of young children in mind, exactly what is involved in planning the curriculum for 3–5s and how this task is to be approached in their classes. In the context of whole-school policy-making, the Foundation Stage teachers are responsible for representing their team's approach to planning the curriculum to the rest of the staff, governors, parents and so on.

Once again, principles are important. If, for example, the team believes that 'what children can do, not what they cannot do, is the starting point in children's learning' (EYCG, 1989, p. 3), they will want to ensure that their planning builds on children's existing interests, needs and experiences, and is flexible enough to enable adults to develop a responsive rather than a directive curriculum. They will resist strongly the pressure to produce neat plans for a year or more's work. They will see planning in terms of possibilities for learning, and not in terms of certainty. It is essential that those who understand the needs of young children are given responsibility for defining what is involved in curriculum development for this age group. Early years approaches provide a firm foundation on which other teachers can build. This is particularly true since the publication of the government's strategy for primary schools (DfES, 2003b), which encourages teachers in Key Stages 1 and 2 to match their planning to children's individual learning needs.

Breaking down the tasks

If they are not to be overwhelmed, teachers need to prioritize. The day-to-day demands of a busy early years setting can lead to a crisis management approach where things are dealt with as they arise. There are times when this approach is unavoidable, since some things need to be dealt with there and then. Generally though, time is more effectively utilized and outcomes more satisfactory if task priorities are set (identifying the task, or part of the task, to be worked on first) and plans made for action (identifying what needs to be done, deciding who will do what, what they will need and by when they aim to have completed it).

It is important that what has been planned is achievable. Teachers have to make difficult decisions about what it is realistic to expect of themselves and others, in the time and with the resources available. It is better to start slowly and on a small scale and achieve something, than to have big ideas which end up being abandoned due to sheer frustration with the enormity of the task. If, for example, it has been decided that some curriculum planning should relate to the staff's observations of the children's interests and achievements, it is better for each member of staff to concentrate on observing one child or a small group of children, and to have something to work from, than to try to observe the whole class and end up observing no one because the task seemed so enormous it was impossible to get started!

Prioritizing is possibly the most difficult part of the teacher's job. All teachers complain that their job is unmanageable and that too much is expected of them. Foundation Stage teachers are no exception.

At times when the pressure to improve or develop ten aspects of practice at once seems totally overwhelming, it is not surprising that prioritizing seems impossible. After all how can you concentrate on developing provision for outdoor play when your record-keeping system needs improving, you need a written policy statement to explain your approach to literacy, and the local authority adviser has just told you you need to change the way you plan the curriculum!

This is why, when experienced early years teachers are asked 'which aspects of your current practice would you most like to develop?' they often answer 'everything!' By saying this they are acknowledging the need to review regularly everything they do, and the impossibility of ever doing any part of their job to their complete satisfaction. This is a problem only if they are overwhelmed and prevented from tackling anything at all. The best teachers recognize that they will never be satisfied with their practice because they will always be able to see ways of developing it.

It is the teacher's job to ensure that the team's achievements to date are acknowledged and celebrated, and to identify the next step. At the same time she needs to keep in mind longer-term plans. Knowing where you have come from, where you are now, where you are going next and where you hope to be in the future is the best way to reassure yourself and your team that progress is being made; and to protect yourself from the pressures. Wise headteachers and inspectors/advisers respect and support teachers who plan for development in this way.

Involving the team in prioritizing

The teacher is responsible for prioritizing, but this does not mean she should do it alone. As well as taking into account external influences, the skilled teacher knows that greater co-operation will be achieved if all members of the basic team are involved in deciding what to tackle first.

There are many ways of approaching this. In a small team of two or three, where basic trust has been established, a discussion is probably the best way forward.

One teacher asked the nursery nurse she worked with to think about the aspects of practice she was pleased with and thought worked well, and which she was not pleased with and did not work well. Both members of the basic team thought about this for a week and made a few notes to bring to a discussion. They then shared their ideas and discovered that the aspect of their provision they were both least pleased with was the lunchtime period. Together they were able to identify what was going wrong, what they would like to achieve for the children and themselves (their aims) and what steps they could take to achieve their aims in practice. The main points from the discussion were recorded by the teacher for future reference. Since organization of lunchtimes involved the meals supervisor, the teacher followed up this meeting of the basic team with a discussion with her, explaining what had happened and asking for her views. In this situation the teacher acted as coordinator – making sure that all members of the team were involved and had a chance to have a say. The outcome of these discussions was a set of policy and practice guidelines to inform staff supervising meal-times. All staff involved were committed to them because their contribution had been valued and included. The guidelines were shared with the rest of the school staff and with parents of full-time children, so that everyone could gain an insight into what the early years team were trying to achieve. They were also shown to, and discussed with, all students and relief staff who came to work in the class.

In a larger team, where some staff may lack the confidence to express their views openly, e.g. in a large nursery school or centre, or large Foundation Stage team in a primary school, a structured questionnaire, filled in anonymously, can be a helpful approach to prioritizing. Dowling (1992, pp. 218–19) includes a sample questionnaire adapted from the Schools Council document *Guidelines for Internal Review and Development in Schools* (1984). Some teachers offer parents the chance to be involved in filling in a similar questionnaire about the strengths and weaknesses of the education their children are being offered. (See also Chapter 3 on action planning).

Prioritizing democratically in this way can produce unexpected results –

the area of practice a majority of the team identifies as being most in need of development may not be the area which the team leader would have selected. In this situation it is important that the teacher remembers the other parts of her leadership role – in particular her team-building responsibilities.

Team-building

If they are to achieve their tasks teachers must involve the whole team. Many a new teacher has come to grief because she has plunged enthusiastically into the task as she saw it, and antagonized the other members of her team in the process.

Teachers need to help all members of staff to understand that they need to work as a team – that they need to reach some shared understandings on which they will base their work. This seems obvious and yet discussions with early years practitioners reveal that this fundamental need is sometimes neglected, leading to situations where individuals function quite separately from each other.

Teachers are not self-sufficient, and depend on the support of their team for the successful running of their class. A basic leadership function is therefore to ensure regular opportunities for team discussion, both formal and informal. These discussions have a triple function. They provide the teacher with insights into the attitudes and understanding of team members – in particular they enable her to identify the stage of development her team has reached. They also offer all team members the chance to put forward their point of view and share in the decision-making process, and finally they reinforce the idea of a shared team approach. It is difficult to see how any sense of collective purpose could be achieved without these regular discussions.

Co-ordination and communication

It is not always possible for all members of the team to meet at the same time, and the nursery teacher has to act as co-ordinator and communicator of discussions. It is through this co-ordination and communication that the teacher constantly reinforces the idea of a collective team approach. She acts as a link between team members, and also between the team and the outside world.

In order to co-ordinate and communicate effectively, the teacher must realize that no two teams are the same and that each team will have 'its own personality, its own power, its own attitudes, its own standards and its own needs' (The Industrial Society, 1969, p. 10). She has to find out about and respond to the particular characteristics of the people she works with. This sometimes means putting her own needs and interests to one side and concentrating on the needs and interests of others. There will be times when she will want to shield the team from outside pressures she knows they are not yet ready to deal with, and there will also be times when she will want to encourage the team to share their achievements with others. At all times she will want to emphasize the unity of the team particularly in terms of practice.

Teams are made up of individuals with different life experience and points of view, and unity comes from working together to reach a shared understanding of the principles and tasks mentioned previously. In Chapter 3 we will see how the policy-making process can contribute to team-building. The teacher is responsible for checking that everyone is committed to translating decisions made at meetings into practice.

From time to time this will involve her in asking why particular members of the team are not working consistently with team objectives. Is it because they were not fully involved in, or did not understand, the discussion? Or because they disagreed but were afraid or unwilling to say so? Or because they have been unable to translate policy into their own practice? Or some other reason? The answers to these questions will provide the teacher with clues for evaluating her leadership skills.

Relating to the team as a group can only work if she also relates to each member of the team as an individual, since it only takes one individual to sabotage (intentionally or unintentionally) the work of the rest of the team. One team's work on encouraging children to be less dependent on adults was hampered by a member of staff who persisted in doing things for the children, which they could easily have done for themselves, such as putting on an apron for water play. The children soon learnt which adult to go to if they wanted to save themselves some effort and other adults in the team became resentful because their colleague seemed to be taking the easy way out. It is often easier and less time-consuming, at least in the short term, to do things for young children than to encourage them to try to do it for themselves. It is the teacher's responsibility to help this individual to understand how she is undermining the work of the whole team.

Teams need to feel that their collective achievements have been recognized by their leader. It can be useful, at the first staff meeting each term, to provide time for reflection on the highlights and achievements of the previous term, before looking at what needs to be achieved this term. This gives the team a sense that they are making progress in their practice and that their efforts are worthwhile.

Developing individuals

While most people enjoy the companionship and support of teamwork, they also want recognition for their individual contribution. The team leader needs to create an environment where individuals can feel a sense of personal achievement, and are offered a degree of challenge and responsibility consistent with their ability. In order to remain motivated, individuals need to feel that their achievements are recognized and that they are making a valuable contribution. A dissatisfied individual can place a tremendous strain on team relationships and can have a detrimental effect on team achievements.

Knowing individuals

The teacher needs to get to know each member of her team as an individual – to find out about particular interests and skills, and also about the parts of their work which they are most and least confident about. This finding-out process involves, first, discovering how each individual sees her role within the team. Nursery nurses may see their role differently depending on when they completed their training, and it would be inadvisable for the teacher to make assumptions based on her view of what she wants from them. While keeping in mind the support she would like and relevant job descriptions, the skilled teacher negotiates responsibilities based on each nursery nurse's perceptions of the role and on her ability to undertake that role.

For example, in one team slightly different responsibilities were negotiated for each nursery nurse in relation to their involvement in record-keeping. All staff agreed that they had a contribution to make to the process of recording children's progress, but they felt they needed different approaches to the task. It was decided that one would record observations to contribute to the children's records, because she felt confident that her training had equipped her well to do this and because she enjoyed this aspect of her work. The other, who had trained many years ago when the NNEB training had placed less emphasis on the educational side of a child's development and on written recording, did not feel confident about writing observations but was keen to make a contribution to the children's records. She was particularly sensitive to children's emotional needs and noticed things, which other staff sometimes missed. She was encouraged by the teacher to share her observations verbally. In this way the different strengths of both were valued, and both continued to feel they had an important contribution to make.

Appraising individuals

Getting to know individuals can only be achieved through regular one-to-one discussions that focus on particular skills and interests, feelings about work and specific needs, such as training needs. These discussions can help team members review their own achievements to date and plan future developments. They can also provide the teacher with an opportunity to acknowledge things done well and discuss any areas of concern.

Appraisal has become more accepted and these discussions have been formalized in many settings with teachers appraising some of their team members. This can take the form of a termly or annual meeting where both parties could identify and comment on the following:

- Particular areas of responsibility, i.e. those held currently, and new areas of responsibility for the future.
- Work that has gone well/been particularly enjoyable.
- Work that has not gone so well/not been so enjoyable.
- Relationships that have been most and least positive, i.e. with colleagues, children and parents.
- Particular strengths and weaknesses (using answers to the above to provide clues).
- Support (both human and training) needed to develop practice.
- Plans for the next few months
- Individual goals or targets for the next term or year

These meetings should be regarded as an opportunity for mutual review. It is just as important for the team member to be able to say what she needs from the leader as vice versa. Offering individuals positive feedback on their work, and identifying suitable professional development opportunities for them, is a vital part of the teacher's responsibilities. When individuals know that their strengths are recognized it is much less threatening for them to acknowledge, and ask for support in tackling, their weaknesses.

Delegating responsibility

It is often possible for the teacher to delegate responsibility. The nursery nurse who is particularly knowledgeable about gardening could be given responsibility for advising the other staff on developing the outdoor area. This responsibility could involve ordering equipment as well as leading a session on planning what needs to be done, when and how. Because the ultimate responsibility for what happens in the setting is still held by the teacher, it is essential that this work is carried out in consultation with her – it is important that the nursery nurse who has been given responsibility is encouraged to keep the teacher fully informed about all developments. Delegation does not mean offloading! Neither does it mean allowing people to take responsibility by default and 'justifying' it afterwards – as in the case of the school secretary who was allowed to handle admissions to the nursery class single-handedly with no regard to school policy because 'she does it so well it would be a shame to take it away from her'. This approach to delegation often masks a real fear of tackling the school secretary!

Effective delegation means allowing someone else to use their skills, but this must be within the philosophical framework already established for the team, and must involve the support of the team leader.

Summarizing the leadership task

In summary, the three main areas of activity for the Foundation Stage team leader are

1   ensuring the tasks for which she is responsible are identified prioritized and achieved;
2   developing a team approach and a shared sense of purpose; and
3   identifying and attending to the individual professional needs of team members.

So far the focus has been mainly on how the teacher acts in relation to her basic team, since this is the foundation on which early years education is based. If this foundation is strong, all members of the basic team will be well equipped to include and involve parents, colleagues, governors and students as part of the wider team.

It is not possible to approach leadership of the wider team in quite the same way, but the general principles remain the same. The aim of the teacher is to extend the shared sense of purpose and commitment to all members of the school community to enable others to understand and become involved in the children's education (see Chapter 3).

Some questions to support further thinking and discussion: what kind of a leader are you?

Think about yourself as a leader of other adults and ask yourself:

- In which situations did I lead effectively?
- What reasons do I have for considering I was effective?
- Why was I able to lead effectively in these situations and with these people?
- In which situations and with which people did I not lead effectively? Why?
- What was difficult about these situations/people? Did I do (or not do) something which made the situation more difficult? Can I trace the difficulties back to a failure to pay attention to any of the tasks of leadership outlined in this chapter, e.g. a failure to establish a shared sense of purpose or a set of ground rules, or a lack of understanding by colleagues that they need to work as a team?
- What could I do to make this kind of situation easier next time?
- In which leadership situations do I feel most/least confident? How can I increase my confidence?

Imagine members of your team were describing you as a leader – what do you think they would say about you? What would you say about your own leadership style? Would you say you are more task or more people oriented? What are your strengths and weaknesses?

Personal qualities of the leader

Although effective leadership depends on the teacher's understanding of what her task involves, there is also a personal dimension – in other words, it is not just what the leader does but it is also the way that she does it (Stubbs, 1985). Rodd (1998 p.3) highlights in broad terms four key elements of effective leadership as being 'the leader's ability to:

- provide vision and communicate it;
- develop a team culture;
- set goals and objectives;
- monitor and communicate achievements; and
- facilitate and encourage the development of individuals.'

She emphasises that leaders of early years teams must place strong emphasis on both the task and on relationships, the style of leadership described by Neugebauer (1985) as the Motivator. Clearly the characteristics described in Chapter I are essential for the leader. Experienced early years practitioners consider experience and personal style to be extremely influential. They identify a number of attributes which are essential for effective leadership:

- Commitment,enthusiasm and humour
- Ability to deal with others
- Good communication skills
- Consistency and a sense of fairness
- Loyalty to the team (putting the team's interests first)
- Ability to earn respect by example

The team leader needs to provide a model of good attendance, punctuality and hard work, since a team will usually adjust its behaviour to match the leader's expectations. If the teacher takes time off for every minor ailment and/or regularly arrives late, then very soon other members of the team will be doing the same. It is difficult for the leader to retain respect in this situation.

All team members need to feel that their leader possesses some skills, knowledge and experience which the rest of the team do not have. It is expected that the leader will be well informed and will be able to act as a role model through example. Team members need to see the leader putting principles into action and being able to explain clearly the links between theory and practice.

Some questions to support further thinking and discussion: what kind of personal qualities do you bring to leadership?

- How would you describe your own personality? Which aspects of your own personality help you to be a leader? Which aspects hinder you?
- How would you assess your own ability to communicate your work/beliefs to others? Which parts of your work do you communicate most/least competently and why?

How well do you listen? Use the criteria for active listening on pages 5–6 to evaluate your own active listening skills

- How do you respond in potential conflict situations? Think about actual situations you have had to deal with and how you responded, e.g. a parent aggressively challenges you to explain why her child needs to use sand. (The parent understandably considers sand a nuisance because it gets in the child's hair.) Were you defensive? Aggressive? Calm? Confident you could cope?
- In which situations are you most confident/least confident? How could you increase your confidence in all leadership situations? What support might you need?
- Is there a personality clash between you and another member of the team? Can you identify the cause(s) of this clash? (You may need to think back to trace what started the problem.) What could you do to improve the relationship? (This will require you to recognize your own responsibility for the clash.)

As indicated in Chapter 1, it is difficult to separate inherent, personal qualities from those qualities which can be gained through experience and practice. However, it is clear that Foundation Stage teachers, if they are to become confident leaders, need to be able to review their personal and interpersonal skills as well as their practice.

This has obvious implications for initial teacher training. When selecting students the future role of the early years teacher as leader of adults should be taken into account. If good communication skills are needed to take on this role, these should be assessed at interview, and opportunities should be given to evaluate and develop these further throughout the course. Many teachers believe that assertiveness training should be included in initial training courses.

Tutors on initial and in-service courses need to act as role models for their students, and offer a responsive, facilitative, reflective approach to training rather than the didactic approach which sometimes dominates. An example of this didactic approach to training was given by a newly qualified teacher during a discussion on young children's ability to make choices. She told how her college tutor had insisted that only one type of drawing implement (e.g. wax crayons or coloured pencils) should be offered to children at any one time. When asked by other members of the discussion group to explain why, she was unable to do so and became visibly anxious. Her college experience had not prepared her well for helping colleagues to develop principles for practice – at least on this issue. Tutors should realize that many of their dogmatic statements will be remembered but the reason for them forgotten! In the long term it is always more productive to support teachers in thinking and reasoning through the issues for themselves.

If teachers are to encourage and support their team they need to be encouraged and supported themselves. They need to be given the skills to enable them to work effectively with other adults. They need to see these skills being demonstrated, and discussed by others.

Leadership challenges

Early years teachers very rarely have non-contact time (i.e. time away from their class teaching responsibilities), and have equally rarely received training in leadership skills. It is therefore not surprising that some teachers run into difficulties. Indeed, it is to their credit that they cope as well as they do!

When asked 'what is difficult about leading?', teachers' responses fall into the following categories:

Fear and lack of confidence

Fear can be 'paralysing' and can discourage the teacher from trying to tackle her leadership role. Inexperienced teachers and those new to a particular situation are most likely to be affected. Those teachers without an appropriate training working with Foundation Stage children are particularly vulnerable. They are often less aware of the needs of young children than the nursery nurses they have been appointed to lead.

The overwhelming nature of the job

Many teachers have excessively high and often unrealistic expectations of themselves and of others. There are also situations where other team members are unwilling to become involved in all aspects of practice, increasing the burden on the teacher, e.g. the nursery nurse who does not see why she should contribute to the children's records and refuses to do so. Thankfully these cases are rare, and it is important to note that sometimes it is the teacher who asks too little of her extremely skilled nursery nurses.

Disputes of this kind have emphasized the need for clear job descriptions for all staff involved.

Fear of unpopularity

Most human beings want to be liked and to receive positive feedback from the people they work with – particularly when they work in close proximity with others as early years practitioners do. The fear of being disliked by other members of their team may prevent them from tackling difficult issues, or encourage them to 'ignore' practice which is inconsistent with their aims. Either of these responses can lead to resentment in the long term.

Handling conflict

Dealing with differences of opinion or handling conflict can be difficult. Fear and lack of time are given as reasons why this is so. Often a tactful, considered response is required and yet the leader is sometimes expected to respond immediately before she has had time to think the issue through fully. Having to respond before her own mind is clear often leads to an inappropriate reaction, which can cause even more difficulties.

Dealing with personalities

Any situation involving a number of personalities will inevitably present challenges. Teachers of older children usually only have to tolerate those adult personalities they find most difficult during breaks and staff meetings. However, early years practitioners spend most of their time together and it would be naive to ignore the fact that there have been situations where two or more quite incompatible personalities have been placed together. Teachers, aware as they are of the need to present a united front to parents and children, go to great lengths to minimize differences but there is no doubt that this can cause considerable stress.

As well as their immediate colleagues, teachers are also expected to involve parents from a wide range of backgrounds and cultures in their work. They will find some of these parents easier to work with than others, but will recognize their responsibility to them all.

Tackling the challenges

Making the job manageable

Some of the difficulties described above can be resolved, at least to some extent, through understanding the tasks involved in leadership, and through learning from mistakes. Teachers will not gain more hours in the day, but they will gain confidence to put some tasks to one side while they and their teams concentrate on others. If the rest of the team feel they have a specific goal, which they can work towards and, most importantly, achieve, they too will be more likely to make an effort. The action planning process described in Chapter 3 can be invaluable.

Similarly, individual team members will be encouraged to give of their best if they are offered the chance to take some responsibility for an aspect of work which particularly interests them and for which they have specific skills.

Through working together, towards clearly identified aims and objectives, all members of the basic team can gain the confidence to articulate their work to others, thereby relieving the teacher of some of the responsibility for communication. In this way she still retains responsibility but does not have to do it all herself.

Making time for leadership

Time will always be the central problem for Foundation Stage teachers. Accepting this, and refusing to use the shortage of time as an excuse for inactivity, is one step towards tackling the problem.

It is particularly difficult for Foundation Stage teams to make time to meet together. They are on duty with the children virtually all the time they are in the setting. Those who offer full-time places do not even get common lunch breaks since at least one member of staff is often on duty whilst the others have a break.

In spite of these difficulties, teams do find time to meet together informally and formally to discuss their work. Some teams, having organized the learning environment in such a way that minimal setting up is necessary in the mornings (see Chapter 5), use this time to talk together. Others have a regular team meeting one afternoon each week at the end of the day. Those who have common lunch breaks use some of this time to talk with each other – in some settings headteachers or managers enable lunchtime meetings to take place by relieving staff of meals supervision one day a week. Headteachers and Managers benefit from this arrangement too, since they get to know the full-time Foundation Stage children.

It is essential that the teacher takes responsibility for ensuring that the most effective use is made of this time. Many teachers write a weekly sheet (or page in a book) of news and items of general interest, such as visitors to the school, for their teams so that weekly meetings are not taken up with basic information giving.

Agendas for formal meetings can therefore be carefully planned to cover the priorities the team has identified. One person – usually but not always the teacher – ensures the team stays on task and allocates time so that they achieve their aims for each meeting. Progress may be slow in these circumstances but it will happen nevertheless.

Making time to communicate with the wider team presents an even greater challenge. The Foundation Stage team need to consider how they organize the daily routine to provide themselves with opportunities to communicate with others (see Chapter 5). Headteachers must also be helped to recognize the importance of establishing this wider network in order that they view requests for non-contact time or additional staffing sympathetically. It is clearly not possible for Foundation Stage teachers to involve parents, governors and other professionals in the team's work effectively without some support of this kind.

The teacher needs to organize her own time as effectively as possible. As the role model for her team she needs to be seen to be doing her job efficiently. She will always have an enormous number of different things to do and to think about. One way of ensuring that everything is done is to make a list in a notebook of things, which have to be done each week, adding to it as the week goes by. By numbering the tasks in order of priority or urgency and crossing them off when they are accomplished, she can gain control of her workload and resist the temptation to flit from one task to another without completing any of them. She can also see clearly whether or not it is possible to fit in an additional task, which is being asked of her.

There are always ways of making better use of the time that is available and many teachers are attending time management courses

---

Some questions to support further thinking and discussion: how can you make time for leadership?

- List the time you spend engaged in formal and informal leadership activities. Is the balance between formal and informal about right, or do you need to make more opportunities for formal meetings of the team or of you and individuals? When could you find this time? (You will need to consider not doing some things to make time for this, and may consider asking for support from your headteacher or manager.)
- Is the time you spend on leadership activities used effectively? (If you have a meeting of the basic team, are you and the team clear about what you are to achieve, or does the meeting just ramble on and become anecdotal?)
- When did you last find time to acknowledge the achievements of members of your team or talk to them individually about their work? How could you make more opportunities for this?
- How can you find time to communicate your work to the wider team (including governors and parents) and listen to their views?

Coping with fear, lack of confidence and conflict

Leadership can be very lonely and can generate considerable self-doubt and anxiety. To a certain extent confidence comes from getting to grips with the leadership task, but this does not account for the fear which comes from personal and interpersonal dimensions. Teachers have identified and developed a number of ways of building up their confidence and counteracting the loneliness of their role:

Developing support networks Having other Foundation Stage teachers, particularly those working in a similar setting, to talk to is essential, since only they have an intimate understanding of the role. Many teachers use in-service courses as an opportunity to meet others of like mind – tutors need to bear this in mind and build in opportunities for discussion and sharing of ideas. Other teachers have established formal i.e. linked to national organizations such as Early Education (the British Association for Early Childhood Education) or National Campaign for Real Nursery Education (NCRNE) and informal local groups, which meet regularly to provide a forum for early years staff in the area. Others have established telephone and e-mail contact with other teachers. These opportunities provide an invaluable lifeline when things are proving difficult. Sharing the problem with someone else is often the best way of finding the beginnings of a solution – but that someone else needs to understand the issues!

Developing awareness of strengths and weaknesses Teachers realize that they can gain confidence from an awareness of their own strengths. It is easy to dwell on weaknesses and never identify the things, which are done well – this applies to oneself as well as to colleagues. An ability to recognize both strengths and weaknesses is essential to effective teamwork. By concentrating on the strengths of all members of the team it is possible to establish a positive base on which to build. Weaknesses can then be seen in the context of already-established strengths. The teacher often finds herself protecting her team from the criticisms of the outside world, e.g. 'Yes, I acknowledge that the music experiences we are offering at the moment are not very exciting, but we have recently worked very hard at encouraging the children's language and literacy development and I believe this is a real strength because …'. If teachers are not confident about their own strengths they are likely to be threatened by, and unlikely to be able to make full use of, the talents of others. Those teachers with the least confidence in themselves, can tend to become defensive and can sometimes seem to withdraw from their team.

Gaining respect and dealing with conflict Successful leaders recognize that they must gain the respect of their team and that this does not necessarily mean being popular or being liked. Their aim is to develop a positive professional relationship founded on mutual respect rather than a friendship.

One way of highlighting, and providing a framework for monitoring, the professionalism of team relationships is to work together to draw up a set of ground rules or expectations to guide staff behaviour. The staff team can be asked to identify the ways in which they want all team members to behave towards each other. Examples of ground rules might include:

- be open – talk about concerns or misunderstandings when they arise – but focus on the problem not the person;
- communicate respectfully with adults and children;
- be consistent – overcome moods or tiredness at work;
- respect team decisions and policies and put these into practice
- ask if you do not understand;
- adopt a positive approach; and
- maintain a sense of humour.

These rules for staff are just as important as rules for children.

There are times when leaders have to make a stand. A certain amount of conflict is inevitable when a diverse group of people work in close contact with each other and adults are not always good at expressing their feelings and thoughts. Analysing problems as they come up, rather than pretending they do not exist is the best way of getting to the root of difficulties and finding a method for dealing with them. Teachers spend a considerable amount of their time observing, listening and acting as evaluators. It is just as important that they evaluate what adults are expressing through body language and through what they are doing and saying, as it is that they observe and listen to the children.

They need to ask regularly questions such as 'Why did S. do that?', 'What could I do to help K understand that?', 'Why did M answer so abruptly when I asked her that?', 'Did B really mean what she just said or was she trying to make a point about something else?' and so on. This kind of analysis of the situation is vital if an appropriate reaction is to be identified. It is never a good idea to respond on the spur of the moment without allowing some thinking time. This will sometimes mean saying to a team member 'I'm sorry but I can't discuss that at the moment, but I would like to talk to you about it after school or tomorrow morning'. Gaining time in this way can prevent outbursts, which are later regretted, or an embarrassed avoidance of the situation.

Stubbs (1985, p. 26) describes the traditional responses to conflict and difficulty as

- fight (aggression)
- flight (avoidance)
- or resentful submission (accommodation).

He suggests assertive behaviour, where all parties are enabled to retain their self-esteem, as an alternative response. This approach relies on leaders being honest with all team members right from the start.

Leaders need to be able to admit to any mistakes they have made rather than becoming defensive in the face of criticism. Often un-cooperative behaviour by a nursery nurse is a way of expressing fear (see Chapter 3 on managing change), or dissatisfaction with the way the teacher has treated her – perhaps she feels angry because she was not consulted or involved in a change the teacher has made. It is up to the teacher to find an opportunity to ask if she has done or said anything to upset the nursery nurse (rather than assuming the nursery nurse is at fault) and to persist gently until the problem has been aired. It is then equally essential that the teacher apologizes for any wrong she has done. Very few people can resist an apology and a genuine attempt to put things right. If the nursery nurse continues to behave un-cooperatively, the teacher may need to take further action and gain the support of the headteacher or manager. However, this is very much a last resort after the teacher has identified and attempted to make up for any wrong on her part. If the problem is not resolved, the team will be unable to move forward in harmony and the teacher's role as leader will continue to be undermined.

When drawing attention to something unacceptable a team member has done a similarly assertive approach is required. Assertiveness requires us to:

- focus on the facts of what happened;
- say how we felt; and
- make a constructive suggestion for moving forward.

One newly qualified teacher needed to confront her two much older nursery nurses who ignored her each morning. She needed to follow the assertive approach by saying something along the following lines:

- Every day this week I have come into the nursery and said good morning to you and you have not responded.
- I have felt hurt and isolated and I dread coming to school each day. I am worried that I might have done something to upset you.
- Can we talk about this please so that we can try to improve our working relationship?

Through tackling (rather than ignoring) the interpersonal challenges, leaders gain the respect of colleagues – a much more valuable commodity than popularity. Experienced teachers agree that however frightening at the time it may be to deal with conflict, it always seems less so after the event. It is a relief to have done something positive, rather than to have used fear as an excuse for inaction. Even if the approach turned out to be clumsy and did not achieve the desired outcome, the teacher will be able to learn from this and use the experience to improve future interactions. A teacher who never tries to tackle an issue is denying herself the opportunity to learn.

Asking for help   There are occasions when teachers will need to ask for help from those with greater authority than themselves. The headteacher or manager is there to offer leadership to the teacher and can be called on to help with particularly difficult problems. One day, a child in a nursery class was called for by a very drunk father who was in no state to look after a 3-year-old. The teacher explained to the father that she could not allow the child to go home alone with him, but was unable to get the point across. She felt unable to take sole responsibility for the situation so she took the father over to the headteacher's office for the decision to be reached.

Similarly, a teacher may ask the headteacher to mediate in a situation where there is a dispute about the duties of a team member. A nursery nurse was persistently late, and continued to be so even after the teacher had reminded her that her contract required her to be in school in time to help set up the nursery environment. The headteacher was asked to clarify the situation for the nursery nurse.

In the case of personality clashes, it can be valuable to talk to an outsider with greater experience who can bring a less subjective perspective to the situation. An experienced nursery nurse felt the nursery teacher in her class undermined her by not communicating effectively with her. The teacher felt she had tried to communicate, but that the nursery nurse always responded negatively. The point had been reached where working relationships had become strained and there seemed to be no way forward. They both agreed to a meeting in the presence of the headteacher, who was able to support them both through the process of realizing how an initial failure on the part of the teacher to include the nursery nurse in her plan to invite parents to borrow books from the nursery library had led to resentment which was now being characterized by the nursery nurse's un-cooperative attitude. Both members of staff could see that they had some responsibility for the current situation and were able to establish a more positive working relationship. They were subsequently more able to talk openly about problems as they arose.

It is vital that grievances are aired as they arise and not allowed to blow up out of all proportion. This requires all parties involved in Foundation Stage teams to behave in a mature, responsible and open manner. While this can be expected of, but not necessarily achieved by, paid trained staff it cannot always be expected of parents who are motivated primarily by their interest in their own child. The parent of the child who had been bitten by another child will not always respond calmly to the teacher's attempts at reassurance. The same parent's angry promise that she will find the perpetrator of the crime and punish him or her is understandable but not easy for the teacher to handle.

The more effective she has been in involving everyone in her work and encouraging them to work together for the benefit of all the children, the less likely it is that serious conflict will arise. Many of the conflict situations which arise can be predicted and can be prepared for and de-fused in advance. Inevitably a child will be hurt by another at some time. With this knowledge, teams can think about how they could prevent this happening, and how they could deal with it when it does happen – perhaps formulating a behaviour management policy which is specific to younger children. Many private nurseries, which cater for children from birth to five, have written guidelines showing staff how to deal with instances of biting etc. and these can be shared with parents. Being well prepared removes at least some of the anxiety from conflict situations.

Positive aspects of leadership

The leadership role makes considerable demands on the Foundation Stage teacher. However, it also has its positive side and it is important not to lose sight of this.

Foundation Stage teachers benefit greatly from having other adults to share ideas with, and to challenge their thinking. Having to explain and defend their views to others in a clear, accessible way, prevents the teacher from becoming complacent and stale. It keeps her mind working and her ideas flowing. Those teachers, who have also taught older children, often say how much they missed this challenge to their thinking when they were working alone with the children in a Key Stage 1 or 2 class.

There are many opportunities for learning together. All members of the team have something unique to offer and each one, including the leader, can learn from and offer support and companionship to the others. Above all, the team can have fun together. They all know the same group of children and can delight together in daily happenings. Teachers and their teams value the time spent together at the beginning and end of each day when anecdotes are shared and plans made. These informal get-togethers provide the leader with a firm foundation from which the more formal aspects of her leadership duties can develop.

In the following chapters the importance of clear principles, teamwork and respect for individuals will be emphasized. This is because the teacher approaches all aspects of her work as the leader of the team. Her effectiveness in all the other roles she has to adopt is influenced by her effectiveness as a leader. This should be fully recognized by those who offer training in early childhood education.

**Some questions to support further thinking
and discussion: how can you get support?**

- What support is currently available to you in your leadership role?
- What support would you like/do you need?
- What steps have you taken or could you take to get this support? For example, start a self-help group with other teachers, ask for training courses, talk to your headteacher/manager and so on.
- Finally, what steps have you taken to help others understand the complexity of the Foundation Stage teacher's leadership role? Have you encouraged the local authority to invite experienced Foundation Stage teachers to talk to newly qualified staff about the leadership role, and to provide ongoing training in leadership skills?

Further reading

MacNaughton, G. (2003) *Shaping Early Childhood: Learners, Curriculum, Context*, Open University, Buckingham.

Rodd, J. (1998) *Leadership in Early Childhood, 2nd ed.* Open University Press, Buckingham.

Smith, A. & Langston, A. (1999) *Managing Staff in Early Years Settings* Routledge, London

3

Co-ordinating early years practice

It is now clearly acknowledged at national level that children from birth to 3 and from 3 to 5 years of age need a distinctive curriculum (QCA/DfES, 2000; Sure Start, 2002). No longer is it considered acceptable for children to receive a diluted version of a curriculum for older children. As we saw in Chapter 1, this has increased the need for specialist teachers to lead teams. In primary schools, nursery and reception classes and sometimes pre-schools and private nurseries on the same or nearby site are required to work closely together as they develop the Foundation Stage curriculum. In integrated early years centres, senior teachers are usually appointed to co-ordinate practice with children from birth to 3, as well as from 3 to 5. Teachers working in private nurseries may also be required to oversee the curriculum for babies and toddlers.

This chapter looks at the challenges involved in co-ordinating early years practice at times of rapid change and development

What is the role of the early years co-ordinator?

The Foundation Stage co-ordinator in the primary school

In schools the early years or Foundation Stage co-ordinator is responsible for ensuring that the Foundation Stage is seen by all members of the school community as a distinctive statutory key stage just as important as Key Stages 1 and 2, and that nursery and reception class staff work together to develop a shared philosophy on which to base their practice. This is no easy task. Nursery and reception class practice has developed differently, and reception teachers have often felt pressured to work in ways, which do not meet the needs of young children. Before the introduction of the Foundation Stage curriculum in 2000 they had often been unable to develop nursery approaches because of poor adult:child ratios, space and resources. Her

Majesty's Chief Inspector of Schools highlighted these differences in his *Annual Report* (OFSTED, 1997, p. 16): 'In Pre-Key Stage 1, the curriculum is generally more fitted to the needs of four year olds where they are in nursery schools or classes than in reception or mixed age classes.' Since 2000, this situation has improved, but many experienced reception teachers have found it difficult to fully embrace the new national requirements. Foundation Stage co-ordinators have been appointed in most schools and a growing number of schools are integrating separate nursery and reception classes into Foundation Stage Units. Inevitably, because the *Curriculum Guidance for the Foundation Stage* was drawn from best practice in nursery education, many of these newly appointed co-ordinators previously worked as nursery teachers. In some cases Key Stage 1 co-ordinators have taken on the role of co-ordinating Foundation Stage practice. This rarely works well, because the Key Stage 1 teacher is usually too removed philosophically and practically from the Foundation Stage team to give a strong lead.

A group of experienced early years co-ordinators working in the Royal Borough of Kensington and Chelsea (RBK & C, 1993) highlighted a number of key responsibilities for the early years co-ordinator based on their own experience of, and vision for, their role – which, even though they pre-date recent initiatives, could offer useful starting points for developing job descriptions for Foundation Stage co-ordinators. Their ideas (ibid., pp. 26–7) have been reorganized under three main headings – the text in italics comes directly from the work of the group.

Encouraging the nursery and reception class staff to work together to develop a shared philosophy

- *to create a co-operative and dedicated team in the early years department*
- *to bring early years staff together so that no-one is isolated*
- *to ensure continuity across the early years phase*
- *to co-ordinate the team of staff and students from different backgrounds who work with the children*
- *to ensure that staff talk to each other about the ways in which young children learn across the whole age range*
- *to highlight, during the policy making process, what learning takes place at each stage.*

Explaining, protecting and promoting early years practice within, and beyond, the school

- *to raise the profile of early years*
- *to promote early years methodology and to raise awareness of early years as a specialism*

- *to ensure appropriate resourcing through taking some responsibility for requisitioning stock*
- *to protect resources for the early years*
- *to be involved in, and advise on admissions*
- *to act as a 'bridge' between the needs of the early years team and the rest of the staff*
- *to liaise with other co-ordinators with a view to helping subject co-ordinators focus on the early years*
- *to ensure that learning processes children engage in during the early years are valued and carried on throughout their time in school*
- *to be involved in policy making with a view to ensuring relevance to the early years*
- *to liaise with parents/communities/outside agencies – communicating early years issues and the curriculum*
- *to liaise with headteachers and governors acting as a representative for the early years team*
- *to ensure that all early years classes are seen as an important part of the school in their own right*
- *to make links with other forms of provision for under 5s and with other schools*
- *to develop links between nursery school and infant/primary schools*
- *to set up support groups for early years co-ordinators and early years staff.*

Monitoring and evaluating practice and staff development

- *to support members of the early years team*
- *to provide school-based INSET [in-service training]*
- *to participate in appraisal*
- *to monitor external INSET provision and make recommendations to staff*
- *to oversee records and to ensure appropriateness to early years staff and children.*

Additionally, the co-ordinator would be expected to observe and feedback on practice within the Foundation Stage, thereby ensuring continuity and progression.

Co-ordinating practice with children from birth to 5

Senior teachers (i.e. those working in nursery schools, integrated centres, private day nurseries and in some community primary schools) may be required to co-ordinate practice with children up to 3 (some of whom may be attending drop-in facilities with their parents), in addition to leading

Foundation Stage practice. Few teachers have received any training to work with such young children and many have little experience of working with them in a group setting. This presents a challenge when leading others who may have more knowledge and expertise. Local authority guidelines (such as Islington Education's *Early Years Curriculum Guidelines from Birth to Five Year Olds*, 1999) and the nationally produced *Birth to Three Matters* pack (Sure Start, 2002), which provides a strong framework for discussing developmentally appropriate practice for very young children, have therefore proved invaluable. Teams working in large nursery schools, centres and private nurseries are generally larger and more diverse in terms of their qualifications and experience. Staff turnover in these settings may be higher than in many primary schools. Also, in some settings where the centre is open all the year round (not just in term time), staff may work to a shift system with some staff operating on part-time contracts. It can therefore be difficult for teachers to find opportunities to meet and plan with the whole team.

In integrated centres co-ordinators work closely with professionals from other disciplines. The benefits of this interagency working are described by Ben Hassan, Deputy Headteacher of the Portman Early Childhood Centre, Westminster:

> Working within an integrated setting is exciting and intellectually stimulating. It provides an opportunity for practitioners to learn about the roles of other professionals who play an equal role in supporting children and their families. For example, the family support team have a greater knowledge and expertise in supporting families across a range of issues, such as abuse, housing and behavioural issues . The Centre therefore enables families to access a number of relevant services, and provides a more holistic approach to the care and education of young children and families.

Whatever the size of the team that co-ordinators have been appointed to lead, their role encompasses everything included in the previous chapter. However, because they are co-ordinating practice in larger, more diverse teams they have additional responsibilities. These include:

- developing a shared vision and philosophy through policy development;
- managing the change and development process – particularly in the light of new national initiatives;
- supporting staff development; and
- monitoring, evaluating and feeding back on Foundation Stage practice.

These additional responsibilities are explored in the rest of this chapter.

Developing policies for the early years

Co-ordinators are expected to to unite their team through policy development. Writing about aspects of early years practice strengthens the understanding of the team and can also communicate philosophy and practice to others. Policy development involves bringing the team together to discuss and document their practice, and then disseminating a first draft of this work to other members of the community so that they can ask for clarification and/or make a contribution.

Why are early years policies important?

Because some workers may believe they are written for OFSTED inspectors, it is important to outline the real reasons for policy development. All establishments have policies whether or not they are written down. It would be impossible to function effectively if a team had no shared ideas. When teachers say 'we haven't got any policies', they are really saying 'we haven't got any written policies'. So why is it necessary to write them down?

Policies should help teams to

- clarify their beliefs, aims, objectives and vision for all aspects of their practice;
- develop shared understanding and expectations and, therefore, work more consistently;
- ensure that all children and parents have equal access to a high-quality educational experience;
- communicate their philosophy and practice to others (e.g. parents, governors, colleagues, new staff members, students, inspectors); and
- monitor and evaluate their practice using agreed criteria.

Policies are working documents, which should inform the early years team – they should not just be filed and ignored.

The process of writing policies helps teams clarify what they believe and intend. Negotiating the words which will be used can highlight misunderstandings or disagreements which can otherwise be overlooked. When we talk, we can seem to agree with each other. It is only when we try to write down the words that we see the inconsistencies or ambiguities. Writing with, and for others, encourages us to be clearer than we would be verbally. Written policies that focus particularly on young children help all members of the community to focus on this vitally important developmental phase and to recognize the features of an effective early years curriculum. Early years staff lay the foundation on which Key Stage 1 and 2 staff build. It is, therefore, in everyone's interest to ensure that these foundations are strong. Written policies can help to raise the status of specialist early years teachers and nursery nurses because they enable others to understand more about the complexities involved in educating young children. At a time when there is too little early years expertise, it is essential that this area is better understood and is not marginalized.

How should policies be developed?

If policies are to be useful, it is important not to rush the process of writing them. It is not effective for one member of a team to write them and present a complete version to the others. Neither is it useful to copy policies from other settings – although it can be useful, when the team has had a go at writing, to look at how others have approached the task.

The process of writing as a team is empowering and, although, the nature of involvement will not be the same for everyone, it is essential that everyone involved in implementation is involved in the development of the policy. The co-ordinator is responsible for ensuring that all members of the team can make a contribution. When developing a policy for supporting bilingual children, the co-ordinator could seek the views of part-time bilingual support staff while they are in the setting and feed their ideas back to the rest of the early years team at the end-of-day staff meeting. The policy can be drawn up at staff meetings, and a first draft given to bilingual support staff to read and comment on.

Much discussion, working towards reaching a consensus, needs to precede writing ideas down on paper. All members of the team need to feel free to express their beliefs, ideas, fears and hopes. This is not easy to achieve. Often one or two more articulate team members dominate the policy-writing process and the others silently appear to support them. Often this silence masks misunderstanding, confusion or even total disagreement, the effects of which are seen later in gaps between policy and practice in the setting. The co-ordinator is responsible for creating a climate of trust and openness where each member of the team knows her point of view will be heard, even if it is not agreed with.

Dealing with differences

Dealing with differences of opinion is a challenge for co-ordinators. Nursery nurses and teachers may have different ideas, whilst nursery and reception class staff may not agree about some aspects of practice. Many nursery nurses have had limited access to in-service training over the years and may therefore cling to out-of-date ideas, whilst the pressure that reception staff find themselves under may have caused them to lose sight of what is most appropriate for young children. Teams may include teachers who are not trained to work with 3–5-year-olds and are therefore not aware of early years issues. In larger integrated centres the team may include staff from a range of disciplines, who do not share the same language and are suspicious of the 'jargon' used by others. Unqualified staff can hold very strong beliefs which come from their life experience rather than professional training.

The co-ordinator is responsible for ensuring that team discussions are conducted in a professional manner, i.e. that points of view are backed up by research evidence and by current thinking in the early years field. She needs to create a climate where all team members recognize that individual personal beliefs or views are not valid in themselves – they have to stand being put to the test against nationally documented expectations and current literature in the field

Researching an aspect of practice

Policy development should therefore give staff an opportunity to research the aspect of practice they are documenting – this could involve reading, in-service training courses and/or focused visits to other schools to examine alternative ways of operating. For example, if a team is developing a policy for learning out of doors, the co-ordinator could, before starting the policy writing process:

- offer books and articles on outdoor learning for staff to read and discuss;
- seek out relevant courses for staff to attend and then give feedback at a staff meeting; and
- arrange visits to other settings to focus on different aspects of learning out of doors, e.g. one or two members of staff could look at how a particular setting develops children's knowledge and understanding of the world out of doors – it is important that time is given for feedback from these visits. In some schools the early years team uses one of its five INSET days for this purpose. All staff visit different establishments (often in pairs) in the morning and then come back together in the afternoon to report their findings.

In this way policy development includes in-service training and enables all staff to feel more confident in their ability to contribute professionally to the writing process.

If staff are encouraged to give professional reasons for their views, they will be less likely to reach the kind of impasse which occurs when purely personal beliefs are expressed. Ultimately the co-ordinator will have to mediate and/or take a final decision and it is essential, therefore, that she has the expertise required of someone in her position.

Involving all members of the team

Where teams consist of four or more it is usually best to ask people to work in pairs or threes (if possible, with a mix of staff in each) and to ask each small group to jot down their ideas about an aspect of the policy (e.g. what they believe about how young children learn most effectively.). Each group can be asked in turn to share one of their ideas with the others, who are encouraged to ask questions, seek clarification or suggest alternative wording. The co-ordinator needs to take a full role in this process, reminding team members of the need to communicate clearly and accessibly, and asking staff to give professional reasons for their ideas if necessary. The agreed words are then written on a flip chart. The process is continued until each small group has contributed all their ideas. This approach works because no team member is singled out and everyone is enabled to put forward views with the support of at least one other person. The results of this session should be typed up as a first draft and circulated to all team members. At a future meeting the draft could be discussed with a view to adding omissions and tidying up the wording. It is essential that whoever types up the initial work resists the temptation to edit – if team members feel their agreed words are not respected, they will not be so eager to participate in the future.

Once the team is satisfied with their first draft they can share it with the wider community such as headteacher, Key Stage 1 and 2 colleagues, governors or management committee and parents. It is often useful to gain an outside perspective by asking a local early years adviser or consultant for comments. It is essential that policies are accessible to all groups, and the redrafting process enables jargon or woolly phrases to be eliminated and greater clarity to be achieved.

What should early years policies look like?

The skill in writing effective policies is to get across the main points briefly. Too often policies are dense, lengthy documents, which are difficult to read and to use. Often this is because early years teams try to cover all aspects of early years practice in one policy – it is usually more effective to think of an early years policy as being a set of short policies, each one looking at a different strand of practice. Sometimes it is because they include more detail than is necessary. This can be avoided if co-ordinators recognize the difference between a policy and a set of more detailed guidelines. Policies need to be seen as public documents, whereas detailed guidelines, whilst they might be of interest to the wider community, are most relevant to the team working directly with the children. A setting might have an induction policy which sets out briefly its approach to admitting and settling in new children. This policy might mention that 'a home visit is made before each child is admitted to the setting to enable parents to talk to a member of staff about their child'. The early years team might also feel the need to write a set of detailed guidelines which indicate clearly how staff should conduct the home visit. These guidelines should be seen as an appendix to the policy rather than a part of it.

Structuring the policy

When writing policies it is important to be succinct. The aim is to produce short policies of approximately two typed sides of A4 paper set out in such a

A FRAMEWORK FOR WRITING POLICIES

(TITLE OF POLICY)

Rationale
This first section should set out the setting's philosophy or beliefs in relation to the theme of the policy and should address 'why' questions, e.g. why do we need a distinctive curriculum for the under 5s? (for an early years curriculum policy); why do we need to take care when admitting new children to school? (for an induction policy), why do young children need to learn through play in and out of doors (in a learning and teaching policy) etc.

It is often useful in this section to include a well chosen quote or two to support the school's philosophy – quotes from national policy documents such as the *Curriculum Guidance for the Foundation Stage* are particularly useful.

Purposes or outcomes
This section should address 'what' questions by setting out as clearly as possible what the purposes or outcomes of the policy should be, i.e. what the setting wants to achieve in this area of practice. These should be written clearly to enable them to be used as an aid to monitoring and evaluating the effectiveness of the policy in practice (see later in this chapter). It is often helpful to record this section in bullet-point format.

Broad guidelines
This section should briefly address 'how' questions, i.e. how the setting sets out to achieve the purposes/outcomes outlined above. Many teams find that, when they are developing a policy, the process of researching an aspect of practice enables them to stretch their vision of what is possible. It is therefore useful to divide this section into two parts:

1   How we are currently working at achieving our purposes.
2   How we intend to develop our practice in the future to enable us
     to achieve our purposes more effectively.

Finally, it is useful to identify how the policy will be monitored and to set a review date.

Continued over

Figure 3.1 continued

1 Rationale

Why do we need a distinctive approach to teaching young children? What do you believe about:

- children as learners;
- the kind of environment which supports children's learning;
- the kind of teaching/adult support which enables children to learn;

and why do you hold these beliefs?

2 Purposes or outcomes

What are the outcomes you are hoping for in your school, i.e. what should effective learning and teaching look like. Consider:

- what the learning environment should look like;
- what children should be doing; and
- what adults should be doing.

3 Broad guidelines

How do/will you ensure your purposes are achieved?

4 Monitoring and evaluation

Briefly identify a few strategies for monitoring and evaluating this policy – include what you intend to do, who will do it and how, and how you will feed back to the whole team. Set a date for reviewing the policy.

Figure 3.1 *Framework for developing a policy for early years learning and teaching*

way that the main points can be clearly seen. A commonly used structure which many early years teams have found useful in helping them develop policies is set out in Figure 3.1. The basic structure for developing policies is given, followed by an illustration of how this could provide a framework for developing a learning and teaching policy. Teams attending short in-service courses on policy development have been amazed that they could complete first drafts of several policies in a very short space of time. However, many teams find writing the rationale section most difficult – probably because they find addressing 'why' questions most difficult (Drummond, 1993).

It is important to ensure that each section of a policy is reflected in the others. The rationale should inform what is included in the purposes, and the guidelines should demonstrate how each of the purposes is being, or will be, achieved. In large settings, where a number of different services work in different parts of the building, experience has shown that the whole team can and should work together to develop a common rationale and set of purposes/outcomes. However, because different services have to operate differently, it is usually more satisfactory if subgroups representing each part of the service use this shared work to develop broad guidelines for their area of responsibility. A team in a large integrated centre worked together to document the first sections of a policy on the learning environment and then subgroups representing family support services, community groups and the nursery worked on developing their own broad guidelines. It was agreed that, as long as all parts of the environment reflected the agreed philosophy and purposes, it was acceptable for practice to differ to take account of the needs and requirements of different groups using the setting. Similarly when Foundation Stage teams in primary schools are developing an induction or admissions policy the broad guidelines for settling children into the reception class might be different from the guidelines for settling children into the nursery.

The sample policy for play in Figure 3.2 has been produced (with permission) by combining and developing the work of early years teams who attended a course in the summer term 1997. It is offered to show what a first draft policy might look like – in particular to show the style in which each section might be written – not to provide a model or an easy option for other teams.

Early years staff often ask for advice on what should be addressed in early years policies. The simple answer to this question is, 'all aspects of early years practice you feel you need to explain to others'. As a minimum, the Foundation Stage policy might therefore be made up of a folder of short policies linked to the following themes (Note: equal opportunities issues, partnership with parents and inclusion of children with special educational needs – themes on which there should be whole-school policies – should be integrated into all Foundation Stage policies):

- Inducting new children into the nursery/reception class (admissions/settling in/managing the transition from nursery to reception class).
- Learning and teaching in the early years (some teams have found it useful to focus separately on play in the early years and on learning out of doors, since these aspects of early years practice are often misunderstood).
- The early years curriculum (this could include planning and assessment or a separate policy could be written to focus on record-keeping) (for a sample curriculum policy, see Chapter 6).

POLICY ON PLAY IN THE EARLY YEARS

Rationale

Play is the young child's work. Through play, the child is able to learn through practical, hands-on meaningful experiences. Play allows children to make sense of the world encouraging them to explore and investigate in a unique and non-threatening way. It provides them with an opportunity to experience real-life situations – this is particularly important at a time when a lot of children's experiences are second hand through television, videos and electronic games. It supports all aspects of children's development.

We believe that through play children can learn at their own level and pace and can explore and experiment without fear of failure.

Through play children and adults discover that learning is fun and enjoyable. It gives the children choice and ownership over their actions and reactions and provides concrete experiences, which provide the foundation for later more abstract thinking. Play enables children to learn individually and with others. We believe that careful planning is required if play is to be of a high quality.

'Well planned play, both indoors and outdoors is a key way in which young children learn with enjoyment and challenge' (QCA/DfES, 2000, p. 25).

Purposes/outcomes

We want:

- each class to offer children a range of well planned play opportunities which offer continuity and progression, e.g. physical play, creative play, imaginative play, social play, play with natural materials;
- to provide a stimulating environment with easily accessible resources;
- to help children to become independent learners and to develop their creativity and imagination;
- to provide play contexts which are well planned and resourced to allow access to the Foundation Stage curriculum and to foster all aspects of children's development (physical, emotional, social and intellectual);
- to provide situations which will enable children to appreciate the multicultural society in which they live;
- to provide appropriate, good-quality materials and resources which reflect careful planning, which enable children to interact at their own level of development, and allow for progression;
- children to show consideration for others and to treat equipment with respect;
- children to be in control of their own learning and derive pleasure from it;

Continued over

Figure 3.2 continued

- to encourage children to explore everyday situations in their play;
- to positively encourage all children to have equal access to all play experiences;
- to challenge stereotyped ideas about play;
- adults who understand the importance of play, who get enjoyment from playing alongside the children and who learn from it;
- adults who respect and value children's play and are able to interact sensitively in it;
- adults to have time to observe children at play and monitor their development in all areas of the curriculum to inform future planning of play provision.

Broad guidelines
- Planning for play includes provision for different kinds of play – the following list of play situations and resources are readily accessible to the children:

outdoor play	creative play
imaginative play	investigative play
small world play	role play
construction kits	writing area
book area (with puppets, story props, etc.)	natural materials

- Resources within these areas are organized so that children can access them independently and take responsibility for tidying away. Resources include bought, collected (e.g. recycled materials, shells) and improvised (old curtains to make dens or shawls) items.
- Planning of play experiences includes clear learning intentions linked to the areas of learning, but also allows for play to arise from children's own ideas. Planning takes account of issues of space, time, provision of resources (including equality issues) and adult interactions.
- Children are encouraged to use materials creatively and imaginatively and to reflect on their play experiences.
- Adults take time to observe children at play in order to make valid assessments of learning and behaviour.
- Activities are planned in response to observations of the children – this enables adults to ensure progression in play.
- Adults interact sensitively with children to heighten the quality of experiences and build upon the children's interests. Men and women are encouraged to take part in all types of play to challenge stereotyped ideas about what is suitable for girls and boys.

Continued over

Figure 3.2 continued

- Adults regularly monitor, evaluate and develop the provision they make for play.

(This sample policy is developed from the ideas within the policies developed by the early years teams at Bursted Wood School, Bexley and Eastbury Infants School, Barking during the summer term 1997.)

Figure 3.2 *Developing a policy for play*

In England, the aims (pp. 8–9) and principles (pp. 11–12) of the Foundation Stage could be included at the front of the folder alongside any mission statement that the setting has developed itself (QCA/DfES, 2000).

This basic set of policies can be supplemented by appendices which include more detailed guidance for the early years team on aspects of practice (e.g. managing assessment, meal times, home visits, etc.) and sample planning sheets and assessment records.

Nursery schools, early years centres and private nurseries need a wider range of policies covering all aspects of the health, safety, care and education of the families they work with. They may also find it useful to develop a policy for each of the areas of learning rather than having one general curriculum policy. However, because every setting is unique and the size of early years teams varies, it is ultimately the responsibility of the co-ordinator to decide what documentation is necessary to ensure continuity and progression of experience for the children and their families.

How can policies be used?

Policies must inform practice. Early years teams need to use their policies to aid professional development, and to monitor and evaluate all aspects of their practice. Inspectors and advisers use policies to 'tune into' a particular team's philosophy and approach, so it is essential that what has been written is reflected in practice. It is better that the early years team identifies any mismatches!

If policies are clearly written, it should be possible to use them as a monitoring tool to check that team members are working in ways which are consistent with the broad guidelines and to evaluate whether the purposes/outcomes are being achieved. It is the responsibility of the early years co-ordinator to ensure that monitoring and evaluation happens, but it is more effective if all members of the team are involved. Ways of using policies for this purpose include the following:

- *Selecting a policy (or an idea within a policy) and gathering evidence (through focused observation) to show that it is being translated into practice.* In one school they decided to monitor children's independence and their ability to initiate their own learning in the nursery and reception classes. Team members focused on children when they were not working directly with an adult. Using these observations, they evaluated the extent to which children were achieving the outcomes in their learning and teaching policy, e.g. to be able to access materials and resources, to take responsibility for tidying away. It is often useful for a member of the nursery team to swap with a member of the reception class team to make observations, as this raises awareness of continuity issues as well as highlighting inconsistencies in resourcing.

● *Discussing a policy at a team meeting and highlighting aspects which the team feel are being well developed in practice and aspects which need further development.* It is useful to give team members notice so they can observe and think in advance and come to the meeting with ideas prepared.

● *Using policies to evaluate and support the development of curriculum planning, assessment procedures, quality of the learning environment – identifying any resource implications.* One school, having identified what they hoped the children would learn in the area of knowledge and understanding of the world, realized that they needed additional science and technology equipment in the nursery and reception classes (rather than in the school's central science store) – they felt this was essential to enable children to investigate and design spontaneously.

● *Using policies as a focus for monitoring and evaluating the quality of learning and teaching – all staff can be involved in this process.* Individual staff members can use policies to evaluate the quality of the children's learning and the effectiveness of their interactions with children. It is now common practice for staff to observe (or video) each other working with children and then to use the observation as a focus for discussion. When policies are used to identify what went well, the person being observed is much less likely to feel threatened and more likely to be able to identify things she could have done differently. Co-ordinators need to empower all members of their team to engage in peer observation using policies as a focus.

● *Asking parents and governors to give their views on how well the policies are being translated into practice.* Staff could design a simple questionnaire to help them focus on aspects of the policy. When governors make visits to the school it can be helpful to give them a clear focus, e.g. in one school governors were asked to look for evidence (in planning and in the classes) of children learning maths in practical contexts. The governors were encouraged to feed back their findings at the next governors' meeting. Governors have a role in monitoring practice. They should gather factual evidence of what is happening. They should not make judgements about the quality of teaching.

Policies are a key tool in the monitoring and evaluation process. Monitoring involves gathering evidence, whilst evaluation involves making judgements based on the evidence collected. Having agreed criteria against which to make judgements makes it easier for early years co-ordinators to deal with ineffective practice. Team members also gain confidence from being clear about what is expected of them. The more policies are used to look at practice, the more likely team members are to feel ownership and confidence.

Why do policies need to be reviewed and developed?

When policies are developed, they reflect the views and aspirations of the team at that time. These views and aspirations may not be so relevant in the future – this is why all policies should be clearly dated and a review date set. There needs to be a planned programme to review all policies to take account of:

- *new legislation and statutory guidance* – changes to the curriculum, assessment procedures, inspection demands, etc.;
- *developments in local policy* – changes in local admissions policies, opening of new types of provision, co-ordination of services, etc.;
- *new research evidence* – on how children learn most effectively, on teaching in specific areas of learning (e.g. literacy), on children's health (which supports the need for outdoor play), etc.;
- *practice developments* – which come from the above research, from visiting other schools, or from local authority guidance;
- *the team's experience* – philosophy and practice develop in the light of experience and many teams find that their policies become outdated as they work and talk together to spark off new ideas and stretch their vision;
- *changes of staff* – new team members or reductions/additions to the staff team;
- *changes in the catchment area or in children's developmental needs* – the admission of children from a new hostel for homeless families or from a new official travellers' site or an increased number of children with language delay or disorders; and
- *changes in the physical environment* – new or altered buildings or development of the outside area.

The changes outlined above should not throw an early years team completely off course. Policy review and development involve staying true to the principles of early childhood education, whilst taking changes into account – for example, the introduction of the *Foundation Stage Profile* in 2003 (QCA/DfES, 2003) highlighted the gulf between nursery and reception class assessment practice. Many reception teachers expressed anxiety about an observation-based approach. It is essential that co-ordinators help their teams place the *Profile* in the context of existing effective early years assessment practice (see Chapter 6; Fisher, 2002; Hutchin, 2003) and ensure that they base the completion of the profile on substantial observation-based evidence.

The co-ordinator needs to be aware that she is responsible for supporting her team through the change process and helping the wider community understand why changes need to be made.

Some questions for discussion

- To what extent has the early years team developed a shared philosophy through discussing statutory curriculum documents and policy writing? Are your policies brief and clear – if not could you work together to edit them using the framework offered in this chapter?
- Which aspects of early years practice do you feel you still need to explain through:

  - written policies;
  - detailed guidelines to inform practice;
  - in-service training sessions (both in and out of school)?

Managing change in the early years

There is a range of influences, which require teams to review their policies. Change in the early years comes about because of these influences, which can broadly be grouped as

- *political* new initiatives or demands from national and local policy-makers;
- *research-based* evidence about young children's learning which has implications for practice;
- *personnel* changes in the staff team (either new staff members or additions or reductions to the size of the team); and
- *interpersonal* changes in the relationship between team members (e.g. the promotion within the team of a team member, or one team member suddenly not pulling her weight).

Change is inevitable, and often imposed from outside. A team's ability to cope will depend on how they function as a team. It is useful here to consider three different types of team which are prevalent in early years work and how each might deal with change. These types are drawn from experience of early years teams and many early years workers will recognize them as ones they have worked in:

- *The cosy team.* The members of this type of team have usually worked together for some time. They have an established way of operating which they feel works well for them. They all feel they know what the others are thinking and see no need to write things down or have formal meetings. They often work hard but their practice is usually out of date. They are largely inward looking and, when faced with suggestions for new ways of working, support each other to argue against these. If a new member of staff joins the team, they may reject all her ideas on the grounds that 'we've tried that and it didn't work'. Their approach to dealing with change is to ignore it. The co-ordinator in this type of team may be part of the problem and needs to recognize this in herself. A new co-ordinator joining a 'cosy team' needs to be aware that it will be a challenge to help the existing staff see the need for change, and needs to proceed cautiously. To impose sudden change on this kind of team would be to threaten their sense of security and, thereby, lose their goodwill. Her priority is to put in place formal structures for discussing practice with a view to developing written policies.
- *The turbulent team (with undercurrents).* The members of this type of team (usually three or more members) can appear to be getting along well on the surface. Team meetings are rarely controversial because the majority accept the suggestions of the few, without dissent. However, outside the meetings, strong disagreement may be voiced behind the backs of those who speak most at the meeting. The dissenters may deliberately ignore policy decisions and subtly work in ways which are inconsistent with agreed procedures. Outsiders visiting establishments with this kind of team may become aware of some of these undercurrents. Occasionally the undercurrents rise to the surface and disagreements between two or more team members become more public. Change is difficult to effect in this kind of team because the structures for reaching shared decisions have either not been established or have broken down. The co-ordinator has almost certainly not established herself as a leader as set out in Chapter 2 – she is possibly ignoring the undercurrents because she is afraid of addressing them. She will need to focus both on her leadership role and particularly on the team-building element

of it. If policies have been developed she will need to monitor carefully that they are being implemented in practice and discuss, with the team members concerned, any deviation from agreed practice. She may also need to identify and deal with those team members who are undermining the others.

- *The rigorous and challenging team*. The members of this type of team see themselves as professionals who want to do the very best for the children in their care. They are outward looking and seek opportunities to learn and develop their own expertise. They have strong beliefs which come from their training and from their reading and visits to other establishments. They have regular formal and informal opportunities to discuss their work with each other. They do not always agree but are able to argue professionally until they reach a consensus – they are all willing to listen to, and try out, each others' suggestions because they have an underlying respect for everyone's commitment. They are never satisfied with what they are doing and challenge each other to develop aspects of practice. In fact, they sometimes find it hard to see what they do well, because they are so aware of things which could be better. Imposed change can worry this team, but more often they are able to cope because they work in a context of ongoing change and development anyway and are able to set change into the context of a well thought-out philosophy and practice. The role of the co-ordinator here is to ensure that they recognize their strengths and do not just focus on weaknesses, and to help them to prioritize developments. She may also need to help them to relax and not work too hard.

These types of team are obviously stereotypical, and many teams have some characteristics from each over time. However, it is crucial, when taking on the role of the co-ordinator, that an analysis is made of the team being led before taking any action to encourage change. Additionally, it is important for the co-ordinator to understand why change may be difficult for all team members – including herself. A useful framework for evaluating the effectiveness of teams is provided by the list of indicators (summarized from the literature by Riches, 1993) which highlights that a successful and effective team:

- is value driven;
- has good communication;
- is collaborative in its dealings;
- maximizes the use of the abilities of its members;
- has the ability to listen to others in an effective way;
- has a willingness to solve problems;

- offers enjoyment of membership;
- has well-motivated people in the team;
- has dynamism;
- has flexibility;
- has the ability to cope with confrontation and conflict;
- relates to other teams;
- has effective quality leadership (at all levels) (see Crawford, Kydd and Riches, 1997 p. 4).

Co-ordinators could ask themselves to what extent the team they lead demonstrates these characteristics perhaps by rating each characteristic on a scale of 1–5 (where a 5 rating means the team demonstrates this characteristic very strongly). This would provide a view of the strengths of the team and areas which need strengthening.

Why is change difficult?

Although change and development are seen by many early years practitioners as positive in terms of personal growth, they may also seem threatening – particularly if the change is imposed by someone else. The skill of the co-ordinator lies in her ability to help her team turn what has been imposed by outsiders into something they actually want to do for themselves. Change then becomes self-imposed and much more likely to be achieved.

The reasons why change can be difficult and challenging include the following:

- *It is often externally imposed and has to be achieved within a short time scale* – this can leave insufficient time for communication and reaching shared decisions and can lead to resentment.
- *Leaders may feel under pressure and try to force change along* – this can lead to the whole team rebelling and the leader becoming isolated.
- *Team members are at different stages in their personal and professional development* – some members are better equipped to cope with change than others.
- *It will inevitably expose weaknesses in team functioning (including weaknesses of the team leader)* – dysfunctional teams cannot work together to effect change, and 'cosy' teams often support each other in resisting change. Leaders who have not spent time on getting to know their team and on team-building will find that they cannot move practice forward.
- *Team members will be required to re-examine their values and attitudes* – all practitioners have developed a set of values and attitudes which

come from their life experience, both personal and professional. These develop as experience broadens. Teams are made up of people from a range of backgrounds, who have had different training opportunities and work experience. Proposed changes will almost certainly require some team members to review, if not abandon, values they have held dear for many years, and to change their attitude to some aspects of their work. For example, some workers, who valued the control they had over children, have found it hard to raise their expectations sufficiently to enable children to make choices and take responsibility. Other practitioners, working in newly integrated centres, have found it difficult to accept the long hours that some children spend away from home, and are unhappy about changes to their working conditions as the centre moves towards all year round opening.

- *It involves feelings which team members may not be able to articulate, but which may affect their behaviour/actions.* There are likely to be team members who feel positive and enthusiastic about the change and others who feel more negative or fearful. There are rarely opportunities to explore feelings and many adults may not be able to articulate the strong feelings which are being provoked. They may therefore behave irrationally.

- *Different expectations are highlighted.* On a day-to-day basis, it is easy to overlook the fact that the values and attitudes held by team members may result in different expectations of their work . Proposing change or development may expose this for the first time. Early years staff seem unusually worried by differences of opinion – during small group work on courses they tell tutors 'well we all agree really – we're just using slightly different words' when, in fact, those 'slightly different words' indicate deep, underlying disagreements. There is a danger that, if these differences are left unexplored, the changes sought by the early years co-ordinator will never happen.

- *It may threaten security and feelings of competence.* Some team members may feel their existing practice is being criticised, others may worry that they will not be able to cope with new ways of working. To propose change implies that what was happening already is inadequate in some way. To an individual team member, it may imply that *she* is inadequate in some way. If workers feel secure with their existing way of working, it is inevitable that they will worry that they may not be able to cope with something new. Some workers may therefore become defensive or aggressive when change is proposed.

- *Extra work will almost certainly be involved (at least in the short term).*

Any new way of working, however welcome it might be, takes time to get used to. What was once undertaken automatically, has to be thought about deliberately and continuously – a bit like when on moving to a new house we find ourselves automatically reaching up in the kitchen to the cupboard in our old house! Many practitioners have found the increase in recording daunting, and this is undoubtedly involving significant extra work. However, most teams recognize that anything new gets easier given time – and, if it does not, the team needs to think again. It should be remembered, though, that nursery nurses and class assistants are paid significantly less than teachers, and will understandably feel aggrieved if teachers are not seen to be taking on more of the extra work and responsibility.

Co-ordinators and practitioners working in large, multi-disciplinary integrated centres (particularly those which are still expanding) may also find the following aspects of change difficult:

- *A rapid increase in team size* – this can lead to staff feeling a sense of alienation and clinging to people and ways of working they knew before. Some staff, who enjoyed working in a small team, may become a negative influence because they constantly refer back to how things were in the 'good old days' – this can sap the energy of newer more enthusiastic members of staff.
- *Communication is more difficult when staff work shifts and miss meetings* – the larger the team the harder it is to ensure that everyone receives information and feels included in what is developing.
- *Leaders may find it harder to retain an overview of the work of their team* – they may also be less aware of sub-groups or factions forming within the team and conflict may pass unnoticed;
- *Tension may develop between staff from different professional backgrounds* – because early years services have been non-statutory, a certain amount of professional protectiveness, rivalry and sometimes suspicion has developed. Professionals are often unaware of how their everyday language becomes 'jargon', which excludes others, in a multidisciplinary service. At worst this tension can lead to one group rejecting or being dismissive of the contribution made by other groups. Adair (1986) highlights the following behaviours between groups which can occur when groups within an organization are in conflict:
  - hostility – members of one group become hostile towards other groups and hostile attitudes may be displayed in aggressive language, tone or behaviour;

>   – communication breakdown – communication decreases and one
>   group may avoid the other(s). Words and non-verbal behaviour
>   may be interpreted in ways which support the group's own
>   position. In whole-team meetings it is likely that each group will
>   only hear that which supports its own views;
>   – mistrust – the less the groups communicate the more their
>   meanings are distorted by interpretations based on assumption or
>   prejudice. Mutual understanding and trust decreases.

If the co-ordinator can be sympathetic to the reasons why team members can find change challenging, she will be in a strong position to lead the development process. Time for communication is essential.

Managing the change and development process

The following tips for managing change and development should prove useful in helping the co-ordinator set a pace which is not too threatening, but which is not so slow that progress is disappointing:

- All staff should be aware of the standards set for practice within the early years and should know what is non-negotiable (i.e. the practice which the early years co-ordinator finds unacceptable and is not prepared to compromise on – with her reasons). As we saw in Chapter 2, the team leader has overall responsibility for everything which happens and therefore needs to be quite clear about the things she cannot allow to continue. (Note: these should be confined to important issues and linked closely to statutory guidance, such as the need for children to have maximum access to the outside area.)
- The idea of change and development as an integral part of early years practice needs to be promoted by the co-ordinator through the action planning process (see Figure 3.3 for a description of this process and a possible action planning pro forma). She needs to be seen to be willing to change herself and needs to guard against trying to impose sudden dramatic change. It is more constructive in the long term to implement a process of gradual, steady development.
- All team members should be offered opportunities to identify aspects of practice needing change and development so they learn to share ownership of the development process – the use of national guidance as described in Chapter 2 pp. 16–17 is an example of how this might be achieved.
- All staff need relevant opportunities for personal and professional

ACTION PLANNING INVOLVES:

- Identifying one or more aspects of practice which need development.
- Setting clear achievable objectives/targets.
- Making a programme of tasks which will enable targets to be achieved.
- Identifying who will do what, when (attaching names and deadlines to each task).
- Identifying resources and funding which will be needed (including staff time).
- Identifying some success criteria which will help to measure progress and achievements.
- Identifying who will be responsible for monitoring and evaluating progress with the plan.
- Setting a review date.

The example below was provided by Sarah Davies, Millennium Primary School in Greenwich and was drawn up by the Foundation Stage team following a course.

Foundation Stage Action Plan – pro forma

Aspect of practice needing development: To raise the profile of learning in the Foundation Stage within the school community

Objectives/ targets (what we want to achieve)	Tasks (what we will need to do)	Who is responsible for each task/by when (identify deadline for completion)	Resources and funding needed	Success criteria (Practice you would expect to see when you have achieved your objectives)	Who will monitor and evaluate – when?	Review date

continued over

Figure 3.3 continued

Parents and colleagues are aware of the recent changes in the Foundation Stage and how they are working in the school	Presentation to the governing body about current practice.	Sarah (June '03)	Digital camera, technology to create and show PowerPoint presentation Preparation time	All members of the governing body understand how the curriculum works in Foundation Stage classes	S.D. (Foundation Stage Co-ordinator Headteacher after governors' meeting	July '03
	Ensure that displays outside classrooms show learning intentions alongside examples of activities across all six areas of learning and show progression from Foundation 1 > 2. Displays to be updated to reflect current interests	S.D. B.A. C.S.	A variety of photographs and examples of children's work Foundation Stage Guidance for stepping stones and early learning goals	Parents are aware that a variety of activities promote learning across the curriculum and that adult and child-initiated activities are carefully planned and supported with specific learning intentions in mind. Main displays show learning intentions. All 6 areas represented over a year	S.D. half-termly	July '04

Figure 3.3 *Action planning process and pro forma*

development. Because of training and status differences between members, not all staff will see the point of, or can be motivated to change or develop their practice.

- It is important to acknowledge openly the feelings which are involved when we are asked to change our way of working, e.g. fear, anger, insecurity, apprehension, being threatened, as well as feelings of hope and excitement. The early years co-ordinator needs to share her own feelings as well as encouraging team members to express theirs. If team members can express their feelings openly, they are less likely to feel the need to talk behind the back of the leader or sabotage developments (Rodd, 1998). However, it needs to be made clear that negativity is not acceptable in the long term. The co-ordinator needs to help individuals to consider what could be done to address issues constructively.

- However crucial change might seem, it is salutary to remember that changing practice often involves changing attitudes. This cannot be achieved quickly. It is necessary for team members to broaden their professional experience through courses, visits, etc. All staff need to be helped to see how they can individually be involved in developments.

- The co-ordinator needs to give regular feedback on what her team has achieved – it is important not to dwell on what has not yet been accomplished. This positive feedback also needs to be communicated within the wider community (e.g. at whole-staff meetings, governors'/management committee meetings, in a newsletter to parents).

- Hardest of all, the co-ordinator needs to accept that she will not always be able to make the changes she wants immediately with the existing team. It is better to concentrate on what can be achieved rather than pursuing the unattainable.

Managing change: a practical example

In the following case study, Ben Hassan, Deputy Headteacher of the Portman Early Childhood Centre, describes his role in managing the change process in the nursery department of a large multidisciplinary centre which offers a range of services for children and their families.

As Deputy Head I am responsible, with the Headteacher, for developing the quality of the curriculum. Promoting change of any kind can be difficult in a large multidisciplinary team. Identifying the need for change is an evolving process, brought about by practitioners being both reflective and critical of their practice. A year ago I was a newly appointed staff-team member with an initial brief to develop both the rigour of 'end of day' evaluations and to establish a more child-centred approach to displays in the nursery. What I found, for example, with the end-of-day evaluations, was plenty of enthusiastic commitment to talking about children, but no systematic way of using that information, nor a solid understanding of how to analyse learning intentions. We discussed my observations and agreed to pilot a structure for end-of-day evaluations.

This structure involved clarifying adult roles. Nursery staff are divided into two teams each comprising a teacher and two early years educators. These teams are supported by learning support assistants, part-time teachers, and two early years educators supporting children with special needs. The staff were divided into the following roles:

- adult responsible for the Focus Activity – leading an experience with pre-defined learning intentions;
- adult responsible for the Curriculum Focus – observing, listening and supporting child-initiated learning within a chosen area of provision; and
- adult acting as the Float – maintaining an overview and supporting children to access experiences and develop self-help skills.

Each of these roles was clearly defined for staff and at the end-of-day evaluation meetings staff shared their observations, using a set of questions to focus discussion. From the information discussed, decisions were made and fed into future planning.

In Figure 3.4 some examples of the questions used to structure the evaluation process are provided.

After piloting the process, it became evident via meetings and observations that some staff were anxious about the changes; in particular, several were concerned with 'getting it wrong'. It was crucial at this point that staff were reassured and ambiguities clarified, involving reiteration of the reasons for the changes and what those changes entailed. This was achieved at a whole-staff meeting and with the team leaders. I discussed it with team leaders to empower them in what was required, as well as 'modelling' how this could be achieved in their respective teams.

What was apparent from this process was that staff required continuous modelling and encouragement for this structure to become embedded in nursery practice. Also, listening to the staff team was important as it provided information and suggestions for change. For example, through discussions I realized that the team wanted a very structured set of questions to facilitate the end-of-day evaluation process; prior to this I felt that such questions would reduce the staff's own level of creativity.

Having worked in an integrated setting before, I was aware that for any process to become truly a part of nursery practice (irrespective of agreement) requires constant repetition, guidance and time for reflection. This is particularly true when a new process appears to challenge previous ways of working. Even after a year, modelling, repetition and praise are still needed to reach the stage where the process is 'owned' and understood by the majority of the staff team.

Working with a multidisciplinary team is exciting, supportive and stimulating. However, it may also involve difficult management issues, requiring not only effective communication and a shared vision – but also a great deal of stamina!

	Focus Activity	Curriculum Focus	Float
Evaluation focus questions	What was your learning intention? Did children achieve it – what evidence have you got?	Which children used the area? How were they using it? What were their areas of interest? How did children want their learning to be extended?	What significant observations did you make? How did you respond?
Questions to enable staff to highlight what needs to be fed into future planning	Does the learning need to be revisited, consolidated or extended? Which children will be targeted?	Should activity in the curriculum focus area become a Focus Activity? Should we change the area for Curriculum Focus? Does the adult need to continue to observe or take on a role as play partner?	How could we further support the children's learning? Do we need to alter the provision in any way? Do we need to change the Curriculum Focus area?

Figure 3.4 *Some examples of the questions used to structure the evaluation process are provided*

Source: From the work of Ben Hassan who acknowledges the inspiration of Bernadette Duffy, Head of the Thomas Coram Early Childhood Centre, Camden.

Supporting staff development

As we saw in Chapter 2, leadership involves enabling individuals within the team to develop their expertise. The co-ordinator needs to take responsibility for overseeing both setting-based and externally organized in-service training for her team and also for members of the wider team (e.g. head-teachers and governors). As part of the appraisal process, the training needs of staff should be identified.

Some staff working in the early years may be unqualified, and a priority should be to encourage these team members to gain a qualification. Possibilities, which involve training whilst working, include National Vocational Qualifications (preferably Level 3), or the Specialist Teaching

Assistant Qualification. Where teachers are not trained to work with children younger than statutory school age, the early years co-ordinator needs to seek out courses which address this need – the government and many local education authorities (LEAs) have acknowledged the need for retraining non-specialist teachers and a growing number of courses have been organized. Other staff, who may have relevant specialist initial qualifications, still need opportunities to update their expertise. Many staff are now pursuing higher-level qualifications such as diplomas, foundation degrees and masters degrees in early childhood education.

The co-ordinator needs to keep an overview of courses and conferences organized by the local authority, EYDCP, university departments and national organizations such as Early Education, and ensure that her team is represented on as many of these as possible. There should be an understanding that representatives feed back to the rest of the team. The whole team also needs opportunities to train together and many co-ordinators in primary schools have argued successfully for at least one of their five INSET days to be spent exclusively on early years issues – sometimes involving Key Stage 1 and 2 staff to raise awareness within the whole school. At a time when funding is increasingly scarce, she will undoubtedly have to argue strongly for funding with the INSET co-ordinator, headteacher and governors. If training needs are linked to staff appraisal and to policy development, a more positive response is often achieved.

Training need not always cost money. Part of the role of the co-ordinator is 'to provide school-based INSET' and this would not just be for the early years team. It is increasingly common for co-ordinators to lead staff meetings, have a slot at governors' meetings or even organize and lead INSET days. Increasingly, teachers who have achieved Lead Teacher or Advanced Skills Teacher status are being asked to lead in-service sessions within their local authority as well as welcoming other practitioners into their setting to look at their practice (see Chapter 9). However, this can be a nerve-wracking experience for some. Using the structure of policy writing can be helpful in providing a clear focus and in giving confidence. The elements within a policy are very similar to the elements required in a successful training session, i.e.:

1 A rationale for the subject under discussion/some theoretical underpinning.
2 An overview of what we should be trying to achieve/what outcomes we should be hoping for.
3 Some examples of what to look for in practice.

Following this format and possibly using the policy as a focus, a short training session on learning out of doors could include:

- a brief review of why children need to learn out of doors (see Chapter 5 for ideas);
- an overview of what early years staff should be trying to achieve in terms of the outdoor learning environment, children's learning and adult involvement; and
- some examples, preferably visual, of what learning out of doors looks like in practice.

The second and third parts need to involve group members. Participants could be shown video material or photographs and asked to highlight:

- what they think the children were learning;
- how the learning environment and resources helped or inhibited learning; and
- what kind of adult support would best extend learning.

Participants could also look at their own planning sheets to see how effectively learning out of doors is addressed. They could also be offered the chance to analyse observations of children learning out of doors. To follow up a session like this in a primary school, subject co-ordinators could be invited to visit the early years classes to see how the children access their subject out of doors.

When running training sessions it is useful to illustrate theoretical points with relevant anecdotes relating to young children, as it helps to make the session more accessible and ensures that the enthusiasm of early years

---

Leading teams through change and development: some discussion points

- What kind of a team are you leading? What are its strengths and weaknesses? Using this information, identify your priorities for leading this team.
- What kinds of changes have the team implemented over the last year or so? Have their work and achievements been recognized by you and the wider school community – if not how could you raise awareness?
- Make a list of the changes you would like to make in your setting (you could ask your team members to make similar lists). What are the most urgent priorities? What would be the best way of initiating these, bearing in mind the characteristics of your team? How could you ensure that team members do not feel threatened or overwhelmed?
- What training opportunities have you offered your team members? How do you identify and respond to training needs?

practitioners is communicated – it is difficult to talk about what young children do and say without sounding enthusiastic. Enthusiasm is usually infectious and, coupled with a confident style, is one of the key ingredients for effective advocacy. Later, in Chapter 9 the training role of the teacher will be further explored.

Monitoring and evaluating Foundation Stage practice

Earlier in this chapter we saw how policies can be used within the monitoring and evaluation process. In this section the complexity involved in monitoring and evaluating Foundation Stage practice will be explored.

Why do we need to monitor and evaluate practice?

Because formal monitoring is still a relatively new initiative, and because it can feel quite threatening, it is important to be clear about why it is necessary. Reasons include:

- *Accountability* – early years staff are accountable first to children and their carers. All children have an entitlement to receive an early education which enables them to reach their full potential. Additionally, because of national concerns about standards and value for money it is essential that settings can demonstrate that the children are making good progress.
- *To raise awareness of quality issues* – it is empowering for practitioners to know what the quality agenda is and to be able to see what they do well and what they might need to improve. If all early years teams had efficient evaluation systems in place there would be no need to fear inspectors, as there would be no surprises (and, if there were, the team would be in a good position to dispute them).
- *To provide evidence to justify practice and to argue for resources etc.* – the monitoring and evaluation process often highlights areas where lack of resources is hindering progress. Many reception teachers have been able to argue for enhanced outdoor facilities as a result of monitoring their practice and evaluating it using the Foundation Stage guidance.
- *To check compatibility of national expectations, setting aims, policies and practice* – it is essential that policies reflect national expectations and that practice reflects both.
- *To identify and celebrate strengths/achievements and to identify areas needing development* – monitoring and evaluation often leads to action planning (see above).

- *To develop a shared commitment to ongoing development* – it is vital that early years practitioners recognize that there is no such thing as perfect practice and that there will always be aspects of their work they can improve. Having an effective monitoring and evaluation system in place is a key way of preventing the team becoming cosy or stagnating!

These reasons or purposes should inform the approach to monitoring and evaluation, and should be used to reassure practitioners that the process will be constructive rather than destructive.

What does monitoring and evaluation involve?

The relationship between monitoring and evaluation is similar to the relationship between observation and assessment. When we monitor something we are gathering factual evidence. This evidence may be:

- *written*, e.g.
  - development or action plans,
  - policies,
  - booklets for parents,
  - plans and rotas,
  - observations and assessment records,
  - displays and notices;
- *verbal* – involving
  - all staff,
  - parents,
  - children,
  - governors/managers; and
- *visual*, e.g.
  - organization in and out of doors,
  - displays of photos or children's work,
  - resources and equipment,
  - staff deployment,
  - what staff are doing/how they are interacting,
  - what the children are doing/how involved they are.

When we evaluate we make judgements about quality based on the evidence we have collected. This is where the difficulties begin to arise. A vast number of people make informal and formal judgements about early years practice and not all of these judgements will be made using appropriate values or practice criteria. These people can include:

- managers, headteachers, co-ordinators/team leaders (including non-specialists), early years practitioners, other staff (such as cleaning and caretaking staff who may be highly critical of the 'mess' in an early years room!);
- children and their carers;
- visitors;
- governors/management committees/owners;
- inspectors and advisers; and
- politicians.

When considering this range of people it is clear that the potential for clashes of values and judgements is huge! Many early years practitioners waste time and energy struggling to please external evaluators – 'Tell me what OFSTED inspectors want to see' they say on courses. Some have completely lost confidence in, or have never developed, their own value position. Some teachers, who say things like 'the parents want to see work on paper' or 'my head won't let us ...', seem to be influenced most by those who put the most immediate pressure on them. A key role of the co-ordinator is to ensure that all the above understand that the values and practice criteria for evaluating the Foundation Stage must be drawn from the statutory guidance. When the setting's policies are consistent with this guidance, they should be used to help everyone develop a shared value position. In primary schools head-teachers, subject co-ordinators and governors need to be shown how to use statutory guidance and policies. The section on learning and teaching (QCA/DfES 2000, pp. 20–4) has a set of useful bullet points in the margins which can provide a starting point for discussing what these points would look like in practice. The example in Figure 3.5, page 71, is based on work produced on a course by a group of experienced teachers. Co-ordinators could encourage their teams to do a similar exercise with all the bullet points and then use this work to monitor whether they can actually see this evidence in their practice.

To summarise briefly, monitoring and evaluation involves:

- establishing a clear value position (with reasons) – clear policy and practice guidelines;
- objectivity – collecting factual evidence. This includes both quantitative data (such as attendance patterns, Foundation Stage Profile assessments) and qualitative data (such as observations of learning and teaching, or scrutiny of the planning or assessment records);
- reflection and analysis – asking why, what and how questions;
- teamwork – gathering evidence and then sharing the process of analysis/making judgements;

- a process which involves planning (what is to be monitored and evaluated), information gathering, reviewing findings and making judgements; and planning future development;
- interpersonal factors:
  - trust in others – this is easier to achieve when the team is confident that everyone will be judging them using the same criteria (it is not surprising that some OFSTED inspectors, who clearly do not understand early years practice, and who are not as familiar as they should be with statutory guidance, are distrusted);
  - some discomfort – evaluation should highlight strengths but should not be too cosy or self-congratulatory; and
  - taking responsibility for findings/judgements – avoiding defensive behaviour (e.g. saying things like "well it's not usually like this").

Externally produced frameworks to aid monitoring are used by many teams. The Effective Early Learning project (EEL, 1994) sets out a series of questions related to 10 dimensions of quality to encourage an exploration of all aspects of practice: aims and objectives; curriculum; learning and teaching styles; planning; assessment and record-keeping; staffing; physical environment; relationships and interaction; equal opportunities; parental partnership, liaison and co-ordination; and monitoring and evaluation. Teams, which have been involved in the EEL project, have been supported to measure the quality of children's involvement and of adult interactions. Increasingly, externally validated quality assurance and Kitemark schemes are being used to help settings evaluate their provision. Whilst there can never be a truly objective approach to measuring the quality of something as complex as learning and teaching, any form of monitoring and evaluation will generate discussion, provide challenges and raise the awareness of all adults.

In Chapters 2 and 3 we have examined the role of the teacher both as leader of her immediate team and as a co-ordinator of work in the early years phase. The importance of these roles cannot be overemphasized. As Rodd (1998, p. 194): concludes. 'The opportunity for community acknowledgement of a new level of professionalism in early childhood hinges on the development of the leadership abilities of members of the early childhood field.'

Some Discussion Points

- What monitoring and evaluation strategies could you implement to check that practice matches your policies?

- How have you ensured that everyone monitoring practice in the Foundation Stage has access to and understands statutory expectations?
- How have you used/could you use statutory guidance to help the wider community develop shared values?

LEARNING IN THE FOUNDATION STAGE

(Ref: p. 20 Curriculum Guidance for the Foundation Stage)

Effective learning involves:	What evidence would we expect?
Children initiating activities that promote learning and enable them to learn from each other.	Good resources organised in an accessible way, to encourage independent choice. Wide range of open-ended resources. Responsive adults who respond to the child's choices in a positive supportive way. Stimulating environment which supports children working together and developing language. Resources which relate to what has been observed as of interest to the child. Giving choices that are real – autonomy. Giving children control. Children knowing the rules/expectations. Long periods of time for play. Investigative activities. Space indoors and outside. Older children working with younger. Opportunities to select own groupings. Confident children to equip themselves for the task in hand. Adult evaluation of activities – is there a need to move on or extend? Use of photos of children at play. Buzz in room. Personal, social and emotional development (PSED) well established.
	Access to outdoors in most weathers – opportunity to move freely in and out. Natural resources. SEN [special educational needs] children have full curriculum access.

Figure 3.5 *Learning in the Foundation Stage*
Source: QCA/DfES, 2000, p. 20

▊ Co-ordination in action: case studies

The two case studies which follow are offered to provide an example of what co-ordination looks like in practice. We see how two teams have worked to develop their practice since the introduction of the Foundation Stage. Their schools, although based in the same London borough, offered quite different physical environments. In the first example, new building was possible to facilitate the creation of a Foundation Stage Unit, whilst in the second the team made links within existing provision. Both identify transition from Foundation Stage to Key Stage 1 as their next priority.

John Ball Primary School, Lewisham

Written by Dimity Dawson, Foundation Stage Co-ordinator

Background

Until 2001 – an off-site, purpose-built nursery class built in 1983 as a 'bungalow'-style building. The outdoor area had asphalt with two fixed climbing frames, a grassy area and a small covered 'terrace' for wet weather or shade.

> 25 children part-time in the morning class (9.00–11.30).
> 25 children part-time in the afternoon class (12.45–3.15).
> One teacher and two NNEBs (the extra NNEB was for the class being off-site).

There were two Reception classes in the main school building, across the road and round the corner. One was on the lower level by the playground and the other was at the opposite end of the building on a higher level! Reception children played in the Key Stage 1 playground. The area has some painted markings, otherwise it is bare. There was a large grassy area next door to the Nursery which was empty.

Catchment area

Blackheath is a very mixed area with two council estates and some very large private housing. The school used to be predominantly white but is now very mixed, both ethnically and racially. There are several families whose first language is not English.

Practice before Foundation Stage

The Nursery was child-centred with all learning through play. The main focus was on PSE, Communication, Language, Literacy, Physical and Creative development. We did home visits prior to children starting in the class and had good parental involvement.

There were *not* good links with Reception classes or the rest of the school.

The Reception classes had one teacher to 30 children. The teaching was mostly formal and focused on Literacy and Numeracy. Children attended daily assemblies, and PE and gym lessons. The two classes were physically very far from each other and teachers planned separately. Work sheets were often used.

In 1999–2000

The chair of governors and the headteacher asked me for a 'dream' scenario for the Early Years. Three annexes were being demolished and therefore 3 new classrooms could be built on the grassy area next to the Nursery!

With the headteacher, I visited Early Years settings in Tower Hamlets and Kirklees to see how they were run and to get advice. We were advised to:

- build our team;
- decide our aims and shared ethos;
- plan our routine;
- co-ordinate our planning and assessments;
- produce a booklet for parents giving information; and
- produce policies on Learning/play, Curriculum, Transition, Settling-in, Behaviour and discipline, and Outdoor play.

We began to plan for an Early Years Unit for Reception and Nursery together on the same site. This was very exciting and challenging. We had many discussions with the chair of governors (who had incredible insight) and the head. With Lewisham Education architects we designed a building on two floors. The downstairs was for the two open-plan Reception classes and the upstairs for a computer suite, kitchen, toilets, and two rooms for the use of the school and the local community.

We planned the outdoor space, which is big, with a parent who is a landscape architect specializing in play spaces. This was the most exciting part. He talked about seeing the area as a journey with boulders to climb on. I insisted on a large sandpit, which we had to justify and argue for with the local authority – but won! We have pergolas and areas for planting.

The Reception classes are interlinked, open-plan with French-door access to outside. The classrooms are small and, in spite of arguing to have bigger spaces, we were assured that the local authority states a regulation size for all new classrooms! There is a sheltered, covered terrace area attached to the classrooms for wet play and shelter.

We needed lots of money for storage outside and many more outdoor resources for an extra 60 children. We had two huge sheds put up and bought new apparatus, a chalet play-house and more planks and A-frames etc. Luckily the building was not completed on time and we had three weeks to build our team and prepare.

Working as a unit

The team

Nursery	One teacher (the EY co-ordinator)
	One NNEB
	One teaching assistant.
Reception	Two teachers
	One NNEB
	One teaching assistant (NVQ Level3).

Two midday meal supervisors for the Reception classes in term 1; three in terms 2 and 3. Support staff for children with statements of special needs.

Last year we had two classroom assistants working in Reception classes half a day for five days per week as there were so many children with special needs!

We now

Plan – long and medium term all together

        weekly and daily plans, Reception classes, together

        weekly and daily plans, Nursery, together.

Assess – we have developed our own profiles to start in the Nursery which reflect the Foundation Stage profiles. We use observations to inform this. Nursery profiles are passed on to Reception teachers.

Meet – we meet for one to two hours each week as a whole team to troubleshoot and forward plan, review practice and pass on our profiles.

Newsletter – we produce a termly newsletter for parents.

Reception class teachers now do home visits to children new to the school.

Daily routine – we seem to be constantly changing this!

On a rota basis Early Years staff set up outdoor apparatus before school starts.

9.00	Reception children go to their bases. Nursery children go to Nursery. Parents welcome and encouraged to settle children in to all bases. Free play in all areas. Reception parents change their children's books. Outdoor table-top activities put out by members of staff, one from Reception, one from Nursery.
9.15	Reception classes have group time for 15+ minutes Nursery children in and outside within coned area. (We put cones across half the playground at times when Reception classes have group time or Nursery have group time.)
9.30	All children use all areas in all classes if they want.
10.45	Nursery children tidy up, have snack and group time. Reception children have snack. Cones put out again. Reception children continue to play in and outdoors.
11.30	Morning Nursery class go home.
11.30	Reception children have group time.
12.00	Reception children get ready for lunch which they eat in the main building.
12.15	Lunchtime, followed by play in Key Stage 1 playground.
12.45	Afternoon Nursery class children arrive, parents settle them in.
1.00	Nursery children can go out (cones out).
1.30	Reception children return and have group time.
1.45	All children access all areas and classes.
2.30	Tidy up outside for everyone. Reception children help with large apparatus as well as their table-tops. Nursery children tidy their table-tops. Then everyone tidies up inside activities. Nursery children have snack and group time. Reception children have group time
3.15	All children go home.

Group times in Reception classes vary in length throughout the year – longer in the summer term. Two to three group times are for Literacy/circle times, one group time is for Numeracy. (We feel some of the group times are too long in Reception classes and will probably be shortened.)

Observed benefits from our changes

The main benefit for the staff is that we are a definite and cohesive team. We support each other, liaise with each other, and all work together towards the same aims and using the same planning and record-keeping. Staff know all the children.

The children, especially the Reception children, have freedom to choose both what they do and where to do it – they can visit each other's classrooms, return to the Nursery or use activities in the Reception classes. Reception children have access to outdoors and well-planned outdoor activities.

Next challenges

To make the transition from Reception to Year 1 smooth and ensure that the Year 1 staff continue to follow the Foundation Stage Curriculum well into the first term in the year.

To continually work to improve the day-to-day running of the Unit to ensure that the Unit evolves naturally, through regular team meetings, attending courses. There is still a long way to go!

Lee Manor Primary School, Lewisham

Written by Joan Thurgar and Rachel Curtin – reception teachers

Background

Our school is a large inner city primary school, with children aged from 3 years to 11 years. In the Foundation Stage, there are:

Nursery: 25 full-time and 10 part-time children
Reception: 60 children divided into two classes.
There is one full-time teacher in the Nursery, one full-time Nursery nurse and some primary helper time.
There are two full-time teachers in Reception and two full-time classroom assistants.

The Nursery and Reception classes are in separate buildings and their outdoor areas are next to each other but divided by a fence. The school is situated in a mainly residential area. The intake of the school is very mixed, both socially and ethnically.

Before the introduction of the Foundation Stage

The Nursery and Reception classes operated separately. The Nursery was seen as something very different from the mainstream school. The children learnt through play and had a well-resourced outside area. They very rarely had contact with the rest of the school. The Reception classes were similar to the rest of Key Stage 1. The children came in and sat on the carpet first thing in the morning, ready for register and followed by a Literacy or Numeracy session. The children were then sent off into small groups to work at activities relating to the Literacy or Numeracy sessions. When the children had completed an activity they could then choose. The day was divided up, like the rest of the school, by set playtimes and daily assemblies. The Reception children were expected to take part in sharing and class assemblies. At playtimes the Reception children had their own sectioned off part to play in, but there was no equipment except balls, skipping ropes and hoops. There was no outdoor cover if it rained, therefore wet play meant children staying in their classroom.

How we wanted to change practice

We wanted to develop practical, child-centred learning. We wanted the Foundation Stage to be seen as important and worthwhile in itself and not as just a preparation for Year 1 and above. We felt we needed to develop the outdoor area and create a free flow between it and the inside. We needed to develop links with the nursery, both in terms of our aims and ethos, as well as for the children and staff getting to know and feel confident with each other. We wanted the transfer from Nursery to Reception to be a natural step and to be as happy and stress-free as possible for the children.

Some of the challenges we needed to address

- The views of the rest of the school. We held after school workshops in, and about, the Foundation Stage, so that staff became familiar with the work that went on and why we were doing it.
- Having time to meet as a team, and not having to attend workshops that weren't relevant. This is an ongoing problem. The teaching staff all have other responsibilities around the school, and have to attend most meetings. We have been allocated some time to meet, and have made arrangements to get together in our own time as well. We also have a supportive head who has actively promoted these changes.
- Changing the structure of the day, so that there were no defined playtimes and no expectation of attending assemblies. This meant that teaching staff could not do playground duty in the main school, and were not on the rota list for assemblies.
- Working as a team, so that all members felt equally valued and supported. This meant that we needed to agree common goals and aims, as well as feeling free to discuss our differences.
- Resourcing the outdoor area. We applied for grants where possible, the children and parents helped fund-raise, the Parents and Friends Association was very supportive, developing the Foundation Stage was included on our school development plan, we begged from anyone we could think of, and we collected any free resources we could such as car tyres, plastic crates, pipes and planks.
- Developing an 'open gate' between the nursery and reception classes. We visited other settings that had already developed this, and we tried it out twice a week. This allowed us to iron out problems and become familiar with how it would work, as well as seeing its benefits. We were able to secure funding that allowed us to build a giant sandpit between the two play areas, and to have a very wide welcome gate that gives easy access for children to ride and pass through.

Working as a unit

We feel we have moved on a lot since the introduction of the Foundation Stage. The Reception classes are very different. The children come in in the morning and are able to choose from a variety of activities, that have been set up with daily learning objectives. They can also self-select from easily accessible equipment, and may pursue their own self-initiated learning. The teacher and primary helper will work with focus groups to develop the learning objectives for the day. The outdoor area will then be set up with the help of the children. The outside activities will reflect the learning objectives and the interests of the children. These will usually be linked to the class topic. The children are then free to move between the inside and outside environments. The gate between the Reception and

Nursery is opened and the children are allowed to free flow between the two.

The Reception class planning is based on the stepping stones to the Early Learning Goals, as well as the Literacy and Numeracy Strategies. Observations and assessments, carried out as the children are playing, inform the planning. Carpet sessions after snack time in the morning, after lunch and just before home time will include these learning objectives. The children will be involved in stories, games, music, circle time etc to develop their skills and knowledge in a fun and stimulating way. Sometimes carpet times are used to model play a specific game or activity, so that the children can use it independently if set out on another day.

We feel proudest of our outdoor area. We managed to raise enough money for a very impressive outdoor shelter, so that we no longer have wet playtimes. The children can play outside whatever the weather. We have bikes and a road painted on the tarmac. There are lots of tyres, crates and other building materials, so that the children can create their own activities. We have the huge sand pit, a shed that becomes a petrol station, or a hospital, or a bear's cave, depending on the books we are reading and the interests of the children. There are tables for books, writing, painting, puzzles. We have climbing equipment and planting areas. In fact we can't think of anything the children do indoors that they can't do outdoors as well. There is a lot more scope for messy, large-scale and very active activities outdoors, and on the whole the children prefer to be outside.

Observed benefits

We have seen many benefits from working in this way:

- The children are happier, more relaxed. They love coming to school, and many parents comment that they want to come in at the weekend and in the holidays. They are learning without the pressure of being confined to a particular activity or inside. This way of working allows for all the different types of learning styles. It doesn't lower children's self-esteem, by telling them to sit still all the time, or to keep reminding them of what they cannot achieve. It builds on what children can do, rather than what they can't do.
- The staff are teaching in a way that supports their beliefs in how children learn. It is exciting, creative, flexible and fun. The children are motivated and their sense of 'awe and wonder' is not dampened by the rigid restraints of the National Curriculum. The children's natural zest for learning and curiosity is used as a starting point.
- The children transferring from Nursery to Reception are happy and confident. The teachers and children already know each other, and children are familiar with their new classrooms.
- The parents are very supportive of the way the children learn, nursery parents are familiar with the reception class before the children transfer.

Next challenges

To ease the transfer of children from Reception to Year 1. We are already trying ways for the Year 1 and reception teachers to work together, and for the children to become more familiar with their new settings before the changeover time.

Further reading

MacNaughton, G. (2003) *Shaping Early Childhood: Learners, Curriculum, Context*, Open University Press, Buckingham.

Whalley, M. (2004) *Management in Early Childhood Settings*, Paul Chapman Publishing, London.

See also the following training videos:

BAECE (1994) *Our Present is their Future*, BAECE, London.

BBC/National Children's Bureau (1997) *Tuning in to Children*, BBC Education, London.

Manchester Metropolitan University (1996) *Firm Foundations: Quality Education in the Early Years*, Didsbury School of Education, Manchester Metropolitan University, Manchester.

OMEP (2001) *Playing to Learn – the Foundation Stage*, OMEP (UK), 144 Eltham Road, London, SE9 5LW.

4

Helping children feel 'at home'

The care and education debate

The separate funding and administration of care and education services for children from birth to 5 in Britain have historically resulted in considerable debate about what constitutes high-quality provision for young children. The younger the children the more vulnerable and dependent they are, and the greater their need for care and supervision. A growing number of parents have to work to survive financially, so there has been a gradual realization that a range of childcare facilities is required.

The period from birth to 5 years of age is a time when rapid intellectual development takes place. Children at this stage are particularly receptive learners. (Brierley, 1984; Carnegie Corporation, 1994) A report by the National Commission on Education (1993, pp. 131–2) concluded that there should be 'a statutory requirement on local authorities to ensure that sufficient high-quality publicly funded nursery education places are available for all 3- and 4-year olds whose parents wish it'. This report was rapidly followed by one from the RSA (Ball, 1994, recommendation 12, para. 7.21) which recommended that 'the Government should immediately prepare legislation to create by 1999 a statutory responsibility for the provision of free high-quality, half-day pre-school education for all children from the age of three, in an integrated context of extended day-care'. These two reports echoed the beliefs of many early years practitioners and campaigners who had recognized that the part-time nursery school or class place meets the needs of very few families. Nursery teachers have led, or been involved in the development of, the growing number of integrated early years centres in the UK and have welcomed the challenges involved in working and learning within the context of a multidisciplinary team. Developments of this kind have in the past been stifled by the lack of political sensitivity and funding rather than by practitioners themselves.

However, government policy since the beginning of the twenty-first century has promoted the idea of 'one-stop shops' for families with young children, where health, education and social services for adults and children are available on one site. A major expansion of integrated provision – first Early Excellence Centres and Sure Start projects and then Children Centres – has taken place. However, there are still concerns that current initiatives are under-funded and are therefore failing to ensure that parents have access to the childcare facilities they need, and children receive high-quality educational experiences.

The nursery voucher scheme introduced in 1996 signalled, for the first time, a government's commitment to offering a funded place to all 4-year-olds. However, the scheme was underfunded, the quality of the places offered was variable and the exclusion of 3-year-olds was damagingly divisive. The main effect of the scheme was to accelerate the early admission of 4-year-olds to reception classes and to make some nursery settings unviable.

In 1997 the new Labour government quickly announced the abolition of the voucher scheme and produced guidance for local authorities on drawing up early years development plans and setting up Early Years Development and Childcare Partnerships (EYDCPs). This guidance required various providers to plan and work together and highlighted the need to integrate early years education with daycare. However, the target that 'a good quality place should be provided by April 1999, free of charge for all four year olds whose parents wish it and targets set to extend that entitlement to three year olds over time' (DfEE, 1997a, Annex A) was unambitious. The continued focus on 4-year-olds further undermined nursery education and it was difficult to see how the vision of a truly integrated, flexible, community-based care and education service for 0–5-year-olds of the kind set out by Moss and Penn (1996) could ever be achieved. With the majority of 4-year-olds in reception classes, and staff in nursery schools and classes struggling to maintain high standards with groups of mainly 3-year-olds the long-established definition of quality nursery education (see introduction) was completely undermined. Even though 99 per cent of 3-year-olds had access to funded places in 2003, many of these places were in the private and voluntary sector. The number of 3-year-olds in maintained nursery schools and classes actually fell, whilst the numbers attending private and voluntary provision rose (DfES, 2003b).

Many children are expected to transfer from one setting to another long before they are emotionally or socially able to cope, and rarely have enough time in any one setting to reap the full benefit of what is on offer.

Although young children and their families are higher up the political agenda, there is still little understanding of the complex issues involved in meeting their needs. There is certainly no acknowledgement of the financial investment required to ensure high-quality provision for all children. The redefinition of the term 'nursery education' has enabled politicians to claim that all settings can provide it – regardless of staff training, adult:child ratios, premises and curriculum.

The Rumbold Committee (DES, 1990, p. ii) claimed that 'education for the under-fives can happen in a wide variety of settings', and used the term educator to describe 'an adult working with the under-5s'. When OFSTED inspectors evaluate the 'quality of teaching' they are referring to all adults in early years settings. The *Curriculum Guidance for the Foundation Stage* labels adults working with young children 'practitioners' and the word 'teaching' is used to include all aspects of the practitioner's role (QCA/DfES, 2000, p. 1). The inference that anyone, however minimally trained, can teach, would be totally unacceptable if applied to the education of older children – indeed the suggestion that unqualified teaching assistants could take over some of the teacher's role has been highly controversial. Why then is there still resistance to the idea that young children, who are at a crucial stage in their development, need appropriately qualified teachers?

Perhaps it is the care or parenting element, which confuses the issue. It is quite possible for people with or without training to care about and for children. In spite of this, most new parents feel ill-prepared to take care of their new baby or toddler, and need support. It certainly requires highly trained staff to combine an appropriate education with sensitive care. When inadequately trained staff try to educate young children, the care element can get lost and a transmission model of education takes over, curriculum content taking precedence over children's personal needs and feelings. This became apparent when workers in some settings tried to comply with the requirements of the voucher scheme and set up 'voucher rooms' to teach the desirable learning outcomes! Following the introduction of the Foundation Stage, some practitioners became early learning goal led and planned rigidly to cover them. They ignored the practice guidance, which sets out how learning and teaching should be approached.

Research on 4-year-olds attending reception classes with inappropriately trained teachers has repeatedly demonstrated how children can rapidly become resentful and unhappy if their social and emotional needs are not met (Barrett, 1986; NFER/SCDC, 1987; Bennett and Kell, 1989; Sherman, 1996). This is why training is so important. Only if the needs of young children are fully understood can an appropriate education be defined and developed. The Education and Employment Committee (2000) recommended that 'every setting outside a home which offers early education should have a trained teacher on its staff' (p. xl). They had been influenced by research (Siraj-Blatchford et al., 2002, p. 14) which found 'in both interviews and observations that trained teachers used the most sophisticated pedagogy' and that less well-qualified staff worked more effectively with the children when they were supervised by qualified teachers. It is now clear that early years teachers are needed to lead teams in providing the combination of care and education which young children need. This and the next chapter will demonstrate how the Foundation Stage teacher uses her knowledge of the developmental needs of 3–5-year-olds to establish an appropriate ethos and learning environment for them

What do young children need?

Blenkin and Kelly (1996, p. 10) argue that 'the prime concern of education should be to develop to the maximum the potential of every child to function as a human being'. Their view of 'education as development' (ibid., p. 1) is common to most early years specialist teachers. It is in their first few years at school that children must learn to function as a member of a large social group outside the family, and must develop the resources they need to cope with the emotional, social, physical and intellectual challenges they will meet as they grow older. Early years trained teachers understand their role in supporting this all-round development and how this support will vary for each child.

Within any group of 3–5-year-olds there are wide variations in development. Children grow and develop rapidly during the first five years of their life – even a couple of days can make a huge developmental difference – and no two children do the same things at exactly the same age. These variations are usually quite normal. They require the teacher to get to know and relate to children as individuals and to be able to identify any unusual variations in development, which may require specialist help.

Through a consideration of two children attending the same nursery class we can see how the teacher needs to apply her general knowledge of 3–5-year-olds to the specific needs of individuals. The following outlines are based on a review of the progress of these children towards the end of their first term.

Natalie and John had settled well and were enthusiastic, well-motivated members of the class. They came from the same council estate and lived in small maisonettes in low-rise blocks. Both had attended daycare provision before joining the nursery class and Natalie was still cared for during parts of the day by a childminder. Both children attended nursery full time.

Natalie (who was 3 years old when admitted) was a tall, physically well developed child. She was very independent in dressing, toileting herself and eating lunch, and strongly resisted any help offered. She was a confident user of the nursery environment. She selected a broad range of opportunities for herself, both in and out of doors, but her favourite activity was home corner play. She spent a great deal of time in this area and particularly enjoyed using the telephone. She could often be seen standing with one foot up on a chair (or even the ironing board on one occasion) and one hand on her hip, having a lengthy and usually very loud 'conversation'. It was impossible to understand more than the occasional word. Natalie's language consisted of one or two recognizable words and a considerable amount of babble of the kind most usually associated with children of a much younger age. She was able to imitate very expressively the intonation patterns involved in a conversation on the telephone. When trying to communicate with adults and other children in the nursery, she became very frustrated because she was unable to express anything other than very basic needs in a way that others could understand. This was difficult for her because she was by nature a sociable child who wanted to join in and share her own experiences with others. Occasionally her frustration led to severe temper tantrums.

John (3 years 10 months when admitted) was a quiet, gentle, articulate child. He was also very capable of attending to his own physical needs but he was less confident about making use of the nursery environment. He sometimes seemed nervous of the other children, particularly the more boisterous ones, and was unable to stand his ground if another child challenged him for a piece of equipment. In these situations he would let the other child have the toy and move quickly away from the area. Most of all John liked to look at books, preferably while cuddling up to an adult. He could 'read' simple repetitive stories such as *Where's Spot?* (Hill, 1980) and *Bears in the Night* (Berenstain, 1981) and was interested in discussing the words in books. During one story-telling session with a teacher he asked 'Where does it say but?' There were one or two children in the group who John enjoyed playing imaginative games with, but he was always watchful of those other children he seemed to consider to be a threat.

Obviously the needs of these two children are quite different. Most early years settings contain children like them plus many others at various stages of development. In Chapters 6 and 7 we look at meeting these needs on an individual basis. Although in this chapter we focus on the general needs of young children, the developmental variations within a group make it essential for the teacher to consider the specific needs of each child she works with.

The teacher needs to consider each child as a whole person and to attend to the needs of each one. It is debatable whether any teacher should focus on academic attainment without considering other needs, but it is certain that the Foundation Stage teacher should not. She knows that if she is to plan an appropriate curriculum for the children she must consider their social, emotional and physical, as well as their intellectual needs (Hurst, 1997; Sylva, 2000; Dowling, 2002; Edgington, 2002a).

As the teacher interacts with the children, she operates at many different levels and may be responding to several different needs at once. These needs are considered separately in this chapter and the next to highlight the skill involved in developing the kind of ethos and environment, that would promote development and learning.

◼ The need for equality of opportunity

Only 28 per cent of 3 and 4-year-olds gain access to an LEA nursery school or class place, whilst 31 per cent of this age group attend infant classes in primary schools. (DfES, 2003a). The idea that equality of opportunity can be achieved by Foundation Stage teachers may seem like a forlorn hope. But when considering research evidence such as that carried out by Osborn and Milbank (1987, p. 206) who found that 'as many as 46 per cent of the most disadvantaged children had received no form of pre-school education, compared with only 10 per cent of the most advantaged group', and Sammons et al. (2003, p. 53) who found that children receiving no pre-school experience were 'more likely to be from ethnic minority groups, in particular Pakistani' and more likely to come from 'larger families and have mothers with no formal qualifications', we begin to see that admission policies may be responsible for consolidating inequality.

Where places are in short supply, teachers and headteachers have con-siderable power to include or exclude children. They can decide whether they will give priority to particular groups of children, such as those with special educational needs, those with working parents or those learning English as an additional language. They can also decide to admit children strictly on a first come first served basis. If this second option is chosen, it is inevitable that some children, whose parents are unfamiliar with, or unable to cope with, the procedures, will be left out. Although the Foundation Stage teacher does not have sole responsibility for admission policies, she can have an influence on them. Her attitude can determine which children are considered positively.

Offering equal access to early education is a start but it is not enough in itself. Teachers also have to ensure that all are given an equal chance to take advantage of the range of experiences on offer, and that they all feel equally valued.

Teachers have to recognize that their own attitudes, policies and practices may discriminate against, and limit the opportunities of, some children because of their gender, class, cultural background or special educational needs. This has been difficult for many teachers to accept, not least for early years teachers, who sometimes used to claim that they treated 'all children the same', or that 'there is no racism or sexism in my nursery'.

These views stemmed from a belief that young children do not notice colour, and that nursery activities are used equally by both sexes. These beliefs have been strongly challenged by researchers. Milner (1975; 1983) and Maxime (1991) demonstrated that young children do notice differences in skin colour, and that they attach value to these skin colours. Increasingly, practitioners are reporting that children in their groups are responding to items in the news such as the events of 11 September 2001 and the war in Iraq in ways which are likely to increase the development of negative stereotypical views (Adams and Moyles, forthcoming). The assertion that activities are equally available to girls and boys has also been challenged by, among others, Whyte (1983), who focused on the different ways boys and girls used the home corner, by Thomas (1988), who worked with nursery and infant staff to discover and discuss the extent of sex stereotyping in their classes, and by Browne and Ross (1991), who showed how girls can sabotage staff attempts to engage them in activities they would not normally choose. Most practitioners will have observed that boys and girls make different activity choices and these studies indicate that settings can unconsciously reinforce stereotypical views and behaviour. More recent research (Holland, 2003a; 2003b) has highlighted ways in which early years practitioners can use (rather than ban) young boys' strong interest in weapon and superhero play and develop their imagination, resourcefulness and creativity. It is interesting (and possibly not surprising given the pacifist stance taken by many early years workers) that, when this research is discussed, many practitioners are deeply uneasy about letting go of their 'we don't play with guns here' rule. However, many teams have engaged in discussion and are finding their own ways of interpreting and acting on Holland's findings.

Research has also shown that working-class children can be disadvantaged within early years settings. Tizard and Hughes (1984, p. 257) found that nursery staff often had low expectations of children from working-class backgrounds putting these children 'at an educational disadvantage in school'. Brooker (2002, p. 111) shows how baseline assessment of the most disadvantaged children in reception classes can lead to teachers developing low expectations of some children – 'there was a risk of children being seen, wrongly, as unprepared and unready for school learning.' Trudell (2002) argues that historically children living in poverty, where they accessed a service at all, have often been denied the opportunity to attend provision of the highest quality. She warns that whilst the move towards integrated centres is to be welcomed, 'there are dangers in that all of these initiatives exist in the context of the problem of poverty and social exclusion, and we may be at risk of repeating old errors' (p. 67). Children with special educational needs are often admitted to mainstream nursery schools and classes. Those with more obvious disabilities will usually have been assessed prior to school entry and additional support may have been made available. Often, however, a child's special educational needs are identified by the nursery staff. It is they who will have to act as advocates for the child, working through the stages of the *Code of Practice* (DfES, 2001) to ensure that the support he or she needs is forthcoming. If children with special educational needs are to benefit from early education and not be unnecessarily limited, it is essential that appropriate, inclusive provision is made for them.

All children need to feel proud of themselves and of their family. They need to feel valued for what they are and they need to feel competent and that they can achieve. They need to feel safe within the setting, confident that they will not be bullied, nor subjected to racist or sexist taunts. But it is not just the victims of prejudice who need the support of the teacher. She also has to help overconfident children to develop the kind of positive identity, which does not depend on demeaning others. Only if she works with the group of boys who dominate certain activities or equipment, can she ensure that girls will have equal access to the curriculum. Similarly a black child will only feel properly valued if he or she sees and hears the teacher confronting the child who has made a racist remark.

Equality of opportunity: some points for discussion

Awareness raising

How have you made (could you make) yourself and your team aware of:

- Inequalities in society?
- Inequalities within the education system?
- Attitudes (your own included) which may lead to discrimination against some children and families?
- Practices within your own school and class, which may reinforce existing inequalities? Think about admissions policies, your own involvement – and non-involvement – with parents and children, and in activities, approaches to initial assessment, availability of translations, etc.
- The children who dominate and those who are dominated by others? Including the children who are given most/least adult attention.
- The children who behave confidently and assertively and those who behave aggressively or timidly?
- Discriminatory language used or remarks made by staff, children, parents or visitors?
- The objective views of visitors to your class?

The Race Relations Act required all schools to produce a race equality policy by May 2002. Work on equal opportunities is an integral part of curriculum development and has to affect people as well as resources. It is not enough to put chopsticks in the home corner – it is also essential that children know what they are, and how they are used. If a child makes a negative remark about Chinese food, this must be confronted. For this reason all staff working with young children need regular in-service training opportunities to help them focus on equality issues – see the training packs on 'Equality' (Save the Children, 1993) and on Anti-Bias Training Approaches in the Early Years (Gaine and van Keulen, 1997) for ideas for managing training sessions.

Only when teachers address the difficult issues, rather than ignore them, can real progress be made towards equality of opportunity. Derman-Sparks (1989, p. x) acknowledges that it is not always easy to implement an anti-bias curriculum on a regular basis. She suggests that early years staff need to be prepared to 'learn by doing: by making mistakes, and thinking about it, and trying again'. As team leader, the teacher has to demonstrate her commitment to positive action. She has to be prepared to tackle the incidents she notices herself, and those which others draw to her attention.

Taking this action is not easy. What, for example, is the best way of dealing with the 4-year-old child who has just told her black friend (who had announced proudly which infant school she was going to) that 'My mum says I can't go to that school, "cos it's full of blacks"'? Or, the best way of responding to the child's mother who, when told exactly what her child had said, replied 'Oh dear, she's got it all wrong. She *is* going to that school. It's … school which is full of blacks'?

This is the reality of tackling racism, and it is important to acknowledge the stress and anxiety felt by those trying to take positive action against it, as well the hurt caused to the victims of it. However, anxiety and hurt are considerably relieved for all concerned once action, however clumsy, has been taken. Skills in dealing with these difficult issues can only develop with practice, and the teacher who does not act because she believes she will not get it right denies herself the opportunity to learn.

Similarly, a nursery admission policy which offers places on a first come first served basis may be easier to administer, and appear fair, but will cause considerable stress to staff when they realize which children they have excluded – the child who has just moved into bed and breakfast accommodation in the area, the child whose parents speak no English and did not know about registering early for a place, the refugee child newly arrived in the UK or the child with special educational needs. A policy which ensures that those children who most need nursery education get places may be more complicated to explain, but is easier to live with in the long term.

Through close daily contact with parents and children, teachers have many opportunities to hear and see evidence of the difficult issues mentioned above. Many of them are trying to promote the concept of equality in all parts of their work. Often they have to discuss these difficult issues with those who hold different values and are resistant to their approach. Unfortunately, work on dealing with these issues has been sidelined by curriculum and assessment initiatives which, at best, have paid scant attention to equality issues. Many teachers are honest enough to admit that they feel inadequate. How teachers can demonstrate their commitment to equality of opportunity is examined in this and the next chapter, as part of the exploration of children's developmental needs.

Equality of Opportunity

Taking positive action – Some points for discussion
Being aware of inequality, the reasons for it and the ways in which it is consciously and unconsciously reinforced is essential if the need for positive action is to be understood. The next step is to work towards a set of beliefs:

- What kinds of opportunities do you believe all children, parents and staff should be offered? Write down your beliefs in the form of an equal opportunities statement.
- Taking each belief in turn ask yourselves: how will we make sure that each of these beliefs is put into practice? For example, if we believe that all children should have access to a broad, balanced curriculum, how will we encourage this? The results of this discussion will form an equal opportunities policy or action plan (see Siraj-Blatchford, 1994).

Monitoring equal opportunities policies
Unless your work is regularly evaluated it is impossible to be sure that what you intended is being put into practice consistently. How will you check that your policy is being put into practice by all team members? (see chapter 3 for evaluation strategies)

The need for security

Parents and teachers tend to interpret the word 'security' differently. Parents are most likely to think about their child's physical safety: is it possible to get out of the building or grounds? Are there any dangers such as sharp edges or climbing frames with no safety surface? Teachers are more likely to focus on the children's emotional security: what are the things which worry children? How can we help the children to make the transition from home to the new setting? How can we help Mark to be more assertive? This difference in perspective does not mean teachers are unaware of physical dangers, or that parents are not aware that their child may feel anxious when leaving the home environment – it merely highlights different initial reactions. Both kinds of security are equally important to the young child. In the twenty-first century, where adults are only too aware that they can sue an institution or person if an accident occurs, and where lawyers openly tout for 'no win, no fee' business, health and safety concerns can predominate. Some practitioners have become so fearful that they will not allow anything in their setting that could pose a risk. However, it is important for the sake of children's physical and emotional development that these concerns are kept in perspective (Lindon, 1999).

The need for physical security and safety

Young children are usually unaware of the range of dangers in the environment. They are physically active and are keen to explore everything they come into contact with. This exploration involves touching, and often tasting, as well as the relatively safer looking and listening. They will not know that an interesting object can cut, or is poisonous or unhygienic. Neither are they necessarily aware that, if they throw this solid wooden brick like they just threw the sponge ball, it could hit another child and cause an injury. They are often quite ingenious at finding new ways of using objects and materials. Most parents and teachers know about the child who put a small piece of equipment up their nose or in their ear, or 'posted' something valuable down a drain!

Some of the equipment in the early years setting will be unfamiliar to the children and will require them to learn new skills. Climbing frames, wheeled toys, hammers and nails at the woodwork bench, scissors, large blocks and so on are all potentially dangerous, and children need opportunities to learn to use them without endangering themselves and others.

During their first few weeks in the setting, some children will even try to go home. Parents have a right to expect that their children will be protected from dangers of these kinds.

Ensuring physical security and safety

Checking for health and safety hazards

Early years settings are regularly inspected for safety, and teachers are used to carrying out risk assessments and monitoring to ensure that no hazards have developed. In many settings an early morning check of the outside play area to remove any dangerous litter is part of the routine. All members of the team regularly check equipment for broken parts and sharp edges, and the kitchen and areas containing cleaning equipment are made inaccessible to children except when they are under staff supervision, such as when taking part in a cooking activity. Toilet and washing facilities are kept as clean as possible, and the children are taught to wash their hands after toileting, before lunch and after handling pets.

The teacher must ensure that children are physically safe and that their health will not be endangered through poor standards of hygiene. However, nursery nurse training usually results in a deeper understanding of health and safety issues than does teacher training, so often the advice of her nursery nurse colleagues is sought. This does not mean that all cleaning and checking is left to the nursery nurse. Routine tasks of this kind are the responsibility of all staff, since they are too vital to be left to one person.

Encouraging safe use of equipment

Helping children to develop the skills they need to use safely the entire range of equipment is given high priority. The philosophy of early years education depends on high expectations of children. One response to potentially dangerous equipment would be to keep it out of the setting! It is to their credit that teachers usually reject this option. However, because of an accident, or the fear of being sued, some local authority guidelines place unnecessarily severe restrictions on early years teams, e.g. one LEA banned woodwork from its nurseries because of one accident involving a hammer. Clearly accidents can happen, particularly if staff are not aware of the need to train children to use equipment safely, but they are very rare and it will never be possible to prevent them all. Our aim should be to enable children to grow up with a healthy respect for potential danger. Indeed Lindon (1999, pp. 9–10) warns that 'a goal of zero risk is unrealistic. In fact the precautionary approach itself entails a different kind of risk, that of an oppressive atmosphere for children. Adults who analyse every situation in terms of what could go wrong risk creating anxiety in some children and recklessness in others'.

In the best early years settings opportunities for woodwork, strenuous physical activity and involvement in projects, such as building a low garden wall, are regularly made available and, with well-planned adult support, very young children develop skills which many adults would be proud of. They also learn from experience that the world can be a dangerous place and that they need to take care of themselves.

Sylvia (3 years and 9 months) was ironing in the home corner in an open-plan nursery school. The ironing board collapsed. Without reference to an adult, she picked it up, carried it to the woodwork bench (which was on the other side of the building) and mended it using a hammer and nail. She then carried it back to the home corner and continued ironing. She was able to do this because the teacher (a keen carpenter) had previously involved her in mending equipment, including the ironing board. This teacher, as well as providing girls and boys with a model of a woman capable of doing what is often seen as male work, had very high expectations of the children. She taught them how to use equipment safely, explaining what could happen if they misused it, and then trusted them to behave responsibly. The children fulfilled her expectations.

Establishing safety rules

To enable children to access a challenging range of experiences, many teachers work with their team and with the children to establish a set of safety rules. They identify potential dangers in their own environment, both indoors and out, and suggest ways of avoiding these dangers. Parents may also be asked to say what they think might be dangerous and how they would like to see staff deal with this. The results of this process are written up as a set of safety rules, to be given to all staff working in the nursery and displayed in prominent places for the benefit of relief staff and parents.

For example, in one school the toilet doors, which were saloon-bar style, were difficult for children to manage and, in anticipation of possible problems, a rule was written indicating that all new children needed to be shown how to use the toilet doors safely. A rule for the outside area of an inner-city class made it clear that the playground should be checked daily for rubbish, small pieces of glass and so on by the member of staff setting out the outdoor equipment. The co-ordinator of a Foundation Stage unit worked with the staff team and children to produce rules for the outdoor area. The children drew pictures to illustrate these rules and these were laminated and displayed as a reminder in prominent places outside.

Keeping the environment and the children safe and clean is something most teams do as a matter of course – they do not always talk about it. However, parents often say they would like to hear more from the staff about safety. It is natural for parents to worry about the safety of their very precious child and it is up to early years teams to demonstrate that they have done everything possible to ensure this safety.

Safety and outings

Sometimes children are taken out of the school grounds. Risk assessments are carried out and parents are asked to sign a consent form giving their agreement. They are often asked to participate. Outings into the local and wider community have a very important role in the Foundation Stage curriculum and are essential to learning within Knowledge and Under-standing of the World. Naturally though, parents will want to know that their child is safe. Most local authorities will give advice on the ratio of adults to children allowed for outings, but common sense usually leads teachers to ensure that all children are held by the hand when going on outings in busy streets. This obviously requires parents to be involved, and the teacher has to ensure they are aware of their responsibility for ensuring children's safety, as well as understanding the aims of the outing and how they can help the children to gain educationally. Sharing responsibility in this way helps parents to understand how seriously the teacher takes the children's safety, and gives reassurance to parents in the process. At Mary Paterson Nursery School in Westminster there is a long tradition of using outings to foster children's personal, social and emotional development and to provide the starting point for curriculum planning and development. Sylvie Gambell explains:

> Our curriculum is developed through visits within the local and extended areas. The school has a long history of outings – both local and bus outings –

as a means of developing the children's confidence and resilience as well as strengthening their sense of belonging and being connected to the world around them.

As part of their daily observations, staff note children's interests and ongoing preoccupations and, based on these observations, visits are organized for groups of six children where it will be possible to extend these interests and develop cross-curricular learning. The visit is documented by the children (and the adults), who take digital photographs and video films as a record. These are shared with parents and the other children in the nursery the next day, the video running as they all arrive, the photos spread out for all to see.

These images are then used as a support by staff who encourage children to describe, retell and recall, then to represent what they saw and experienced using a range of media from blocks to modelling with paper, clay, boxes, plaster, to drawing and writing (see Figure 4.1 and Figure 4.2). Children's words and comments are faithfully recorded by the adults, and the work is documented daily for parents and other adults and children. The visit being a shared experience between adults and children, they recall and share ideas about the same event. The visual nature of film and photograph supports the less linguistically fluent children and parents and offers opportunities for all to share our work.

In this way, the curriculum develops in a very organic manner, the links between all areas are easily made. Children measure and use mathematical language as they explore texture and describe changes in materials whilst representing a building using plaster that they spread on boxes covered in newspapers. They recall the place they went to and compare the architecture of a Victorian building compared to a modern structure like the nursery.

This way of working has created stronger links with parents who feel informed of the daily progression of the project; it has involved the children as it is based on their interests, needs and overwhelming preoccupations, it has motivated staff and generated an atmosphere of excitement in all.

Work of this kind reassures parents that the early years team have their children's best interests at heart. Parents trust the staff and are impressed by their children's achievements. (See Chapter 7 for further discussion of outings.)

Coping with accidents

Parents who have gained confidence in the early years team are more able to cope with the inevitable accidents which happen to children. Lindon (1999) emphasizes that it is essential to explain to parents at the earliest opportunity, the setting's approach to health and safety and how accidents are dealt with. Three to five-year-olds are still learning how to control their

Figure 4.1 *Back at school, children chose photographs of details of St. Pancras station and represented them using a variety of media. This child drew the details of the windows and presented her work by sticking it next to the original photograph.*

Figure 4.2 *Following a trip to St Pancras station, Aureta looked at a digital photo she took of the tracks and is reproducing them using rolled newspaper and masking tape.*

bodies, and they will sometimes bump into things, trip or fall over as they practise and refine their physical skills. Most accidents are of the scraped knee variety but occasionally a more serious injury is sustained. Rachel, while walking along a relatively low and very stable wooden box set up in a large space in the carpeted area of the classroom, was suddenly distracted by something across the room, and walked off the edge of the box before the teacher could do anything about it. She fell awkwardly on her arm, which fractured. In this situation teachers need to ensure that parents are given clear, calm and accurate information about what happened. This is never easy, since no parent copes well with seeing his or her child hurt in any way, and teachers inevitably feel responsible even when it would have been unrealistic to expect that the accident could have been prevented.

Coping with aggression

Even more difficult to cope with are the injuries inflicted by one child on another. Young children have to learn to share with others and take turns. Often their attempts are unsophisticated and even brutal. They still have to learn how to sort out their problems verbally, and the more limited their language skills, the more they will resort to other methods of communication. Biting, kicking, scratching and hair-pulling are sometimes the only methods they can think of to get what they want. When explaining to the parents of the victim or the aggressor, it is important that the teacher explains the reasons for this behaviour. It is easy for a young child to be labelled a bully, and even for that child and his or her family to be made scapegoats. This situation may reinforce the child's aggressive behaviour. It is very important that this does not happen, since all children have to be given the chance to outgrow what is essentially immature behaviour. As well as dealing with the child who hurts another, it is important that early years staff help more timid children stand up for themselves. This can involve helping them to say 'no' loudly or to go straight to an adult for support. In one early years centre the staff had clearly helped children to verbalize their feelings. A 3-year-old boy who had been pushed by another child, faced up to her and said 'don't do that to me, I don't like it when you push'. It is vital that all children can see that staff will not tolerate any behaviour that intimidates or hurts another child. The increased concern about bullying has emphasized the importance of the role of early years staff in taking positive action to influence children's behaviour at this formative stage in their development. Siraj-Blatchford et al. (2002, p. 12) found that the most effective settings had 'adopted discipline/behaviour policies in which staff supported children in being assertive, at the same time as *rationalising and talking* through their conflicts'. In the next chapter we see how children are helped to negotiate with each other.

Coping with risk

The Play Safety Forum (2002) reminds us that young children would never learn to walk or ride a bike if they were not motivated to take a risk. It is of great concern that in the twenty-first century many children are over-protected. They are therefore denied the opportunity to make their own judgements about risk in the way that children did years ago, when they had considerably more freedom to play outside with older and younger children. Deciding whether or not to do something another child suggested enabled many children to learn, from an early age, to stand up to peer pressure. If children do not have this experience until they have reached adolescence, and have to be given some freedom, it is not surprising that many find it difficult to say no.

The Foundation Stage teacher needs to foster the kind of ethos that will encourage all members of the community to accept that growing up involves taking risks and sometimes getting hurt. She has to help all adults to put this risk-taking into perspective and deal with it constructively. Children can be helped to learn from the consequences of their actions. The child who was bitten because he snatched a toy from another child can be taught to ask for a turn, and the biter can be encouraged to talk about her anger or tell an adult what has happened. Similarly, the child who fell because her attention wavered could be helped to learn that she needs to concentrate when climbing. Through sharing these strategies with parents a more consistent approach to discipline can be achieved. Risk assessments should give teachers confidence that they have taken the appropriate steps to minimize risk.

Dealing with conflict between parents and staff

Conflict can arise when parents and teachers disagree about the most appropriate strategy. Some parents encourage their child to hit back if they have been hurt, for fear that any other strategy will lead to the child being bullied. This is not a response which early years staff would encourage, yet neither do they want to seem to be dictating to parents how they bring up their child.

This conflict can usually be resolved through a discussion of responsibilities. The teacher is responsible for what happens in her setting. She will listen to the views of others and will take these views into account but, ultimately, she has to make a professional decision on what is in the best interests of the group as a whole and must be able to explain her reasons to others. Parents have a similar responsibility to decide what happens in their home. Children quickly learn that each social context has its own set of rules or expectations and that what is allowed in one setting may not be allowed in another. They learn to adapt their behaviour according to the social context they find themselves in – just as adults do.

Generally, parents are quite happy to accept the setting's rules if they:

- know them, understand them and were asked for their point of view;
- trust the teacher and other staff to ensure that these rules are fairly and consistently enforced;
- are confident that their children will be protected (through the enforcement of the rules) from bullying, and will develop strategies for standing up to those who seek to dominate them;
- are able to see that their children's behaviour is maturing; and
- witness a calm, caring atmosphere when they come into the setting.

The creation of a physically safe environment depends, at least to some extent, on the teacher's ability to help children understand and cope with their feelings and to express them in socially acceptable ways (i.e. in ways which do not frighten or hurt anyone else). Many dangerous situations develop from frustration, anger or from feelings of inadequacy.

Health and safety: some points for discussion

- What steps have you taken to ensure that the nursery environment is clean and safe? Does everyone understand his or her responsibilities? Do parents know how you make sure the setting is kept clean and how you ensure their child's safety?
- What are the rules in your class? How do you ensure that staff, children and parents know them and understand the reasons for them? How do you reinforce these rules on a daily basis?
- Are there any areas of conflict between staff and parents? What are the reasons for this conflict? Is there any way of resolving it?
- How do you enable children to accept challenges and learn to make their own judgements about risk?

The need for emotional security

The first aim of the Foundation Stage curriculum is to support, foster, promote and develop children's 'personal, social and emotional well-being: in particular by supporting the transition to and between settings, promoting an inclusive ethos and providing opportunities for each child to become a valued member of that group and community so that a strong self-image and self-esteem are promoted' (QCA/DfES, 2000, p. 8). When admitting children to a Foundation Stage setting teachers need to be aware of their emotional vulnerability.

Emotional security for both adults and children stems from:

1 knowing what to expect from a situation (it helps if the situation is one which has been successfully coped with before);
2 being well prepared for the new experience, and being motivated to take part in it;
3 knowing someone in the new setting;
4 being able to understand what is going on;
5 being allowed to take things at our own pace and not being singled out or pressured; and
6 being encouraged by others and not made to look foolish.

Often adults are inhibited from trying something new because of previous negative experiences.

The main difference between adults and very young children is that adults have a wealth of previous experience to draw on, which either helps them to cope with new situations and expectations or inhibits them – as adults we can often avoid or opt out of those experiences which generate most fear. The younger the child, the less life experience he or she has. Much of what happens to him or her is happening for the first time and there is little choice involved. When children encounter a new situation they generally have no negative feelings about it – unless adults or older children have transferred their worries to them or unless they are tired or ill. They are open to the new experience and their feelings about it will develop positively or negatively depending on how they are treated.

Consider the 3-year-old boy starting at a nursery. Often this is the child's first separation from his family, which has provided the setting for his development so far. Within this familiar setting he has been known and valued as an individual, his identity, language and culture have been developed and reinforced, and he has learnt the rules for functioning. By the time he is old enough for nursery he has already built up a view of himself and the world – his own world. Most children are confident and competent operators within their home setting (Wells, 1986).

He is expected to move from this relatively secure environment into one where there are many more children than he has seen before, with whom he has to share equipment and adult time; where he has to relate to unfamiliar adults who do not always understand his approaches and who may not even speak his language; where he does not know what is expected and keeps getting things wrong; and where there are adults who do not always seem to understand or value the things he has learnt at home. It is hardly surprising that many children find the transition from home to nursery difficult, at least to some extent. Similar challenges and difficulties face children starting in the reception class. Even those who have attended a nursery have to adjust to the out-of-class experiences such as assembly, PE, playtime, lunchtime and even going to the toilet (which is often down a corridor), which many find the most stressful parts of the day (Cleave, Jowett and Bate, 1982). This is why, since the introduction of the Foundation Stage many teachers in reception classes have been considering how they can support children with these out-of-class experiences and also questioning whether they are appropriate at all. The early weeks in the reception class are very important. Children, who operated confidently in a nursery setting, may become anxious again in the reception class – particularly if they are one of the youngest in the group – and yet many reception teachers still assume that if children have been to the nursery class they do not need a second settling in period. It is true that, because of the Foundation Stage, nursery and reception classes should offer a seamless continuity for the child but, in reality, many do not (Adams et al., 2004). Fabian (2002) highlights a number of physical, social and philosophical discontinuities children may experience which can impede their progress. The establishment of Foundation Stage units in a growing number of schools (see Chapter 3) has been an attempt to minimize transitions and offer stability and consistency for children in their first few years at school.

Young children starting both nursery and reception class need support to enable them to adjust to temporary separation from their family. They need to feel that they are a valuable competent member of the new social group, and they need to develop positive attitudes towards the range of new experiences they will encounter. They need to be helped to retain the self-confidence and self-respect they have already gained. This is easier for children whose experience at home matches, at least in part, the expectations of the setting. However, as Brooker (2002, p. 111) points out:

> the preparation some had received at home bore little resemblance to the curriculum or pedagogy of the school. For some children, their primary habitus, and the knowledge they had acquired in their communities were unhelpful in the classroom, and 'learning to be a pupil' meant learning to be someone different altogether.

Encouraging emotional security

The early years team needs to build on the work of the family and take steps to ensure that the child is valued as an individual in the setting. This sounds a considerably easier task than it actually is. Children enter school from a variety of backgrounds and respond to it in many different ways. The teacher may not always know about worries the child may have, since these worries sometimes surface at home rather than at school. Caroline (3 years) told her mother that she never used the toilet at nursery because the toilet paper was 'scratchy on my bottom'. She had become quite anxious about needing to go to the toilet and not wanting to go. The problem was resolved when her mother talked to the nursery staff, and the teacher was able to use this child's anxiety to argue for softer toilet paper for the nursery children. Joshua, who had been admitted to a reception class at the age of 4 years and 2 months, started wetting the bed again during his first half-term in school. On investigation this seemed to be due to general anxiety rather than any specific worry, but it was a sure sign he needed support and reassurance from his family and teacher.

If she is to help children retain their individual identity, the teacher has to ensure that the ethos and learning environment she creates are responsive and flexible to cater for the entire range of needs.

Sharing information

Parents can provide a wealth of knowledge about their children and are generally very keen to share this with the early years staff. Through talking with parents, teachers gain the insights they need to make the transition from home to the setting as smooth as possible. Getting to know the child and planning for admission to the setting require parents and teachers to engage in 'an equal partnership in which both learn from each other'

Emotional security: some points for discussion

- What opportunities do you provide for all parents to tell you about their child, and to find out from you about what goes on in your setting?
- Think of yourself spending time in a place which is not your home:
  - What does it take for you to feel welcome?
  - How do you make all parents feel welcome in your class? (Think about dads, parents with babies and toddlers, parents who speak little or no English, etc.)
  - How could you find out whether all parents feel welcome?
- Think about each individual child starting in your setting – what will this child find that connects with his/her previous life experience?
- How do you continue to give parents time to tell you what their child is experiencing at home?

(Hazareesingh, Simms and Anderson, 1989). Teachers can learn from parents how to respond to a particular child, and parents can learn from teachers how they can contribute to their child's security in the setting.

In spite of lack of time, teachers regard this sharing as vital, and have built a variety of opportunities for this kind of communication into their practice. Some nursery classes and schools have toddler groups attached, which teachers and nursery nurses visit regularly, so links are built up from a very early age. Visits to the class prior to a child's admission are also arranged. During these visits the child becomes familiar with the new situation, and the parents and teacher have the chance to share information and concerns. Some teachers offer to visit families at home (always respecting the parents' right to say 'no thank you'!), to give parents the chance to talk in more detail about their child and to ask any questions about nursery education, and also to demonstrate to the child the close link which is developing between his or her parents and the teacher. Other teachers offer the parents an appointment to come to the setting to talk about their child. Usually teachers will share these responsibilities with nursery nurses. In this case, the member of staff who has visited the family will maintain the link during the settling-in period. Whichever member of staff is involved in initial communications, the teacher is responsible for ensuring consistency of approach, and all members of the basic team (see Chapter 2) need to have information about the child.

Each team, in consultation with parents, will decide what information would be useful to them and how they will record it. This aspect of record-keeping is explored in more detail in Chapter 6.

Establishing a welcoming environment for parents

How willing parents are to share what they know about their children will depend on the kind of environment the teacher offers them. Parents need to feel that their presence is welcomed. Many of them have memories of school, which make them feel apprehensive about entering educational establishments and approaching teachers. Pugh (2002, p. 113) highlights 'how damaging it was to parents' confidence and to their capacity as educators if schools made them feel their role was unimportant or misguided – "We don't like them to come to school reading", or "We don't do capital letters yet"'.

Collaboration with parents is a vital part of an early years worker's role as carer and educator of young children (Whalley and the Pen Green Centre Team, 1997; 2001; QCA/DfES, 2000). Many teams have worked very hard to create the kind of relaxed, informal atmosphere which will encourage all parents to participate.

In order to achieve the kind of collaboration which will support the child at times of transition, teachers:

- must organize their time so that they are free at the beginning and end of a session to welcome and talk informally with parents (Kenway, 1995) – particularly those who are least confident in the school situation;
- need to be flexible so that all parents have the chance to contribute to, and participate in, their child's learning. This requires them to make opportunities to talk with working parents, and seek the support of translators and interpreters to ensure that all parents, whatever language they speak, are given equal access to information and equal opportunities to share their knowledge of their child. Many teachers have had to acquire the skill of communicating via an interpreter;
- must demonstrate their respect for parents' knowledge by asking for their views and by listening to what they say. They must believe that all parents are capable of contributing valid views and need to be aware that children do and say things at home that we see no evidence of at school; and
- need to help parents to gain the confidence to contribute within the setting. It is also necessary for teachers to make their expectations clear to parents. For example, if a home visit is proposed by the teacher, she must ensure parents understand the purpose of such a proposal, as well as respecting the parents' right to reject the suggestion. Tizard, Mortimore and Burchell (1981) found that parents welcome this kind of involvement if they have a clear understanding of the purpose.

Establishing an atmosphere of trust and equality takes time. Teachers recognize that, if parents have confidence in, and understand, the educational aims of the staff, the children will benefit. An investment of time before the child is admitted generally results in a much smoother transition from home to the setting because parents are better equipped to support staff before and during the settling-in period.

Supporting children before admission

Both parents and staff want children to enjoy starting nursery or primary school, and they see the need to work together to support children to cope with new experiences. Through pre-admission visits and home visits parents and children begin to know what to expect from the setting, and the staff get to know the family.

Sometimes teachers will make photo books of life in the setting for parents and children to borrow and discuss at home. These books include photos with captions of all areas of the nursery including toilets, and show what happens during the day, from hanging up coats on personal pegs, to going home at the end of the session. Through discussing the book with their parents, children gain a much clearer view of what will happen and some possible anxieties are minimized. For example, many children are concerned that they will be left overnight, and are greatly relieved when their parents emphasize the section of the book, which deals with going-home time.

Parents and staff can anticipate any aspects of life in the setting the child may find difficult and can plan to help the child cope with these.

Settling children into the class

Admissions should be organized on a staggered basis so that the person who has made the closest contact with the family is available to greet them personally and give time to them on their first day. Although the family will know at least one member of the nursery staff, young children, who often find it difficult to express their needs verbally, also need the support of their parents or regular caregiver during the settling in period. This needs to be explained to parents well in advance so that they understand why their child needs them and can make appropriate arrangements. How long this support will be needed depends on the child and is generally negotiated between the parent and the teacher. During the first few days the assigned staff member will make sure that she gives time to the child and parent, if necessary with the help of someone who speaks the family's language, so that both develop confidence in the relationship.

The early years setting offers a bewildering array of tempting opportunities for the child. Teachers work with their team to ensure that, during their first few days, each child finds something familiar within the class, which he or she can relate to, as well as new and stimulating opportunities. Teachers also have to create an environment which reflects the society the children live in and which questions stereotypical ideas about the roles which men and women, black and white people and people with disabilities can take. The environment teachers create gives important messages to children and parents about what they value. They need to ensure that children will find the familiar resources they need for security and self-esteem within the new situation. Anyone who has seen the expression of joy and excitement on the face of the child who has spotted the book, poster or dressing-up outfit which reminds him or her of home, will understand the importance of resources to the child's emotional security. It is as important for the child who lives in a high-rise flat to find books and pictures of tower blocks, as it is for the Chinese child to find books and pictures of Chinese people in Britain. If children are aware that their background is acknowledged and valued they will be well equipped to acknowledge and value backgrounds of other children.

Teachers are powerful role models for the children. If the staff are seen to cook, and to encourage parents to cook, a wide variety of foods and then to eat these foods enthusiastically, children are more likely to want to try them and less likely to reject anything unfamiliar.

Small children are reassured if they find equipment in the setting, such as Lego or a favourite book, which they have already used at home. Using the knowledge, which parents have shared with them, early years staff can help children find familiar resources in the class.

To cater for a wide range of needs and interests the teacher has to organize her class so that equipment is easily accessible to the children (see Chapter 5). She must ensure that children with specific special educational needs are not excluded and can access the full range of experiences with or without support from adults. Parents are often asked to help their child get used to making choices, using equipment safely and taking responsibility for their actions or for clearing away. Right from the start children are encouraged to feel powerful members of the group, secure in the knowledge that they have some choice and control over what happens to them within the framework of a set of consistent safety rules.

Once a child is able confidently to use all parts of the setting and feels at ease with at least one member of staff, parents can feel quite happy about leaving him or her. Usually, teachers will advise parents to leave their child for just a short period at first, in case the child should become distressed, building up the time gradually until the child stays contentedly for the full session. This kind of gradual separation is very important for young children if they are not to suffer stress and anxiety.

Supporting bilingual children

The transition from home to a Foundation Stage setting can be particularly bewildering for children who are learning English as an additional language and for their families. It may take bilingual children longer to feel settled and secure, and it may be even more inappropriate for them to be expected to transfer early from nursery to the reception class. Amina started nursery school when she was just 3. Only after four terms did she begin to operate totally confidently in this very secure setting. During her fifth term she blossomed and was often to be seen explaining how the nursery worked to new children and to visitors. If she had been expected to transfer before the sixth term she would have lost this opportunity to increase her confidence and to function as one of the oldest members of the group – her development would almost certainly have been negatively affected as she tried to make sense of another new situation. Extended time in one setting is of particular importance to young beginner bilinguals.

The need for bilingual support staff, who are able to interpret and translate, has already been stressed, and early years staff need to be aware that families for whom no such support is available will be disadvantaged. Members of the early years strand of the Intercultural Education Project, who were asked in a survey what strategies they had found useful for helping young bilingual learners to access the curriculum, identified offering children support in their home language as the most helpful strategy for supporting children when they start nursery or infant school (Lally, 1993). They identified the advantages of this support as follows:

- Children's confidence and sense of identity increases – children talk more in their home language and in English at school, and they settle into school more quickly when there is a bilingual worker present.
- Parents understand more about, and become more involved in the school – a number of schools and LEAs have found that the involvement of Asian parents is dependent on having workers or community members who speak their language.
- Children are helped to gain access to the curriculum when bilingual adults are involved in the development and adaptation of resources, and in involving children in stories and experiences in their home language. Opportunities to use their home language at school also support children's concept development.

This survey revealed that although some schools are fortunate to have bilingual teachers, nursery nurses or assistants, many others were success-fully involving parents or other family members (including older siblings), members of the local community and students as well as the local translation and interpreting service. All teachers need to look at their setting from the point of view of someone who is learning English as an additional language – how do families know how to apply for a place, how welcoming is it, how effectively is information communicated (parents to staff as well as staff to parents)? They also need to be aware that it is easy to underestimate the competence of children whose first language is not understood by any of the staff, and that they are not likely to be able to make a valid initial assessment of these children unless they have support from a bilingual person.

Managing the transition from home to setting: some points for discussion

- What kind of admissions policy would enable you to get to know and respond to each child as an individual?
- Which aspects of life in your setting are likely to be stressful for a young child starting in your group for the first time? (Think about toilets, noise, numbers of other children, unknown adults, care of personal possessions, etc.)
- What steps could you take to minimize stress? How do you ensure that the child adjusts gradually (i.e. without shock) to the new environment and to new expectations? Are your settling-in procedures flexible enough to cater for individual needs?
- How could you involve each child's parents or carer in supporting the child during the transition from home to early years setting ? What opportunities do you provide for parents and children to discuss their concerns with you during the settling-in period? How do you encourage both children and parents to discuss their feelings openly with you throughout their time in the setting?

Maintaining emotional security

So far the focus has been on the teacher supporting the child emotionally during the potentially traumatic transition from home to setting. It is helpful to hold a review meeting with parents after about half a term to discuss how the child is settling in – it is often at this meeting that parents will ask questions about their children's learning. A positive start is vital but the teacher has to continue to foster emotional development throughout the remainder of each child's time in the Foundation Stage . She has to:

- help each child express and cope with his or her feelings in constructive rather than destructive, assertive rather than aggressive or passive, ways. This will be examined in further detail in Chapter 5;
- make sure that each child's achievements are recognized and encouraged so that all children retain positive attitudes towards learning. By acknowledging each child's individual effort and progress, she encourages a sense of achievement rather than a sense of failure;

- provide opportunities for children to come to terms with their fears and anxieties through their play experiences. Jane's baby sister was seriously ill and had been taken into hospital. Jane's mother (a lone parent) was temporarily living in at the hospital and Jane was being cared for by her grandmother. Jane's teacher noticed her pushing a baby doll in a pushchair. As Jane passed she told her teacher, 'She's really, really sick in her tummy. I got to take her to the hopital'. The teacher played the part of a concerned friend and helped Jane to express some of her fears about what was happening in her family. At the end of the session she told Jane's grandmother what had happened so that she too could offer Jane some support;
- help children to develop the skills they need to stand up for themselves and challenge aggressive, racist or sexist approaches. This work has been developed to help children protect themselves from abuse by adults (Pen Green Family Centre, 1990); and
- notice changes in behaviour which may signify worries or insecurity. One of the times when behavioural changes are most likely to occur is after the birth of a sibling. Parents and staff can work together to help the child respond positively to the new arrival.

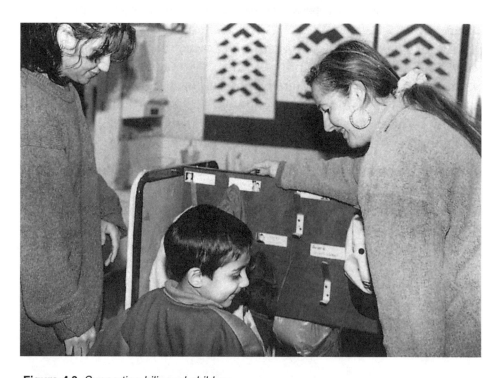

Figure 4.3 *Supporting bilingual children*

Teachers need to create an atmosphere of respect and trust with children and also with their parents. Children will only initiate discussions with adults who have demonstrated their willingness to listen, and to respond to what they say.

The teacher needs to be able to share power with children and their parents. She cannot adopt the role of all-knowing professional. Power-sharing is only possible if teachers feel secure in and confident of their own skills. As we saw in Chapter 2, lack of confidence often leads to defensiveness, and an unwillingness to share with others for fear of being made to seem inadequate. Well-trained teachers are confident in their skills, and aware of their own strengths and weaknesses. The less well trained admit that they worry about working with parents because they are afraid of being challenged. Trainers on initial and in-service courses need to ensure that teachers develop confidence in their knowledge of child development and are able to articulate clearly and assertively their approach to others. The self-esteem and confidence of teachers directly affect their ability to offer an environment which enhances the self-esteem and confidence of children and their parents.

Ongoing emotional support: some points for discussion

- During their time in the early years setting children will be encouraged to take part in a variety of new experiences and new challenges – how do you help children to approach these with confidence rather than fear?
- How do you monitor how well each child is coping with being in the setting and with new experiences?
- How does the early years team work together to ensure that the child's next transition is as stress-free as possible? How have you highlighted possible discontinuities between nursery and reception classes?

Further reading

Brooker, L. (2002) *Starting School – Young Children Learning Cultures*, Open University Press, Buckingham.

Derman-Sparks, L. and the ABC Task Force (1989) *Anti-Bias Curriculum: Tools for Empowering Young Children*, National Association for the Education of Young Children, Washington, DC.

Dowling, M. (2000) *Young Children's Personal, Social and Emotional Development*, Paul Chapman Publishing, London.

Fabian, H. (2002) *Children Starting School*, David Fulton, London.

Roberts, R. (1995) *Self-Esteem and Successful Early Learning*, Hodder and Stoughton, London.

Save the Children (1993) *Equality: A Basis for Good Practice*, Save the Children, London.

Siraj-Blatchford, I. and Clarke, P. (2000) *Supporting Identity, Diversity and Language in the Early Years*, Open University Press, Buckingham.

Whalley, M. and the Pen Green Centre Team (2001) *Involving Parents in their Children's Learning*, Paul Chapman Publishing, London.

5

Helping children to 'branch out'

The need to develop social strategies

Admission to the Foundation Stage requires children to extend the range of interpersonal strategies they have already built up at home. The skill involved in supporting this development through a well-planned settling in curriculum is often underestimated. Teachers of older children may not realize the demands which are made on Foundation Stage teachers as they help children to develop a range of behaviours appropriate to a group setting. Teachers in reception classes may underestimate how much support children, starting in their class, need. They are more likely to find children's natural behaviour difficult or even naughty and are less likely to use appropriate strategies (Sherman, 1996) – it is therefore not surprising that children are being excluded at younger ages from primary schools.

Teaching style and the development of social strategies

Young children are physically small and usually eager to please their teachers (Katz and Chard, 1989). It is therefore relatively easy to control them and make them conform within an adult-directed environment. Effective teachers do not take the easy way out. They are aware that domination by adults may lead to some children modelling this controlling behaviour, and dominating or bullying other children. This would not be a desirable outcome.

There is now evidence that formal education in the early years actually impedes both social and academic progress (Nabuco and Sylva, 1996; Schweinhart and Weikart, 1997; Sharp, 2002). The controlling approach, which encourages dependence on others, is now seen as inappropriate. In fact, the *Curriculum Guidance for the Foundation Stage* actively promotes an approach where children are encouraged to take responsibility for their own actions and learning. In this guidance learning is defined as follows: 'Learning for young children is a rewarding and enjoyable experience in which they explore, investigate, discover, create, practice, rehearse, repeat, revise and consolidate their developing knowledge, skills, understanding and attitudes. During the Foundation Stage, many of these aspects of learning are brought together effectively through playing and talking' (QCA/DfES, 2000, p. 20). Child-initiated learning is strongly promoted throughout the document.

If all children are to become self-motivated and able to initiate and take responsibility for their own learning, they need a teaching style which empowers them and encourages autonomous behaviour. As Blenkin and Kelly (1996, p. 8) make clear, autonomy is not an end-state 'towards which we must strive' but a procedural principle 'by which it is suggested we should live, and, as teachers, help our pupils to live'. In order to encourage children to live autonomously teachers need to inspire them to:

- believe that they have the power and ability to control their own lives;
- make informed choices;
- get involved and enjoy challenges;
- be prepared to take a risk and learn from mistakes;
- plan their own time;
- use others as a resource;
- take responsibility for their own actions and choices; and
- respect others (living autonomously does not mean pursuing one's own interests without regard for others).

These are complex abilities, which many adults have not developed themselves. If children begin to develop these abilities in the early years, they will be well equipped to gain maximum benefit from early education and also to cope with the challenges of later life: 'the early education experience may change children from passive to active learners who begin to take the initiative in seeking information, help, and interaction with others' (Lazar and Darlington, 1982, p. 63). Autonomous or 'mastery'-orientated children (Dweck and Leggett, 1988) are more likely to persist in the face of challenges or problems and are less likely to be discouraged by failure. Sylva (1994, p. 93) concludes that:

Successful early education must do more than instil a few facts or simple cognitive skills. Its curriculum can be explicit about means to nurture positive beliefs about one's talents, and learning orientation rather than performance orientation. Pre-school learning must help children acquire resources for dealing with the stress of failure and the belief that achievement is not God-given but is, instead, acquired at least in part through effort.

Although the importance of personal, social and emotional development in the early years curriculum has been acknowledged within national documentation, it has been marginalized by the continuing emphasis (some would say overemphasis) on literacy and numeracy.

Supporting social development

In an early years setting young children are required to develop as individuals and also as a member of their peer group. These two aspects of development are interrelated: the growth of self-awareness is closely linked with the 'sense of others, their needs and their sometimes conflicting impingement on our own personal space and identity' (Blenkin and Whitehead, 1996, p. 36).

In order to be able to interact harmoniously within a group, young children need to feel confident and secure about their own rights and position. They need to feel valued, respected and cared about so they can value, respect and care about others.

Children are required to share equipment and adult time, make choices and compromises, take turns, take responsibility for their own actions and take into account the needs of others in the group. These are complex skills and children need a great deal of support if they are to acquire them.

Learning to share equipment and take turns

The Foundation Stage setting offers a treasure trove of delights for the 3-year-old on his or her first visit. Children's response varies. Some want it all at once and race from area to area sampling the activities and equipment on offer. Others seek out one piece of equipment which attracts their attention – often something they are already familiar with – and stay with this to begin with. Others appear totally bewildered and refuse to leave their carer's side.

Children have to learn that they have the right to choose from and use all the equipment, but that it does not belong to them exclusively – they cannot take it home, for example. This involves discovering that some pieces of equipment, such as construction kits or the climbing frame, are to be used simultaneously by more than one child, while others, such as headphones or a sand spade, are to be used by one child at a time.

Most children will never before have been expected to share so much with so many. Merely putting children together will not in itself ensure that they learn this social skill. It is a major part of the role of the teacher to help all children to operate confidently, to select and make use of the equipment they need while respecting the needs of others.

Helping children to share equipment and take turns

The teacher's first responsibility is to ensure that the learning environment is adequately resourced and that suitable storage systems are available to enable children to access materials and tidy up after themselves. Resources should be available as much of the time as possible and there should be sufficient to encourage imaginative use. Better to have a large quantity of one construction set, which several children can use productively at once, than small quantities of several different sets, none of which offer even one child the chance to build in depth. Reception classes have not always been as well resourced as nurseries and it is essential that schools monitor carefully to ensure that children are offered both continuity and progression as they move through the Foundation Stage – later in this chapter we will see the range of provision which is required to develop a high quality curriculum for 3-6-year-olds.

Making as wide a range of equipment as possible available for children to choose from every day is the best way of encouraging sharing and turn-taking. In classes where staff limit the activities on offer, or the time available to use equipment, there is often an air of desperation about the children, who know that if they do not get a turn now, they may not get one at all before the equipment is put away. If they know that what is available today will still be available tomorrow they are certain to be more relaxed about their involvement. Teachers need to decide what will be available every day and what they will need to add to the provision from time to time to extend children's interest and learning.

Children are less likely to hoard all the equipment for themselves if they can see that there will be enough for them even if others use some, or that they will have plenty of time to have a turn after other children have finished. Sometimes teachers help children to understand that there is enough for everyone by offering them a similar, alternative piece of equipment. This is a useful interim strategy as children are learning but, ultimately, teachers aim to help children consider the interests of others as well as their own. They have to judge when each child is able to begin to identify and empathize with others in this way. Communication skills are important, since children need to be able to make sense of the teacher's verbal explanations.

The ways in which young children express their frustration when others take their toy, or will not give them a turn, have already been discussed in Chapter 4. The teacher talks each situation through with the children involved and helps them to reach a solution to their problem which is appropriate to their level of understanding.

Samantha and Wahida (two 3-year-olds) were playing alongside each other at the sand tray. Samantha was filling a bucket using a spade, while Wahida was piling sand up in the corner of the tray with her hands. Wahida suddenly seemed to decide she needed a spade to pat down the top of her pile of sand and grabbed the spade, which Samantha was using. A brief 'tug-o'-war' ensued and both girls screamed loudly. The teacher who had been observing the incident intervened at this point. She talked quietly to the two girls explaining to Wahida that Samantha was using the spade to fill her bucket and that if she wanted a spade she could choose one from the trolley next to the sand tray. She proceeded to help Wahida make her choice and the play continued smoothly.

Because the girls were both new to nursery, the teacher's main priority was to draw their attention to the choices available to them. However, she also began the process of signalling to them the need to respect the activities of others.

As children gain in experience and maturity, teachers use such situations to model ways for the children to negotiate with each other. Caroline and Natalie were both well settled at nursery school and often played together. One morning Caroline had been playing on the tricycle for some time and Natalie wanted a turn, so she tried to push Caroline off the tricycle. The teacher helped her to find an alternative way of receiving a turn by working through a negotiation process with her. She encouraged Natalie to say 'Can I have a turn?' and when Caroline said 'I haven't finished yet', helped her to negotiate a timescale which would give Caroline one more circuit of the playground before it was her turn (sand timers are sometimes used to help children see when their time is up or when it is their turn). The teacher stayed with the girls long enough to ensure that Natalie got her turn, and also observed the girls over the next few weeks and supported Natalie's subsequent attempts to negotiate. This ongoing support is important if children are not to get discouraged. They need to be able to see that alternatives to aggression can be just as effective.

Of course, just because a child asks nicely they may not get a turn there and then. Children also have to learn when it is inappropriate to expect another child to give up something he or she is using – when the child has just begun to use it, or when the piece of equipment is central to a lengthy project, for example. This is where children on both sides of the situation can be helped to reason with each other and begin to understand how it feels to be the other person. So, when Natalie several days later approached another child who had just got on the bike and asked for a turn, it was necessary for the teacher to help her to see how she would feel if she had just started to use the bike and someone wanted her to get off.

Naturally, children will try to test out how far they can go in this situation. It is not long before a child asked to give up the tricycle after two more circuits realizes that she can prolong her ride by cycling very slowly – causing great frustration to the child waiting for a turn and testing the patience of the adult. A sensitive teacher can use these situations to help children become more self-aware and also more aware of the feelings of others – for example by saying to the bike rider 'I know you would like to ride the tricycle for much longer and don't want to give it up, but ... hasn't had a turn at all, and you know how unhappy you would be if you hadn't had a turn'.

In this way, teachers offer some verbal strategies for children to employ and help them to empathize with others. Before long children are able to invent their own strategies for other situations – it was not long before Natalie was overheard suggesting to another child that she should be given a turn with a sand wheel 'when you've tipped that bucket in'. Older children will also delight in helping younger ones to develop the skills they have already learnt.

This is why Foundation Stage Units where 3-5-year-olds are educated together have an advantage. Nursery teachers who lose their 4-year-olds to reception classes comment that the remaining 3-year-olds are at a disadvantage when they have no slightly older role models. In the same way, reception classes or nurseries where predominantly 4-year-olds are admitted do not offer the children a chance to care about and take responsibility for the younger ones. When children have a substantial period of time in the same setting, their personal, social and emotional development is enhanced. National and local policy-makers, governors and headteachers urgently need to be helped to understand the negative effects on children's learning and development of separating 3, 4 and 5-year-olds.

Supporting children's development in the ways described above is a time-consuming process, and requires both vigilance and patience on the part of all members of the early years team. Only when consistent efforts are made will children really be able to feel confident that aggression does not pay. Above all, adults must be seen to be fair. Even the very youngest children are quick to notice unjust treatment.

Encouraging assertive behaviour

The domination of certain areas of provision by particular children has been discussed in Chapter 4. An important aspect of the teacher's role is to help children stand up for themselves in the face of intimidation or bullying by others.

Both passive and aggressive children are at a disadvantage. Indeed, aggression thrives on passivity. With increased awareness of child abuse children need to be aware that adults are not always to be trusted. Assertive behaviour is most likely to be encouraged in a situation:

- where aggressive behaviour is not rewarded (even unintentionally);
- where adults treat children as people with equal rights who are entitled to put forward their opinion and challenge adults if necessary;
- where passive or withdrawn children are actively encouraged to develop in confidence – this requires teachers to take time away from the more demanding children in their group, and concentrate on the needs of the least demanding individuals; and

> • in an informal environment where adults, including parents, see their role as empowering rather than controlling children – offering children strategies and reasons rather than telling children what to do and expecting unquestioning obedience.

Some staff have begun to formalize this work through written policies or booklets (Pen Green Family Centre, 1990). However, as mentioned earlier, this kind of climate is more likely to be found in nursery settings than in reception classes. Sherman (1996, p. 74) found that reception class children describe their classrooms as places 'where conformity is essential and a systematic, paper and pencil style of teaching reigns'. These children knew that their schooling was to prepare them for the future but the future they describe

> is based on an education that is no more than practice for queuing, the development of an unquestioning attitude towards authority, the under-standing that to be the same is acceptable and to be different is not, and the acquisition of basic proficiencies in maths and languages that require little if no creative thinking and problem-solving ability. (Ibid., p. 74)

Three years after the introduction of the *Curriculum Guidance for the Foundation Stage* in England, many reception teachers still report that they are struggling against top-down pressure, and have not been able to implement fully the statutory guidance (Edgington, 2003; Adams et al., 2004).

Early years teams need clear aims and expectations for children's personal, social and emotional development and need to give these high priority when children start in their setting. They also need regularly to assess the progress the children are making to see how far all children are being helped. Pascal and Betram (2002) assert that, if we wish children to develop as lifelong learners, it is vital to assess their emotional well-being and their dispositions to learning. (See Chapter 6 for further support with assessment.)

Interacting with adults

Children need to be able to approach adults and use them as a resource. This is why the initial personal contact with early years staff is so important.

Some children find sharing their 'special adult' with other children very difficult, especially if they have been used to a close one-to-one relationship with an adult at home. Paul had been brought up on a farm on the fringes of a northern new town. He was the only child of older parents and had spent most of his pre-school life in the company of adults. He found it difficult to relate to the other children in his class who all lived in the new town and did not share his enthusiasm for farming. Consequently, he stayed very close to his teacher's side during his first few weeks at school and needed a lot of support to develop relationships with his peers.

Some children relate happily to the other children but are less confident about approaching the staff. Claudia, an articulate child with her peers and mother, refused to speak to any adult in the setting. The staff had to wait patiently for her to feel comfortable with them. They were careful not to pressurize her by asking questions, but talked to her in the course of activities. One day, nearly three terms after she had been admitted, Claudia started to talk to her teacher as if she had been doing so all her life and from that day onward there was no stopping her. In this case patience was rewarded. If the staff had put pressure on Claudia in any way it is unlikely that this outcome would have been achieved.

Children have to learn to share adult time. They have the right to expect that they will receive some individual attention, but have to learn that others have the same right. Some of the disruptive or withdrawn behaviour which children exhibit is their attempt to gain attention from the adults. It is not surprising that this behaviour is more common, and sometimes more extreme, in reception classes where there are fewer adults to respond to the children. Rather than blame the children for their behaviour, we should recognize the effect of placing such young children in large groups with poor staffing ratios. All young children have a right to adult attention and they will not get what they need unless they are placed in groups which conform to national guidance for nursery classes (i.e. at least one teacher and one qualified nursery nurse for every 26 children). When reception teachers ask how they can meet the children's needs when they are working alone with 30 pupils they (and the governors and headteachers who have put them in this situation) have to be told firmly that they cannot. It is very clear that at least two trained adults are needed to implement the indoor and outdoor Foundation Stage curriculum effectively, and less generous ratios must not be condoned. In 2000 the Education and Employment Committee recommended (p. xiv) that 'the adult:child ratio should be no more than fifteen-to-one in Reception and Year 1 classes'.

Helping all children to establish positive relationships with adults

It is easy to make the mistake of responding to children on demand. This enables some children (the more dominant ones) to take up most adult time at the expense of the quieter, less demanding ones. It is the teacher's responsibility to ensure that she monitors how she and her team spend their time – where, with whom and for what purpose.

Children need an environment where staff have time to listen to their concerns and where they are encouraged to use adults as a resource. Adults need to be free (at least some of the time) from the management and control of resources and activities, and children need to be encouraged to develop their own interests using readily available and accessible materials.

Children very quickly learn whether or not it is worth trying to tell an adult something. They are not likely to engage in conversation with an adult who is constantly 'busy'. On the other hand, they are very likely to approach again the adult who expresses an interest in their activities, and who shares her experiences with them. This kind of equality in interaction offers children a secure base from which to develop the confidence to tell, ask, question and discuss. The development of communication skills will be discussed later in this chapter.

Learning to care and take responsibility

Children starting in the Foundation Stage need to understand that they are responsible for their own actions and choices, and that they share a collective responsibility for the environment and equipment. As they get older, the children are helped to empathize with and take some responsibility for younger members of the group.

Children will only learn to take responsibility if they are given responsibility. Teachers, who with their teams, have organized their classes to encourage greater autonomy and independence, have often been surprised by the children's achievements. They have seen that children do live up to adult expectations (Miller, 1997) – even though they may sometimes make a mistake or not realize the consequence of their actions. Similarly, parents are often surprised to discover that their child can cope with self-help tasks, such as going to the toilet, dressing and undressing, etc. However, patient support from adults is crucial.

Taking responsibility for own actions and choices

Whichever social group we belong to, certain individual and collective responsibilities are inevitable. Children should be encouraged to make choices but need to learn that they are responsible for the outcomes of these choices. They need to understand that the choices they make should not limit the options of others. They also have to learn that they share responsibility for maintaining a clean, orderly environment.

For example, when they have finished using a piece of equipment, they are expected to put it back ready for the next child. If they choose to work with art materials, they are expected to clean up the area when they have finished and, if they play with sand, they need to sweep up any spills. These responsibilities are seen by teachers as a central part of life in a Foundation Stage setting. The beginning of each new term is spent reminding the older children of expectations they may have forgotten during the holidays, and supporting the new children as they adjust to the new social situation.

Young children generally enjoy taking on adult responsibilities. At home they enjoy helping their parents with household chores, such as washing up or dusting. Teachers and nursery nurses who see tidying up as a powerful learning experience are able to build on this natural enthusiasm and turn chores into fun for adults and children alike.

The learning environment has to be resourced in such a way that it enables children to take responsibility for 'their' setting. Everything must have a permanent, clearly marked place. Labelled storage areas ensure that children can quickly see where to return equipment and they take great pride in doing this and great delight in telling when someone gets it wrong. Brooms and mops with short handles enable children to clean up safely (e.g. without poking someone in the eye with long handles), and dustpans and brushes and cloths strategically placed encourage them to tidy up for themselves. Children need to be shown how to brush sand into the dustpan, and how to wipe up spilt water with a cloth, but they are remarkably quick learners if shown what to do. In one nursery school, a bucket with a small amount of water and a sponge was placed near the painting easels and children were taught to squeeze out the sponge and wipe down the easel when they had finished painting. This became part of their painting routine and the children generally took great pride in completing this task without getting water on the floor. This pride was encouraged by the staff, who praised and encouraged the children's positive achievements and dealt sympathetically with their mistakes.

This approach is based on the belief that children are capable, and that learning to take responsibility does not have to be a battleground where adults demand and children resist. It also recognizes that some children find taking responsibility harder than others. Many teachers report that girls are keener to be involved in cleaning and tidying than boys. This is not surprising in view of the adult male and female role models most children see around them. Staff need to ensure that the willing girls are not always the ones to clean up and that all children see these responsibilities as a part of their life in the group. In some settings the whole group is drawn together just before tidying up time and responsibilities are allocated to ensure that everyone takes a full role in the process.

Teachers also have to be aware of what can realistically be expected of each child. A new child who has just got out all the bricks would get maximum help from the adult while being expected to be involved in the tidying-away process, while an older, experienced child doing the same thing would be expected to clear away with much less support. The important aim is to encourage each child to take at least some responsibility for the consequences of his or her actions and choices.

The main tidying up happens at the end of a session when both staff and children are tired. For this reason plenty of time needs to be given so that the tasks can be undertaken in a relaxed manner, and humour and fun need to be injected into the proceedings. Children will get involved more willingly in clearing away a huge amount of bricks if an adult approaches the task with enthusiasm and leads them in singing to the tune of 'The farmer's in the den':

> We're clearing up the bricks,
> We're clearing up the bricks,
> Ee ei addy oh,
> We're clearing up the bricks.
>
> Darren's got some square bricks,
> Darren's got some square bricks,
> Ee ei addy oh,
> Darren's got some square bricks. (etc., etc.)

Tidying up like this takes longer than if the adult were to do it unaided, but it is time well spent, and by the time children transfer to Key Stage 1 classes they are generally very competent and responsible. It is essential that this competence is recognized, encouraged and further developed in the primary school. Many nursery teachers have in the past expressed dismay when they see the competent, independent children they worked with being made dependent again in reception and/or Year-1 classes. However, since the introduction of the Foundation Stage and the Primary Strategy (DfES, 2003b), some schools are developing environments and teaching approaches for Key Stage 1 children, which build on effective Foundation Stage practice and enable children to transfer, and develop, the skills they have acquired in their first years of schooling.

Taking responsibility for the environment

Children learn to take pride in their environment through the discussions they have with the team while tidying up and cleaning. For example, children who attend for the morning session or all day are encouraged to 'make the nursery look nice for the afternoon children'. As they play they are encouraged to think about actions which may damage or have already damaged equipment: 'Is it a good idea to bury the magnifying glass in the sand? Look what has happened to it.' Young children cannot be expected to know that some equipment is fragile and need adults to explain and discuss the reasons why this is so. Children can understand that some resources can be used creatively whilst others have to be used in one correct or safe way.

Involving children in ordering equipment, talking about it when it arrives and explaining that some pieces of equipment cost a lot of money and/or need very careful handling, all help the children to understand something of the cost involved in their education, and of their responsibility in relation to the care of resources. Often, though, they have to learn the hard way. Being deprived of the cassette recorder for several weeks while it was repaired, because someone had forced all the buttons down at once and jammed the controls, was a powerful learning experience for one group. On its return they were reminded of what had happened and why, and shown again how to use the machine properly. The thought of not being able to listen to story tapes for another long spell was an effective incentive not to mistreat the tape recorder, and older children were observed to be carefully monitoring the behaviour of younger ones.

This kind of caring attitude towards equipment will only develop if adults act as role models. If no one seems to care whether a puzzle is put away with pieces missing, or that a book is torn or that all the pencils are blunt, then neither will the children. Adults who talk to children about maintenance tasks will encourage them to be vigilant too. They will quickly learn to bring broken equipment to the adults' attention and will enjoy being involved in its repair. If puzzles with missing pieces are left out where everyone is reminded of them, the pieces are much more likely to materialize than if the puzzles are put back on the shelf incomplete.

Through this involvement young children learn that equipment has its cost, that there is not an unlimited supply and that it must be respected and looked after. Early years teachers are extremely resourceful. They are often to be found looking in skips and outside shops to see if they can find any safe, useful recycled materials for the children to use. This resourcefulness is transferred to the children in the classroom.

A modelling session had come to an end and the teacher was encouraging the children to tidy away a wide range of materials. On the table where the children had been working were several boxes, pieces of cardboard tubing and scraps of paper and fabric. The teacher asked the children to 'think whether any of these pieces are big enough for us to use another day'. She encouraged the children to keep useful materials and throw away any pieces which were too small or too messy with paint and glue. In this way she turned a routine chore into an interesting sorting activity, encouraging the children's mathematical awareness as well as sharing with them her concern about not being wasteful.

This can be extended to involve children in thinking about improving the environment they live in. Involving children in the development of an attractive outside play area helps them to understand that we have the power to improve our environment. Planting flowers, growing vegetables and picking up litter all help children to take a pride in and take responsibility for their living environment.

Care and respect for living creatures

While investigating and improving their outdoor play space children inevitably come across a variety of small creatures. Some children are afraid of spiders, flies, beetles and so on, and others are fascinated and want to hold them. Teachers have the opportunity to create a culture where all living creatures are valued by sharing in children's interests and helping them to gain an understanding of the needs of particular insects. An important early lesson is that insects are tiny and our hands are big! Children need to understand that insects can be harmed during handling and that it is best to look at them through a magnifying glass.

If children decide that stamping on insects is fun, then teachers can talk to them about the need to respect life. The most effective way of fostering respect for living things is to create a natural habitat for minibeasts. Many Foundation Stage settings have established 'wild areas' in the grounds where wild flowers and plants are grown to attract butterflies, and where logs and large stones are provided as homes for other creatures. Carefully lifting logs and stones provides a structured opportunity for learning about minibeasts, and for talking about the need to respect their home environment.

Some teachers offer children the opportunity to care for pets such as rabbits, guinea pigs, gerbils or hamsters in the class. This can only be done if staff and parents all understand the need to commit themselves to caring for these animals at school and during the holidays. Children benefit greatly from having the opportunity to take responsibility for the care of a creature much smaller than themselves.

Learning to care for and respect the rights of small creatures is directly relevant to care and respect for other humans. Children are less likely to bully within a caring environment of this kind and more likely to want to care for and help younger, smaller members of their social group. The teacher helps children to express their own feelings and empathize with the feelings of others. The child who puts an arm around another child, who has fallen and scraped her knee and is crying, and says 'That really hurts, doesn't it?' is remembering what falling felt like. Similarly, the older child who tells a new child, who has just started to miss her parents and has started to cry, 'You want your mummy don't you? She'll be here in a minute', is probably remembering her own separation experience.

This kind of responsibility is both reassuring and empowering. Children are reassured that other children feel as they do, and delight in offering comfort and support. They are even more delighted when they can offer comfort and support to adults. Often adults try to hide their feelings for fear that small children will be unduly worried. The fact that adults are often not successful is a tribute to the observation skills of young children. They are very quick to notice when adults are behaving differently or when something is wrong. Obviously, there are some worries which it is unwise to share with children, but saying something like 'I didn't sleep very well last night and I feel grumpy this morning' or 'I've got a headache today and the noise you are making is making it worse', reassures children, and offers them an opportunity to help by, for example, being quieter. However, it is essential overall that adults work consistently with children and their families and do not allow moods or external influences to affect their relationships with them.

Learning to co-operate

Early years education is a co-operative venture founded on mutual respect and collective responsibility. Teachers aim for children to learn to play together co-operatively and to collaborate on tasks. This does not happen straight away. As Moyles (1989, p. 142) points out, children may pass 'through a process of spectating, peripheral play and parallel play before engaging fully in social play'. Sylva (2000, p. 133) recommends a move towards a 'more social curriculum' for young children.

The Primary Strategy (DfES, 2003b, p. 54) states that 'Citizenship in primary schools ... can have a powerful impact on behaviour, and teach children practical lessons about responsibility and respect and care for others'. 'Good citizens' were defined by Edgington (2002a, p. 26) as:

> those who feel connected to, and are motivated to make (in collaboration with others), a contribution to the community in which they live. They have a strong sense of responsibility to themselves, as well as to others, and show interest, respect and tolerance in their social relationships. They can show maturity by working for the common good, even if that is not what they originally wanted themselves.

Early years teachers aim to create within their Foundation Stage community an ethos and environment which positively encourage co-operative rather than solitary ventures and where children can begin to develop as 'good citizens'. Involving children and adults together in projects promotes the idea that doing things together is both fun and productive. Creating a 'hill' in an otherwise flat outdoor area involved children, staff and parents in planning and executing a major operation. No one had done such a thing before, so everyone was involved equally in making suggestions and solving problems, and took equal pleasure in the finished result. Just as large-scale projects need more than one person, so do some pieces of equipment. Teachers consciously select equipment to encourage co-operative play – for example, some will only buy wheeled toys which more than one child at a time can ride.

Children need to learn how to work together to complete a task – to be able to make plans together, offer ideas, listen to the ideas of others and solve problems. Given that many adults have not mastered these skills teachers have a complex role to play in supporting this learning. They have to help children to take the time to plan what they intend to do, including who will do what, encourage them to listen to each other and help them to deal constructively with frustration when things go wrong.

One of the ways to do this is by initiating projects in response to the needs of a small group. A group of four children wanted a 'fridge' in the home corner. Their teacher asked them to think about what they could use to make one, and helped them to work through the process of deciding what to use, and actually making the fridge. She offered support only when needed,

---

Monitoring behaviours: some points for discussion

To what extent are you encouraging children to operate autonomously?

- What is your attitude to the children? Do you really believe they can do things for themselves and take responsibility or, if you are honest, do you do things for them because it is quicker and requires less patience?
- Does your classroom organization encourage autonomy and independence, or does it make children dependent on adults?
- How much of your time is spent doing or getting things for children and/or telling them what to do? How much of your time is spent observing and listening to them? How much time do you spend explaining/reasoning/ conversing with them? (The best way of discovering the answers to these questions is to ask someone else to observe you.)
- When children are first admitted to your class how do you help them to become aware of
  - the choices available to them?
  - their responsibilities such as tidying up, respecting other children and caring for equipment? The daily routine? The rules for behaviour?
- How do you reinforce this awareness throughout the children's time in your class (particularly after holidays)?
- Are you clear about the kinds of behaviour you wish to encourage? How do you make sure that children are encouraged to behave in these ways, and guard against unintentionally reinforcing the kinds of behaviour you wish to discourage? (For example, if the aggressive children gain a disproportionate amount of adult attention, it may seem to the other children that this behaviour is worth imitating.)
- Do all adults working in your class work consistently towards the same aims? How do you involve parents in your approach?

How autonomous are the children?

- To what extent do children find constructive activities for themselves? Do they use their own initiative or wait to be told/ supported?
- Can all children find the equipment they need for themselves or do they have to ask adults? Can they clear away after themselves with/without support?
- Are the children able to use adults as a resource?

---

and this mainly involved making sure each child's suggestions were listened to, and encouraging them to think in more detail about the features of the model they were making, e.g. at one point she said 'My fridge at home has a special place for putting the eggs. Has yours?' This comment inspired the children to attach an egg box to the inside of the door with Sellotape, and then, because there were no eggs in the home corner, to make some with clay.

Developing social strategies involves children in a complex intellectual process, just as coming to terms with feelings does. It is only when the intellectual demands of this kind of learning are understood that the skills involved in Foundation Stage teaching are fully appreciated. If children do not develop positive attitudes and social competence, they will be less able to take advantage of the full range of opportunities for more academic learning.

The need for an appropriate curriculum

Some of the, arguably most important, components of an appropriate curriculum for young children have already been explored. Foundation Stage teachers encourage security, self-esteem, self-discipline and positive social interactions. They recognize that the personal, social and emotional development of each child underpins his or her overall attainment. They take responsibility for creating a positive environment, and for interacting with their pupils in such a way that all children feel valued and encouraged to make progress at their own rate. This does not mean that teachers are not interested in academic curriculum content.

The introduction of the National Curriculum and the desirable learning outcomes challenged teachers to demonstrate how the experiences they offer to 3–5-year-olds provide a foundation for later learning. Because the desirable outcomes were published without any real practice guidance, and with no examples of stages which might precede the outcomes, teachers were left to their own interpretations. The least well-trained teachers did not rise to this challenge and gave in to perceived or real pressure to work in inappropriate ways. These teachers were not in a strong position to implement the *Curriculum Guidance for the Foundation Stage*. In order to keep their perspective at times of change, teachers have constantly to remind themselves that young children need a curriculum which is appropriate to their current needs, and that early childhood education is not simply a preparation for the next stage. They need to remember the principles on which early childhood education is based (Bruce, 1997; QCA/DfES, 2000) and that, in the words of Holt (1989, p. 160), 'Learners make learning, learners create learning'.

The *Curriculum Guidance for the Foundation Stage* (QCA/DfES, 2000, p. 11) identifies that practitioners need to consider child development and how children learn effectively as well as curriculum content – the 'early years curriculum should be carefully structured. In that structure there should be three strands:

- provision for the different starting points from which children develop their learning, building on what they can already do;
- relevant and appropriate content that matches the different levels of young children's needs;
- planned and purposeful activity that provides opportunities for teaching and learning, both indoors and outdoors.'

In the rest of this chapter and the next, these strands will be further explored.

How do young children learn?

Since birth, children learn from their interactions with people and their environment. They learn a great deal about the world they live in, and are beginning to develop many of the skills they need to operate in their world. It is the task of the teacher to build on this past experience, to recognize and value what children already know and can do, and to support and extend their learning.

Foundation Stage teachers are privileged to work with children whose spontaneity, natural enthusiasm, curiosity and motivation make them a pleasure to teach. Approaches to the early years curriculum have developed to take account of how young children respond to the world they live in. Observations show that 3–5-year-olds need to:

- be actively (both physically and mentally) involved in first-hand experiences;
- use their senses to explore the environment;
- experiment with ways of using equipment, space and time;
- practise and refine their social and physical skills;
- talk about their experiences with others;
- set and solve their own problems (with and without support);
- observe, question and imitate others;
- represent their ideas in a range of ways using a variety of media;
- make connections between, and sense of, all aspects of their home, community and school experience;
- be offered a wide range of materials and experiences and the time to explore them in depth; and
- have access to adults who are interested and share in their experiences and achievements.

Skilled early years teachers have for many years developed a curriculum rooted in these natural qualities and needs. The approach to learning and teaching promoted for the Foundation Stage is entirely consistent with practice developed by these leading early years settings. There is now widespread agreement that young children will not learn effectively if they are expected to be passive recipients of a curriculum (David, Curtis and Siraj-Blatchford, 1992). They need first-hand experience, play and talk (Education and Employment Committee, 2000; QCA/DfES 2000; POST, 2000) and the early years curriculum must be planned and resourced to provide these experiences.

Teachers are also becoming more aware of the need to cater for different learning styles. Research by the Campaign for Learning (Rodd, 2001) indicates that children as young as 3 do exhibit preferred learning styles and that these appear to be developmental, with younger learners favouring a kinaesthetic or active style. This is followed by the visual and then auditory learning styles. Boys tend to respond positively to kinaesthetic learning opportunities. This means they will be particularly disadvantaged by an overemphasis on activities which involve sitting and listening. The *Curriculum Guidance for the Foundation Stage* (QCA/DfES, 2000, p. 16) urges practitioners to 'accommodate the different ways children learn by planning for the same learning objective in a range of different ways.'

If gender inequality is to be avoided, teachers also need to pay attention to emerging brain development research. Scans of young children's brains are indicating differences in the way boys' and girls' brains develop. Boys' brains generally develop more slowly in the first few years of life and it is therefore not appropriate to expect them to achieve the same as girls. This is particularly the case with literacy. Boys tend to have a thinner corpus callosum - the strip which links and aids co-ordination between the left and right sides of the brain – and their language is generally slower to develop. Many boys in the Foundation Stage will therefore find reading and writing more difficult than girls. In addition to stimulating experiences, all children need movement (involving both sides of their bodies), fresh air and drinking water to aid brain development.

The need for first-hand experience and play

Adults may not realize the importance of hands-on experience and play for human learning. Yet, when facing a new piece of equipment, most adults will admit to pressing a few knobs before consulting the manual or asking someone else. They will also admit that they are most likely to be receptive to learning how to use a new machine when they are motivated to do so (i.e. when they need to use it), and if a more experienced person supports them through the process. Most adults do not grasp things straight away and need time alone to practise and consolidate learning. It is often necessary to go back to the experienced person for advice. When adults are competent to use the machine (e.g. a computer) they are able to be creative and play with it. For young children, for whom so much knowledge is new and exciting and so many physical skills still have to be acquired, the need for exploration, experimentation and play is even more important. Interaction with a variety of materials in a range of physical and social contexts provides the perfect vehicle for learning because it naturally motivates young children.

Play, because it draws, and elaborates, on first-hand experience, is intellectually demanding. Vygotsky (1978, p. 102) asserts 'the child always behaves beyond his average age, above his daily behaviour. In play, it is as if he were a head taller than himself'. He regards play as 'a leading activity which determines the child's development' (Vygotsky, 1932, p. 552). However, the word 'play' is open to many interpretations, and early years teachers regularly complain that parents and their colleagues teaching older children think it is a soft option. Nursery teachers working in primary schools sometimes have to put up with sarcastic comments like 'have you had a good morning playing' from colleagues, or 'when is my child going to do some real work' from parents and, not surprisingly, feel dispirited. This is also the reason why many reception teachers feel they cannot allow the children to play – even when they know this is what the children need, and when research is warning that an early years curriculum 'which is too formal will lead to poorer performance, disincentives to learn and low self-esteem' (Sylva, 1997, p. 4).

A simple definition of play has been difficult to come by (Moyles, 1989), and may not even be a realistic aim (Smith, 1984). Bruce (1996, p. 7) sees play as being a part of 'the network of development and learning' which also includes first-hand experience, games with rules and representations. She argues that 'children make sense of what they have learnt through their play' (ibid.) and that 'play co-ordinates learning' (ibid., p. 8). This helps teachers to see that play is both one of, and a co-ordinator of, a range of learning strategies, and strongly emphasizes its importance in early years education. Jennie Lindon (2001, p. 2) defines play as including 'a range of activities, undertaken for their own interest, enjoyment or the satisfaction that results'. This is a useful working definition for the early years practitioner. Children must feel motivated and that they have ownership and control over their play. If an adult starts to take over the activity it stops feeling like play to the children (and often the adult finds herself playing alone!). Play must also be open-ended. There should be no required outcome for everyone to achieve. Instead, each child should be able to explore in his or her own way, and come to their own conclusions or achieve their own goals

The *Curriculum Guidance for the Foundation Stage* (QCA/DfES, 2000, p. 11) stresses that 'children do not make a distinction between "play" and "work" and neither should practitioners'. It states that 'well-planned play, both indoors and outdoors, is a key way in which children learn with enjoyment and challenge' (ibid., p. 25).

Play experiences involve children in a range of learning strategies. They offer children the chance to:

1   *Explore and discover*. During their play, children explore the properties of materials, find out how they behave and discover what effect they can have on them. This exploration involves all their senses as they handle, taste, smell, look at and listen to everything in their environment, and encourages the development of a range of physical skills. Young children also explore feelings during play (Hurst, 1997): they discover what it feels like to be the baby, mummy, dog, etc., and also get the chance to explore their own concerns, such as a hospital visit or the arrival of a new baby.

2   *Construct*. Before children can use materials creatively they have to learn how to put them together. Children enjoy joining Lego pieces together, or sticking paper and boxes together without any particular creation in mind. If asked by an adult what they have made they will sometimes think for a moment and say what they think the adult wants to hear, but it is usually the process and not the end product which is important to them. Similarly, children construct ideas about the world they live in based on their own first-hand experiences and observations. Listening to these ideas provides Foundation Stage teachers with valuable insights into a child's level of understanding.

3   *Repeat and consolidate*. Repetition is an important part of the learning process because it helps us to consolidate our learning. Children will often repeat the same activity over and over again to test out and consolidate skills – making a sand castle over and over again, or returning to the same role-play scenario day after day.

4   *Represent*. From a very early age children will use one object to represent another in their play, e.g. the rectangular brick used as a telephone. Much of what is required of children during the later stages of education depends on them being able to understand the use of one abstract symbol to represent another – the written word to represent the spoken word, the = sign to represent equals, etc. Young children's early representations, and their early scribbles, which they proudly tell us represent mummy or their name, are important signs of this developing understanding. It is perhaps this aspect of play's potential, which is most underestimated with some children (particularly 4-year-olds in reception classes) being expected to cope too early with formal approaches to abstract symbolism. Whitehead (1996, p. 71) warns that children need an environment where they are encouraged to represent their experiences in a wide range of ways. She argues that 'In the process of doing these important things young children become more literate; without these opportunities they are less literate' (ibid.).

5   *Create.* An important development occurs when children deliberately use and combine materials to create something they have seen (e.g. a house, bus, car, television, ticket machine, etc.) to use as what Bruce (1996, Ch. 6) calls 'places to play and props for play'. Selecting appropriate materials from the range available, fixing them together and seeing how they could be used involves children in complex physical and intellectual challenges – more so if they are working collaboratively with one or more other children to whom they have to explain their ideas.

6   *Imagine.* In their play, children take on a whole range of roles and enter a variety of imaginary situations. This can involve the re-creation and exploration of roles and situations within their direct experience, e.g. pretending to be mummy feeding the doll or child baby, and also entry into imaginary situations outside their first-hand experience, e.g. pretending to cross a crocodile-filled river. Moyles (1989) highlights the value of this kind of play in developing concentration and creative thinking.

7   *Socialize.* Although most children need to have opportunities to play alone and in parallel to other children, play is most challenging when they can talk and interact with others – both with their peers and adults. It is obvious that children need language skills in order to be able to socialize in play – perhaps less obvious is that they need to play to help them develop the language skills they need. This is because play, especially self-initiated play, inspires talk – witness the frustration on the face of the child who is unable to make herself understood to those she wants to share an exciting experience or discovery with. Play also allows children to take on different social roles – to be in charge, at least for a short time, in an adult-dominated world, or to be the baby and to have a safe forum for regression.

Play experiences will only reach their full potential if children are offered enriching first-hand experiences related to everyday living (e.g. visits, visitors, shared experiences) and if their imagination is fed with with stories, poems and songs. When adults say children cannot play they are actually highlighting their need for support and enrichment. Edgington (2002b) reminds us that children growing up in the twenty-first century have fewer opportunities to play outside with friends and are more strongly influenced by television, video, computer games and commercial toys than previous generations. In early years settings many young children need encourage-ment to become creative, imaginative and resourceful. Teachers need to ensure that they provide a range of open-ended resources such as wooden blocks, cardboard boxes and tubes, crates, and natural materials to encourage improvisation and innovation.

The role of talk

In the UK, compared with most other European countries, children are hurried towards reading and writing before many of them are fluent speakers (David, 1993). The role of talk (of speaking and listening) in young children's learning is often underestimated. Holdaway warned in 1979 that a 'traditional error of thinking about reading and writing was to see them as discrete subjects isolated from the world of language and spoken culture and then to teach them as if they had no relationship to listening and speaking' (p. 12) and yet this is what is happening to increasingly younger children in many Foundation Stage settings as teachers try to meet, often unrealistic, targets. Talk (i.e. a shared means of communication, which can include sign language) is vital in young children's development because it:

- enables them to communicate more accurately to others their feelings, ideas, hopes and expectations and to form positive relationships;
- enables them to make connections and to consolidate and extend their own learning – through trying to put their experiences or requests into words children extend their vocabulary and use previous experience to help themselves describe something new (e.g. Nicky wanted her grandmother to knit her a pink elephant and, because she did not know the word wool asked 'have you got any pink sewing stuff');
- is their main way of recording their learning and provides the foundation for literacy; and
- enables adults to tune into their thinking and developing understanding – helping with both planning and assessment.

Vygotsky (1986) asserts that it is impossible to separate language and thought, and that those who have a good grasp of language also have a sound ability to think. Teachers need to ensure that they create a talk-rich environment, which motivates children to speak and listen and which offers them the time and support they need to develop further. Beginner bilingual children need opportunities to use their home language when talking about their experiences – if they only have the chance to express themselves in their, at this stage, limited English their conceptual development will be underestimated by teachers. Amina could make scientific predictions to a bilingual support worker who spoke her language, but was only able to name some of the objects she was using in English. Her conceptual development, and ultimately her development in the use of English, depended on interaction with the support worker. Monolingual and bilingual support staff must work closely together when planning for and assessing language development.

Although most teachers are aware of children's need to talk they are not always confident when planning for or supporting language development. Coles (1996, p. 14) asserts that 'Teachers will have to radically overhaul their conception of their teaching role and will need specific curricular time to develop productive talking environments'.

Organizing for children's learning

There is now a clear recognition that children need a broad balanced curriculum and that areas of learning and development interlink and are interdependent (QCA/DfES, 2000). They need a balance of child-initiated and adult-led experiences.

The approaches to classroom organization and to the children's development as responsible, autonomous learners previously described have required teachers and nursery nurses to reassess their roles. Freed from many of the supervisory tasks they used to undertake, they should have more time to observe and listen to children and to extend and support child-initiated learning. Children learn as much (if not more) from their own self-imposed challenges as they do from those posed by an adult – indeed, adults can cut across children's self-motivation with insensitive intervention (Bruce, 1997).

The teacher has four main responsibilities when developing the Foundation Stage curriculum:

1   She must organize and resource the environment for learning through first-hand experience, play and talk.
2   She must demonstrate through her planning and organization her awareness of the potential for cross-curricular learning within the range of experiences she provides (see Chapter 6).
3   She must use her observations of children responding to the environment she has created to inform her interactions with them and her future planning (see Chapters 6 and 7).
4   She must organize her own and her team's time, so that all children and all areas of experience have access to adult support.

In this chapter, which is concerned with the creation of an ethos and environment for learning, the focus is on organization, resourcing and some aspects of planning – other areas of responsibility will be explored in following chapters.

Organizing for learning through first-hand experience, play and talk

How early years teams organize space, equipment and time reflects their priorities (i.e. what they value) and their attitude to young children's learning. Early years teams working in identical buildings can, and do, create totally different settings for children's learning. Some teams use difficulties associated with the building as an excuse for limiting the provision they make, while others see the same difficulties as a challenge to be tackled and overcome. Reception teachers sometimes say their rooms are too small to offer children access to play, but the real problem is that they have too many tables and chairs!

Blenkin and Whitehead (1996, p. 43) stress the need for the learning environment to encourage children's active involvement in their learning to 'enable them to develop their capacities to act upon the materials which are provided and the situations which they meet in a purposive way'. They also emphasize the need for children to be encouraged by the learning environment to set up their own inquiries and to make independent choices. This requires a shift away from the kind of closed organization where adults select and limit the experiences, to one which emphasizes the child's intrinsic motivation, choice and partnership between adults and children.

Developing a sense of community: some points for discussion

- Do all children express their opinions with confidence to adults and to other children?
- Do the children initiate conversations with adults? Do they ask the adults questions about their learning? Do they reason things through with an adult?
- Do children negotiate with each other and with adults – or do they dominate or allow themselves to be dominated?
- Do the children play co-operatively and show concern for other children's points of view? Which children can/cannot share and take turns?
- Are certain areas of provision dominated by some children, or are all children confident about using all areas?
- What would happen if you stood back at the beginning of the session and did nothing? Would all children cope? Which children would you need to support and how would you need to support them?

Organizing space and resources

Active learning requires space both in and out of doors – this is why small rooms, with no self-contained outdoor space, are totally unsuitable for young children. The way teams organize their classroom and outdoor area will either facilitate or hinder learning. Classroom sizes and outdoor areas vary, and teachers are challenged to make the best use of the space available. Clear principles or beliefs are important – teachers who believe that young children need to be active do not fill their classrooms with tables and chairs. It has become clear since the *Curriculum Guidance* was introduced that many early years practitioners only have a scanty view of what it entails to offer an environment which promotes independence and responsibility. It is also clear that the quality of the environment determines the overall quality of learning and teaching. It is no coincidence, therefore, that in the *Curriculum Guidance for the Foundation Stage* (QCA/DfES, 2000, p. 22) the definition of teaching starts with 'planning and creating a learning environment' and 'organizing time and material resources'.

Teachers need to decide with their team areas of provision to which they think children should have access in an ideal world. They then need to work out how they can best make these opportunities available in their own situation. Even though the world is not ideal, it is essential to establish a vision, to avoid settling for second-rate provision, and to give a focus for future development. The vision may not be achieved immediately or ever, but at least there is something to strive towards. Teams who approach decision-making in this way are likely to achieve more for the children than those who start from the physical environment and allow that to limit their aspirations. Planning to create or re-create an environment provides a chance to think afresh about what would be the best for children. Visits to other establishments are essential to see other possibilities.

A list of provision for Foundation Stage children should include the following if children are to access a broad exciting curriculum:

- *A comfortable self-contained book area* where children can look at books; listen to stories read or told by adults or on tape; make up or retell stories using puppets or cut-out figures (with magnetic tape which can be used on a whiteboard); and experiment with writing using magnetic letters. Books should be invitingly displayed with some covers facing outwards if children are to make informed choices.
- *Sand (wet and dry) and water* with a range of accessible bought and improvised equipment. Labelled, stacking vegetable racks make space-saving storage for water and sand equipment, if shelf units are not available.
- *Malleable materials* such as clay, dough, cornflour and water, etc., with a range of utensils. Food preparation (e.g. making sandwiches or salads) and cooking opportunities should also be regularly planned.
- *A graphics area* to encourage mark-making and early attempts at writing. Children should see examples of a variety of scripts and of the different purposes of writing (e.g. letters, lists, forms, greeting

cards, menus, bus and train tickets). Home-made books, envelopes and order forms can supplement blank sheets of paper, and tools could include pencils, biros and felt pens. Office resources such as paper clips, staplers, Sellotape, ink pads and stamps can be added to extend experience.

- *Role-play areas* which enable children to experiment with different roles and relationships. It may be possible to have a permanent home corner and an additional role-play area such as a shop, hospital, clinic, café, etc., but, in smaller rooms, areas have to be alternated. Role-play areas should include as much real-life equipment as possible, which offers children opportunities to gain experience within all curriculum areas (i.e. phone directories, diaries, pads and pens, and recipe books to encourage early reading and writing, sets of cutlery, different-sized dolls and dolls' clothes for mathematics, etc.). Small-world equipment such as doll's houses, garages, railway, etc. also enable children to explore roles.
- *A creative workshop area* with a range of materials to choose from for painting, sticking, printing, joining, etc. Children should be able to develop their own creative ideas and should be given opportunities to select and mix media.
- *Music and movement opportunities* including singing, playing and listening to a range of home-made and bought sound-making instruments, and listening and moving to recorded music. Flowing dressing-up clothes, scarves and ankle or wrist bells can inspire movement.
- *Small and large construction materials* including bricks made from different materials (wood, plastic, foam), a variety of kits which connect in different ways and woodwork using real, small tools such as hammers, saws and screwdrivers.
- *Specific mathematical and scientific equipment* such as scales, matching, sorting and measuring equipment, games, puzzles, magnifiers, magnets, mirrors and collections of interesting things to handle (e.g. shells, buttons, pebbles, old radios, etc., to take apart). Children should also be able to explore growing and living things and technology such as a computer and/or programmable toys.
- *Interactive displays* relevant to what the children are learning about. These should include pictures, captions, artefacts to handle, books, etc. (see Chapter 7).

Teams should identify what kind of space each area needs – how much and what kind of space (e.g. floor, table), and what it could usefully be sited near. Taking into account all the physical limitations of the environment such as radiators, doors, etc., teams can start thinking about where in their room/s areas could be established, making some compromises if necessary, and what equipment should be included to give children cross-curricular learning opportunities.

The learning environment must be well organized. The room should be divided up into clearly defined areas – furniture and/or screens can be used to create boundaries – and equipment and materials should be stored in units and containers which children can access easily. Storage units should be labelled with pictures and words, and shelves can be marked out with silhouettes of the items to be placed there, to help children and adults see quickly where things belong. It is easier to maintain an orderly environment if teams avoid overcrowding areas or storage units. Where space is limited, it is more effective to offer a small selection of equipment, which is available every day, and then to add to this provision with carefully planned selections of materials which are rotated to give a variety of learning opportunities over a period of time. For example, one week water-play equipment could include a good selection of different-sized jugs, bottles, beakers, spoons and ladles to focus on filling and pouring, whilst the next week the focus could change to movement of water and the equipment could include bottles with holes in, sieves, tubing, water wheels, etc. Resources need not be expensive if good use is made of real household equipment and recycled materials such as plastic bottles, boxes, fabric, computer paper, etc. The more children are involved in setting up and labelling areas the more they will understand staff expectations. Time will need to be spent helping children understand how the new environment works. Community Playthings (2002) and Lewisham Early Years Service (LEARN, 2002) have published helpful guides to developing learning environments.

Foundation Stage children are entitled to an outdoor curriculum. Planning the outside environment is therefore equally important (Ouvry, 2000; Bilton, 2002; 2004; Edgington, 2002b) and a similar process needs to be followed. The first task is to identify the strengths and weaknesses of the outdoor environment/s available (including safety issues) and to think about how strengths could be exploited and weaknesses overcome. For example, are there areas which are difficult to use or to supervise, which could be enclosed, for use only by small groups with an adult? Next, it is essential to plan use of space by thinking about the kinds of areas which need to be created and where each could be situated. Examples of the kinds of areas some teams have created include:

- *a defined quiet area* where children can be apart from the more boisterous activities (particularly important for younger children and those with special needs). Growing fragrant plants in this area provides an additional sensory experience;

- *spaces to be active and/or noisy* (e.g. to use wheeled toys, play ball, run and climb). These spaces need to be clearly defined so that boisterous activities do not inhibit other learning. Painting parking bays on the ground encourages children to put away their wheeled toys when they have finished using them;
- *places to hide in* – either natural (e.g. a space in the hedge or a willow tree), or created by staff (e.g. a tent or a blanket over boxes);
- *shady areas to shelter from the sun* – carefully sited trees or umbrellas and child-size garden furniture need to be included; and
- *areas to explore natural interests* (e.g. a wildlife area where children can carefully look for creatures under logs or stones; tubs or a patch for gardening; a digging area, a sand-pit).

Bilton (2002) provides useful guidance on developing zones in outdoor areas. Above all teachers should ensure that the outdoor environment is **natural**. If children only have access to rubber surfacing and plastic climbing frames they will gain few of the educational benefits of being in the natural world.

Once the area is established, similar types of provision as will be found indoors need to be developed outside. These need to be offered in a different, complementary way. For example a small trolley or tool-box can be filled with mark-making equipment (e.g. clipboards, paper, pens, pencils, rulers envelopes etc.) and made available on a daily basis outside to complement the graphics area indoors.

In very small outdoor environments it is not possible to have a full range of permanent areas every day, but they can be planned on a rotational basis over a week or so. Similarly staff can plan to visit other outdoor environments within the community (e.g. parks, city farm) to extend the children's experience of the outside world. Outdoor developments take time to establish and patience and stamina are required (particularly in areas where vandalism causes setbacks). Enlisting the support and vigilance of the local community can be helpful. In one nursery, vandalism decreased noticeably after pupils from a local secondary school had been involved in helping with the development of the garden as part of their technology course.

It is important to remember that outdoor experiences should not simply replicate what happens indoors and that children should be enabled to work on a more active, larger, messier and louder scale. They can:

- climb and gain first-hand experience of what it feels like to be up, down, under, over, inside, etc. – equipment should be selected to maximize opportunities to extend children's spatial awareness and to develop arm as well as leg strength;

- construct larger models with crates, tyres and big boxes as well as with large construction kits;
- paint with decorating brushes and rollers on large rolls of paper, or with water on walls or paving slabs;
- make pictures or patterns on the ground with large, smooth stones, logs, shells, etc.;
- see and feel the force of the wind using streamers, flags, windmills, etc.;
- dig in the earth with real, but child-size, tools and plant and grow vegetables and flowers;
- be part of a marching band playing percussion instruments, or make music by striking large metal pipes and saucepans hung from a wooden frame or washing line (one nursery team hung the pipes from an old wooden clothes horse);
- engage in role-play with more children (ideas for outdoor role-play contexts include a fire, ambulance or police station, a garage, a market stall, a building site, an airport, a drive thru' McDonalds or railway station, a camp site);
- squirt water from squeezy bottles and watch it flow down pieces of guttering or through plastic pipes; and
- blow bubbles and watch the wind move them. The list is endless. Basically early years teams need to think about the kind of experiences children are offered indoors and consider how these could be extended out of doors.

In order to consolidate and extend their learning, children need to know that they can return tomorrow to something they were playing with today (Lindon, 1997). Teachers report a dramatic increase in motivation and concentration when children are able to pursue a project or activity over several days at a time.

The quality of early years provision depends on the teacher's awareness of the need to maintain resources (both in quantity and condition), and of the importance of adapting and developing the provision in response to the children's use of it (Bruce, 1997). What children learn from using the provision also depends on the amount of time they are given to develop their ideas and the ways in which adults support play by valuing it and involving themselves in it.

Teachers developing Foundation Stage practice in reception classes have been challenged to develop the kind of environment and ethos, which has more usually been associated with nursery education, but which offers progression for the children. The following case study illustrates how one team used their nursery experience and their observations to review and develop an aspect of provision in ways, which inspired the children and raised standards of achievement.

Case study

Adamsrill Primary School in Lewisham has 451 pupils from diverse cultural and linguistic backgrounds. An above-average number are eligible for free meals and a high proportion have special educational needs.

Lynn Hand the Foundation Stage Co-ordinator writes:

I have been at Adamsrill School for 17 years, 11 years in my current role as an Early Years co-ordinator. I taught in Reception for nine years and in the Nursery for three years. I returned to teach in Reception in 2002. My experience of going back into Reception from Nursery made me reflect on my practice in Reception. My Nursery Nurse and I, having worked together for the last five years realized how different our attitude was to certain areas of the curriculum.

Developing provision for knowledge and understanding of the world – designing and making   We had previously selected certain tools each week and provided an activity – the table set up each day with resources with which we wished children to develop certain skills. From our time in the Nursery we had discovered, by making resources readily available and leaving the table blank, children began to plan for themselves and initiate their own ideas. We transferred this to Reception and found the children making a wide variety of things like picture frames which stood up, drink machines, jewellery, hobby horses, all their own ideas. We found that by allowing them to choose they would work in a group, of sometimes up to six, for at least 45 minutes to an hour on one model. This started to become an incentive for tidying up quickly as it meant that they had time to show their models to the rest of the class, talk about how they had worked together, who had contributed ideas and most importantly how it worked.

Key lessons learnt by adults   I now realize how important observing is and that the process of learning is not the finished product but the journey the child has taken to achieve it. I have also realized that the provision of good quality resources and appropriate time given for children to express themselves and develop their ideas results in learning. The adult's role is to observe children, how they learn and to provide the right atmosphere for them to grow.

Organizing time

A key element within the action research described in the case study above was the management of time. In this reception class, children were able to spend 'at least 45 minutes to an hour' developing their own ideas and projects. In spite of the introduction of the Foundation Stage, reception teachers still complain that whole-school routines impinge on their ability to offer children uninterrupted time to work in depth. Nursery teachers have usually developed a more fluid daily routine. They have tended to offer children more choice in how they use time and have therefore achieved a more effective balance of child-initiated and adult-led activity. Siraj-Blatchford et al. (2002) found that the excellent settings in their study tended to achieve an equal balance between child-initiated and adult-led experiences. Time is used flexibly to enable children to pursue interests at length and in depth, and to decide for themselves when they want to play outside, have their milk or go to the toilet. Reception teachers need to build on the foundations laid by their nursery colleagues and consider carefully if and when children should attend assembly and PE, and whether they need a 'play-time' if they have access to an outdoor learning environment.

Of course routine is important. Children need to understand the structure of the day so that they can make informed choices rather than random ones. They need to know, for example, that if they start building here now, they will have to clear everything away in 10 minutes because lunch will be served in that area.

The routine should be more concerned with the establishment of flexible daily patterns rather than with set times for whole-group activity. A whole-class approach is clearly not consistent with a developmental approach where individual needs are of paramount concern – as any teacher who has tried to get the attention of 25 3- and 4-year-olds at story time will confirm.

Because of their varying needs, young children should not be expected to conform within a large group, but should be able to operate at their own pace. A set drink or snack time has been replaced in many classes by a time-limited (e.g. for about an hour) self-service system where children can help themselves when they are thirsty or hungry and when they have reached a convenient time to break away from their activities. Often this involves the child in finding the drink with their name label and then posting the label when they have finished – a valuable literacy activity. Similarly, story times are now less likely to involve the whole class, and more likely to involve all members of the team offering stories to smaller groups at the set story times, and also to individuals at different points in the day. Teachers who understand children's needs are well able to resist requests from primary colleagues to take the whole class into assembly or PE from their first week in school. They resist because they know that it is these times out of their class which can cause most anxiety for young children. A gradual introduction to whole-school activities is essential.

Of all the daily routines, registration sessions (particularly if they are extended to include whole-class counting or sound recitation) can be the most time-wasting for young children. They can also cause anxiety for children who have found it hard to separate from their carer, or who are intimidated by the pressure of having to answer to their name. When young children arrive at school each day they, and the adult who brings them, need to receive a personal welcome. Staff taking register sessions cut themselves off from parents and carers and give a message that parents are not welcome to stay. Children separate more easily from their carer, if they can be supported by this familiar person to choose and get involved with an activity or experience. Their carer can be encouraged to ensure that the child registers him/herself on arrival. This usually involves finding his/her name label and putting it in the designated place (e.g. sticking it on a felt board with Velcro). Once the children have arrived, a member of staff quickly ticks off names on the register. This is much less time-consuming than sitting the whole class on a carpet, waiting for latecomers and calling names.

Flexible, fluid use of time enables all children to develop their own learning styles and patterns. If they are offered real choice within an environment, where staff value the full range of activities, children are encouraged to meet their own needs and invariably choose a broad experience for themselves over a period. The learning process often requires us to do things over and over again, and to do one thing before we tackle another. No one learns to order, so why is it that adults expect children to learn when they make them come and sit down and do something? If our motivation were taken away, and someone else's learning style imposed, we would be unlikely to learn, so why should children be any different? If the activities we initiate are interesting enough there will be no shortage of children wanting to take part.

Some less experienced teachers worry that some children spend too much time at one activity. The answer to this concern is clear. If all areas of provision and all planned experiences are resourced to encourage cross-curricular learning, and staff are observing and extending the child's experience and thinking, there is really no problem. What these teachers are really saying is that they think some kinds of experience are less valuable than others – they are unaware of the many kinds of learning which can come from each experience and need to engage in the kinds of long-term planning outlined in Chapter 6. Skilled teachers encourage (through their resourcing and involvement) children to pursue their interests, and inspire them to extend one interest into another (see Chapters 6 and 7).

Another aspect of time which some teachers worry about is time spent out of doors. Some supposedly early years trained teachers are still leaving college with only a hazy view of the importance of outdoor play, and those who trained originally to teach older children may not understand that young children need more than a playtime to 'let off steam'. Some put their ignorance or negative attitude into practice by limiting the amount of time children are able to use in the outdoor area (in extreme cases this can be as little as a 20-minute playtime with all the children having to go out at once). There are many reasons why this is regrettable and they are worth outlining here:

1   Three and 4-year-olds are growing and gaining control over their body movements. Fine motor skills involving the use of pencils, hammers and rulers are generally acquired later than, and are refined from, gross

motor skills such as running, jumping and climbing. If we want children to develop one set of skills, we must give them opportunities to develop the others. Movement aids concentration and brain development.

2   Young children growing up today are often denied opportunities for safe, outdoor activity. In cities many children live in flats with no garden, and the parks are full of broken glass and dogs' mess, while those living in rural areas are often driven everywhere (ESAC, 1989; Education and Employment Committee, 2000). In all areas, worries about traffic and children being abducted are very real and most parents will not let their children out of their sight. The challenges involved in vigorous outdoor play in the early years setting are, therefore, more important than ever – most children do not have the outdoor opportunities their parents enjoyed and benefited from when young (Edgington, 2002b).

3   A rapidly growing number of young children is overweight or obese. This is believed to be due to a lack of exercise and to the increased consumption of junk foods with high fat and sugar content. Attention to diet and increased opportunities for vigorous physical exercise are recommended to promote healthy heart development

4   Some learning can only take place out of doors. Work on a large scale, such as construction, painting and role-play involving a large group, requires space. Environmental studies, such as gardening, noting and experiencing weather changes, studying living creatures in their natural habitats, are also only possible outside.

5   All other learning can happen as well outside as inside as long as the provision is made for it. For some children who, because of the cramped accommodation they live in, or because they are kinaesthetic learners, thrive on playing out of doors and are reluctant to come inside. In the interests of equality of opportunity it is vital that rich, cross-curricular provision is made in the outside area. It is certainly not productive to make these children come inside – unless we want to make them resentful. Teachers need to stop regarding an early years setting as inside and outside and see it as one learning environment – this is certainly how children see it. This position is supported by the growing recognition that primary children also need to learn out of doors and many schools have been developing their playgrounds to offer a more productive educational environment. (Learning through Landscapes, 1990).

Time needs to be carefully planned to maximize staff involvement in children's learning. Children need extended periods of time (at least an hour) when they can choose whether they work in or outside, as this enables them to make links between indoor and outdoor learning and offers staff the chance to work with small groups. If the children all have to go outside at the same time, space becomes overcrowded, supervision is difficult and learning opportunities are lost. Outdoor experience is just as important in winter as in summer – it is inactive adults who feel cold, not children! Many early years settings are investing in all-weather clothing to enable children and adults to learn outside throughout the year (see Figure 5.1).

Teachers need to consider the issues raised here to see if they can professionally justify the way they organize space, resources and time. The crucial question is am I organizing for the convenience of staff or to suit our inflexible attitudes, or because of what I know children need? Reception teachers in particular need to review their practice to ensure that it conforms to the *Curriculum Guidance for the Foundation Stage* (see Chapters 2 and 3 for ways of doing this).

Exploring the wider outside world

Some of the most innovative settings, inspired by the Forest School movement in Denmark, are enabling their children to have the opportunity to experience the freedom of exploring forests and woods. These developments have been prompted by the recognition that children today do not have the same freedom to play outside as previous generations.

Becky Wood describes how this was achieved at Wingate Community Nursery School in County Durham.

Figure 5.1 *At Wingate Community Nursery School, County Durham all children and adults have access to all-weather clothing*

In 1999 the staff from Wingate Community Nursery School visited Denmark to learn about their pre-scool provision. There were certain memorable visits, which had significant impact on our own practice. Arriving at Spilloppen Pre-School Centre one cold, wet morning, we were met by a group of eight children with two staff, a man and a woman. They were setting off for a day in the forest, with their cart loaded with the materials and food they would need to build a shelter and cook their midday meal in the woods. For the Danish group this was a normal regular experience, but for us it gave a powerful message about competent children in their natural environment.

Several days later we visited an outdoor after school facility for 7–11-year-old children. It was a large, interesting site with woodland, a river and a hilly pasture. Here we saw 100 children with 10 adults, mostly men, deeply engaged in a huge range of challenging, real activities: building rafts, making fire, imaginative play in tree houses, exploring nature in an outdoor wooden classroom, creating an obstacle cycle course, and talking together respectfully and confidently. We were moved as we compared these children thriving in a stimulating open-air environment, with similar aged children in the UK, practising for their SATs in stuffy classrooms as the spring sun shone outside.

These experiences strongly reinforced for us our existing belief that children need space, time and opportunities to play and learn freely outside. We already offered our children open access to the school garden and regularly went for walks to the woods, but we were now determined to take the woodland experience that step further and establish our own Forest School.

The Danish Forest School philosophy was introduced 20 years ago to encourage children to have an appreciation of the natural world and develop a sense of responsibility for the conservation of nature. Children gained confidence in the stimulating woodland environment, with very positive developments in their social skills and behaviour too.

Fully committed, we explored training opportunities and sought the funding to facilitate this. Bridgewater College, Somerset, has developed a unique BTEC Advanced Award in Forest School Leadership, which we found we could access through an intensive condensed training course.

Two members of staff, Kath and Glynis embarked upon the programme which involved residential training, outdoor first aid training, major assignments, keeping six-week detailed logs and on-site assessments. Of course, qualifications are of no use without a piece of woodland!

We wanted our Forest School to be within walking distance of the nursery, so that it would be easily accessible for the children. We were very soon in discussions with a very supportive, benevolent landowner, who was extremely enthusiastic about the great benefits to be gained from the Forest School. There followed discussions about insurance, liability, rights, access and agreements, which are all very real issues given the potentially high-risk situations that children may experience. The whole school staff participated in the selection of 'the perfect wood', an acre of mixed woodland, 20 minutes' walk from the nursery, and Kath and Glynis began the task of clearing some of the undergrowth and briars to make it more accessible to the children. Regular risk assessments are an integral part of Forest School, where safety of the children is paramount. Parents were involved in the initiative from the beginning and were kept updated with each small step that we took. We talked with them about the educational value of the Forest School, emphasizing the benefits to be gained, calming any concerns they had and gaining their written consent.

Figure 5.2 *Wingate: into the woods*

Towards the end of the summer term, parents are invited to join the children in a Family Day, when the children demonstrate their new woodland skills!

Each week two staff with eight children visit the Forest School, whatever the weather (see Figure 5.2). All children are given this opportunity, with the possibility of a whole day for the enthusiasts. The children quickly learn to respect their environment and the boundaries within which they need to work – rules, expectations of behaviour, respect for each other and working together. Within the rules laid down to ensure their safety, the children have a real sense of freedom as they are encouraged to move away from close adult interaction and become more responsible for each other and for themselves.

They explore and use natural materials they find in the woods, sometimes building a fire with the sticks they find. They collect and observe, use real tools for real purposes and recall their experiences back at nursery. Each week a range of structured, achievable activities is planned and offered to the children in the woods. As their confidence and competence grows, the children will take on more responsibility for their activities. The walk to the woods is just as important for the children's physical development and understanding about their community, as the woodland activities themselves.

The freedom and independence that we can give children in the woods is unique. When we respect them and see them as competent people, children gain independence and the ability to organize themselves and their environment. They are able to make choices, to be flexible and cope with change, to have positive self-esteem and take responsibility for themselves and their actions. Giving our children self-confidence, emotional well-being and a sense of self-worth is probably the most powerful, lasting asset that we can offer.

In this case study an individual school took the initiative, but in some areas, such as Oxfordshire and Kirklees (Lockett, 2004), local authority personnel have developed forest school programmes, which a variety of settings can access.

The teacher's intentions

The Foundation Stage teacher's responsibility goes beyond merely putting out a range of materials for the children. Through her planning she makes clear her intentions for the children's learning. Only if teachers and their teams have clear intentions for the children's learning will they make rich provision and see the potential for development. Well-planned provision guides children towards the things we want them to learn, but they also have their own ideas.

Many teachers, having observed children beginning to operate autonomously and use the learning environment in creative ways, have recognized the importance of being flexible and allowing children to move equipment between areas where practical, since in the words of one teacher 'this allows children to create their own broad curriculum'. In this way, children would not be discouraged from filling shopping bags (from the home corner) with recycled boxes (from the art and craft workshop area), and taking them outside for a picnic, as long as they put them away again at the end of the session. Observation also gives staff clues about their provision – the

---

The organization of learning experiences: some points for discussion

To what extent does the learning environment you are offering indoors and out encourage children to

- become actively involved in first-hand experiences?
- engage in sensory exploration?
- set up their own experiments with a wide range of materials and equipment?
- practise and repeat their developing skills?
- work in depth over extended periods of time indoors and out (including the chance to continue tomorrow something started today)?

- converse and share ideas with other children and adults?
- set and work through their own challenges and problems, observe, ask questions, and learn through imitation of others who have more experience?

What kinds of experiences do you think children should have access to daily, weekly, occasionally? Why? Take a critical look at the provision you are making from the child's point of view – why are things organized in this way? Are you making best use of space, resources and time, i.e. best for children? Can you think of other ways of organizing?

To what extent does the learning environment you have created reflect the personal interests and previous experience of the children in your class? How do you ensure that high standards of provision are maintained?

How do you regard the outdoor provision? Do you see it as an extension of the classroom or as a less important area where children 'let off steam'? Do you feel it is only for summer use or do you value it all year round?

Ask yourself honestly: what messages are you giving children about the activities you value and those you regard as less important by the provision you make and by your own involvement in activities? How do you encourage all children to take advantage of the broad range of opportunities on offer indoors and out? (Without coercion!) How could you offer a broad, balanced curriculum to those children who choose to spend most of their time out of doors?

How could you use your observations of children more effectively to inform organization?

---

children who regularly took dough from the dough table to the home corner were giving their teacher a message about how they wanted to extend home corner play, and the teacher responded by making dough available in the home corner and organizing cooking activities there from time to time. The teacher needs to keep an open mind to prevent stifling creative thinking or imagination – these are the qualities children will almost certainly need in their adult lives.

Further reading

Adams, S., Alexander, E., Drummond, M.J. and Moyles, J. (2004) *Inside the Foundation Stage – Recreating the Reception Year*, Association of Teachers and Lecturers, London.
Bilton, H. (2002) *Outdoor Play in the Early Years*, 2nd edn, David Fulton, London.
Bruce, T. (1996) *Helping Young Children to Play*, Hodder and Stoughton, London.
Community Playthings (2002) *Spaces*, Community Playthings, Robertsbridge.
Edgington, M. (2002) *The Great Outdoors*, Early Education, London.
Featherstone, S. (2001) *The Little Book of Outdoor Play*, Featherstone Education, Lutterworth.
Featherstone, S. (2003) *The Little Book of Outside in All Weathers*, Featherstone Education,

Lutterworth.

Featherstone, S. and Bayley, R. (2001) *Foundations for Independence*, Featherstone Education, Lutterworth.

Fisher, J. (2002) *Starting from the Child*, 2nd edn, Open University Press, Buckingham.

LEARN (2002) *A Place to Learn*, London Borough of Lewisham, London.

Lindon, J. (1999) *Too Safe for their Own Good*, National Children's Bureau, London.

Lindon, J. (2001) *Understanding Children's Play*, Hodder and Stoughton, London.

Ouvry, M. (2000) *Exercising Muscles and Minds*, National Children's Bureau, London.

 ## Website

Contact Learning through Landscapes at www.ltl.org.uk.

6

Keeping records: planning and assessment

The *Curriculum Guidance for the Foundation Stage* promotes a flexible and responsive approach to curriculum planning and assessment. It emphasizes that the curriculum should be developed in response to, and to cater for, the varied needs, interests and learning styles of the children. Assessment, including the statutory *Foundation Stage Profile*, must be based on evidence gained from observation (QCA/DfES, 2000; QCA/DfES, 2003). This clarification of approaches to record-keeping has been widely welcomed within the early years field. It is now recognized that a ticklist approach to assessment can narrow the curriculum in favour of those skills which are easily seen, and does not take into account the wonderful spontaneity or creativity of young children. Nor does it allow for the child who, in using materials or expressing ideas in unexpected ways, demonstrates levels of thinking way beyond our expectations. Three to 5-year-olds regularly give strong messages through their behaviour and comments, which teachers can either learn from and act on or ignore.

Just because teachers offer learning experiences does not necessarily mean that children will learn, and just because children do not seem to learn in one context does not mean they are incapable of learning. Teachers must observe and listen to children in a range of contexts in order to challenge their own assumptions. If they do not do this they run the risk of switching children off from learning.

A developmental approach

The highest priority must be given to the needs and development of the individual child. The teacher needs to value the contribution each child makes – to recognize that she does not have a monopoly on knowledge about children, or about the kind of approach to learning which will work best for an individual child. She can gain clues from other adults who know the child, and from the child him or herself.

Teachers' own learning will have been inhibited in some ways, which may limit their view of the possibilities for learning available to children. For example, teachers' negative feelings about subjects such as science, or about the value of learning through play, can limit their approach to curriculum planning. Similarly, teachers who hold negative views of children from particular social or cultural backgrounds may see these children as incapable of achieving high standards. Many teachers find that exploring and discovering alongside, and from, young children can be the most effective way of reversing their own negativity and prejudices.

A developmental approach demands that teachers learn from others (both adults and children), and that they regularly test out, through observation, their assumptions about children and the provision they make. Observation has traditionally been a feature of effective early years practice. However, the *Study of Pedagogical Effectiveness in Early Learning* (Moyles, Adams and Musgrove, 2002, p. 132) found that:

> Developmental records are more common than formative or diagnostic records and these show minimal links to planning for individual children. The links between planning>assessment>recording and the cyclical process of using records to inform planning and assessment of progression, appear not to be well understood or well used in many settings.

Although this study included the full range of early years settings, not all of which would employ qualified teachers, it is clear on training courses that many teachers, particularly those working in reception classes, need considerable support to develop an approach to record-keeping which is consistent with national expectations. The *Foundation Stage Profile* was introduced late in the 2002/03 academic year and many teachers did not have the evidence they needed to make secure judgements about children's stage of development. There is a danger, because of this unfortunate start, that the Profile statements will be seen as a checklist, which could seriously narrow both assessment and the curriculum. During the 2003/04 academic year, there is anecdotal evidence that some reception class teachers are only assessing what is on the profile and are narrowing their teaching accordingly. Some are also seeing the Profile as being the only record they need and are therefore not building up a full enough evidence base. It is to be hoped that this will be challenged by the moderation process.

Why keep records?

Groups of early years staff identify the following main reasons for keeping records:

1 *To find out about children as individuals.* Focusing on each child's personality, life experience, learning style, interests, developmental characteristics. Celebrating each child's successes and achievements.
2 *To monitor the progress (or lack of it) of individual children.* Ensuring that all children make progress whatever their starting point. Children's achievements need to be regularly reviewed so that plans can be made to support progress and any special educational needs can be identified.
3 *To inform curriculum planning.* Recognizing that planning and assessment are interrelated ensuring that one influences the other. Teachers need to discover how the curriculum they have offered has been received and to use this information to help them plan future approaches. Record-keeping highlights the difference between the intended and the received curriculum – the difference between what teachers plan for children to learn, and what children actually learn.
4 *To enable staff to evaluate the provision they make.* Finding out how effectively they are working with the children. Concern about inequality has encouraged many teachers to monitor their policies and practice in order to identify possible discrimination (Lally and Hurst, 1992), and to ensure that they are providing a curriculum for equality (Siraj-Blatchford, 1994).
5 *To provide a focus for communication with others.* Using records to open up communication with other adults, such as nursery nurses, parents, speech therapists and infant teachers, and with the children. Record-keeping is seen by teachers as a shared initiative, to which everyone can contribute, and as a way of explaining and justifying their work to others who have the right to ask.
6 *To make the job more enjoyable.* Finding out about and talking about children enlivens the teacher's work. Children make the job worthwhile and provide, through their unexpected responses to adults and materials, the intellectual challenges, which make teaching young children the exciting, collaborative venture it undoubtedly is.

Although 'to monitor progress' is one of their reasons for record-keeping, few teachers feel comfortable with the idea of measuring children's attainment and giving numerical scores which can be used in later value-added analysis of children's progress. At the end of the Foundation Stage in

England, children are assessed and scored using a range of nine-point scales covering the six areas of learning within the Foundation Stage curriculum. Summary scores for each child are sent to local authorities and overall summary data, and a sample of child level data is sent by each LEA to the DfES.

Although there were no plans in 2003 to produce school performance tables showing either Foundation Stage outcomes or Foundation Stage to Key Stage 1 value-added data, many teachers are worried that inappropriate use may be made in the future of the scoring element of the Profile. They are also concerned that these scores are being used to set targets within the context of teachers' performance management. At the end of the Foundation Stage some children are still 4 years old (i.e. those born at the end of July and in August) whilst others born in September are almost 6. This age difference is very significant at this stage in a child's life, when human development is at its most rapid. It is unrealistic and unfair to expect these children to achieve similar standards. There is a danger that the Profile scores could disadvantage further the most vulnerable children in each group.

Teachers, and some parents, are rightly concerned that assigning numerical grades to children so young is meaningless and may lead to low expectations of some children who are developmentally less mature and who have significantly less life experience. Furthermore, if primary schools are motivated to show how much 'value' their teaching has added within the Foundation Stage and from the end of reception to the end of Key Stage 1, there is a danger that children will be scored as low as possible.

On the other hand some teachers are reporting that their performance management targets require them to ensure that a percentage of children achieve particular points on the scales (often the ninth point which is beyond the early learning goals) for literacy and numeracy by the end of the Foundation Stage. This is usually a panic reaction to low Key Stage 2 results and has involved working backwards to decide where children need to be at 5 if they are to achieve Level 4 or beyond at 11. Since each cohort of Foundation Stage children is likely to be significantly different from the last these targets are nonsensical. A few more summer born children, children with English as an additional language or special educational needs can make a dramatic difference at this stage.

It is more important than ever that early years teams do not lose sight of the real reasons for keeping records outlined above and that they ensure their practice matches these, rather than any externally imposed, purposes. Foundation Stage co-ordinators need to ensure (with the help of LEA advisers if necessary) that headteachers and assessment co-ordinators understand the complexity involved in assessing such young learners.

What information should records contain?

A potential weakness of any record-keeping system is an overconcentration on some children or some aspects of development at the expense of others. Team members need to be clear about what is to be recorded for each child, since only then can gaps be identified.

Taking the purposes outlined above into account, teachers have highlighted the need to keep a record of

1   each child's experience prior to school entry;
2   the learning opportunities and provision which are offered both to groups of children and individuals;
3   each child's social, emotional, physical and intellectual responses to the experiences offered;
4   the use of the available provision by the group as a whole (particularly noting whether children gain equal access to the curriculum on offer); and
5   each child's developing knowledge, skills and attitudes – what children know and can do at particular points in time and how they are approaching the learning process.

This information provides the basis from which teams can plan, implement and evaluate their practice and each child's experience.

Who should contribute to the records?

The teacher needs to encourage all members of the team to contribute to the assessment and planning process (QCA/DfES, 2001). Before admission, children may come into contact with parents and other close relatives, childminders or nannies, day nursery, pre-school, playgroup or toddler club staff, health visitors, social workers, speech therapists and GPs; while after admission many adults could be involved alongside teachers and nursery nurses (see Chapter 2).

Although all these adults may have valuable information to offer, the logistics of involving so many people in record-keeping leaves the teacher with a difficult, if not impossible, task. How each one makes a contribution will depend on who they are, and on the involvement they have had with the child. All the teacher can realistically do is get to know who is involved with each child, and create the kind of atmosphere and opportunities, which would encourage the sharing of information.

The teacher who shares her ideas and shows that she is interested in the ideas of others is likely to gain the broadest view of the children in her class.

She must accept that others have a valid point of view. If a teacher believes that parents cannot be trusted to tell the truth about their child, she closes off the possibility of finding out what the child does at home – and, in any case, there is almost certainly going to be more than one 'truth' for each child. Children often demonstrate skills at home, which they never display at school (Tizard and Hughes, 1984; Wells, 1986).

Just as parents like to hear about their child's achievements at school, so should teachers be keen to hear about the children's home and community experience. Hurst (1996, pp. 95–6) stresses that 'we need to involve parents in their children's education in school because without this connection between home and school schooling can become cut off from the child's deepest and most influential experiences'.

The teacher has overall responsibility for ensuring that appropriate, meaningful information is collected, and that the contributions of all adults are valued and included. The children's viewpoints are also valued. Clark and Moss (2001) describe how practitioners can gain a deeper under-standing of children's perspectives through using a multi-method or 'mosaic' approach (including children's own photographs, tours and maps as well as observations and conversations). It is particularly important that early years staff listen to children when child abuse is suspected, since a child's comments may confirm that a bruise or burn the staff have noticed was not an accident and requires further investigation. Teachers need to ensure that the atmosphere they have created encourages this kind of sharing of confidences. A partnership approach to record-keeping is likely to result in a rounder, more flexible view of children than a solo approach.

This is a potential weakness of a system where each member of the basic team takes responsibility for the records for a set number of children. This approach can lead to a possessive view of children and a tendency not to focus on those children 'who are not one of mine'. It therefore loses the advantages which are gained when adults challenge each other's per-ceptions. It is particularly valuable for several adults to observe the same incident in the nursery class, and then to discuss what they saw and how they interpreted what they saw. Not only will each adult see the incident differently (each one focusing on different parts of it) but they may also interpret the same events differently according to their own values and attitudes (Drummond, Rouse and Pugh, 1992). In sharing these differences in perception, adults come to a deeper understanding of children and of themselves – and in the process become less sure that anything involving young children can be certain. Perhaps this experience should be made available to local and national educational policy-makers. It might help them to see what young children really need.

How can assessment information be recorded?

In developing their approach to record-keeping, teachers have taken note of published material such as, local authority guidelines (e.g. LEARN, 2000; Tower Hamlets Early Years Service, 2000; City of Salford EYDCP, 2002) and methods adopted by colleagues in other early years settings . Some have also been influenced by the approach to record-keeping adopted within other countries (e.g. methods of documentation used in Reggio Emilia in Italy and Learning Stories developed in New Zealand – see Carr, 2001). However, most feel that the work involved in developing their own methods is vital to the team's commitment to them.

In any case, no one method, or combination of methods, could necessarily serve the many different types of early years setting. One teacher, who had recently taken a post in a double, open-plan nursery unit with two teachers and two nursery nurses, commented that her record-keeping had 'gone to pot'. She went on to explain that in her previous post she had been responsible for a class of mainly full-time children, and had been able to develop what she felt were comprehensive and useful records. In her new position where the majority of children attended part time (resulting in large numbers passing through the class every day), it was impossible to keep up with her old methods and she was having to think again. She was dis-appointed to discover that she no longer felt efficient. Teachers working in reception classes face an even greater (arguably impossible) challenge if they have a large class without the support of a qualified nursery nurse. Whilst many classroom assistants are very keen and able, if they are untrained, they cannot be expected to contribute to record-keeping in the same way as qualified staff.

There are lessons here for those responsible for admissions and staff appointments. It may seem like a good idea to double the numbers of children able to attend by offering mostly, or exclusively, part-time places, and it may save a little money to employ unqualified assistants. However, the negative effects on the quality of record-keeping and curriculum planning based on children's needs must be recognized. Foundation Stage teachers would be relieved to discover that their difficulties were acknowledged, especially since many of them already use a range of methods of record-keeping without rival in the education system. They are also the pioneers as far as involving parents in record-keeping is concerned.

The assessment methods currently in use are briefly as follows (further detail on these methods is to be found in Lally and Hurst, 1992; Hutchin, 1999; Tower Hamlets Early Years Service, 2000):

1   Profiles of each child completed before admission to nursery class in conjunction with parents and others who have known the child well.

2   Written observations (both quick jottings and longer narrative style observations) organized into the six areas of learning

3   Dated samples of work, photographs, tape or even video recordings with written comments giving contextual information and providing a record of the children's experience and progress.

4   Checklists to record developmental achievements, children's involvement in activities, e.g. how often a child uses sand, books, etc., or takes part in cooking or other group activities, and adult involvement in activities and with children.

5   Regular summaries of children's achievements leading to the identification of future learning priorities – these summative records are used as a focus for discussion with parents and others interested in the child's development.

The importance of observation

Observation is the key to all these approaches. The effectiveness of any of them relies on the teacher's ability to:

- observe each child as an individual and as part of the group and record evidence as factually and objectively as possible;
- analyse and evaluate each observation (Lally and Hurst, 1992; Fisher, 2002a; Hurst, 1997);
- identify the aspects of each observation which are significant in terms of the child's development (Hutchin, 2000); and
- use the information gained to inform her approach to each child.

The teacher acts as a role model for the rest of her team and encourages others, including parents, to observe and learn from the children (Athey, 1990).

Types of observation

There are three main types of observation used by effective Foundation Stage teams:

- *Informal noticing (or having eyes and ears everywhere)* – Early years staff regularly comment that they are 'observing all the time'. There is some truth in this comment, but it also requires qualification. What early years practitioners do all the time is notice the things which draw themselves to their attention – the cry or laugh, the conflict developing, the wonderful construction, the child who speaks to them for the first time, the fight over a toy, the child happily saying goodbye to mum, dad or minder for the first time, and so on. These are important happenings to notice, respond to and sometimes record. Often these 'noticings' are responded to immediately (as in the case of conflict) or sometimes the next day. For example, one team had observed children phoning for pizzas in the home corner. That evening they planned to develop this further. One team member passed a pizza takeaway on her way home and called in to get some boxes and menus. The next day they set up a table near the home corner with a phone, order pad, menus and the boxes. They adjusted their planning by recording these ideas on the relevant day in a different coloured pen. In this way they could show how their daily planning was influenced by observation. Informal noticing cannot be planned for. However, practitioners can ensure that they are in a position to notice things at least some of the time.

● *Participant jottings (quick jottings made when the adult is working directly with the children)* – often these are planned and made within adult-led experiences but they may also be unplanned and be recorded when adults join in with child-initated play. These jottings should record what Hutchin (2000) refers to as significant achievements for each child. The adult records anything she has never seen or heard the child do or say before. These jottings need to be dated and could also include (for ease of reference) the initials of the area/s of learning they relate to (see example below).

Name: Daniel   Date: 27.11.03
Jotting:
Daniel selected a long piece of paper made a line of o shapes on it, punched two holes in it and tied it on to his tricycle with string as a number plate.

Significance:
First independent writing. Evidence of independent designing and making.

                                                            CLL KUW

Many staff use post-it notes or sticky labels to make these jottings and to record anything they notice informally, as they can be stuck into the child's record without being rewritten.

These quick observations will form the bulk of the evidence of learning collected for each child. However, they depend on which child and which contexts adults choose to notice and therefore do not provide the complete picture. What about all those things which happen quietly – the wonderful drawing completed without reference to an adult which goes straight into a pocket for mummy, the subtle, verbal bullying by the child who knows better than to let an adult hear, the body language or facial expression which indicates anxiety or boredom, the sexist comment during home corner play, or the incident which led up to the cry? It is frustrating to acknowledge that we will never see or hear everything that happens. However, we can sharpen our observation skills through a third kind of observation.

- *Focused observation (this involves standing back from what is happening, and writing down as factually and objectively as possible what takes place and what is said)* – the focus of these observations needs to be a child and generally it is most effective and illuminating to observe children when they are initiating their own learning without an adult. Obviously teams will want to make as many focused observations as they can, but in busy reception classes with inadequate staff:child ratios, it may only be possible to observe each child once a term. Many teams select a small number of children each week that they will focus on. All members of the team make a focused observation and then they meet to discuss their findings, make some assessments and consider next steps. Plans to support the development of these children can be included in the next week's planning. In this way every child will be specifically focused on at least once a term. Focused observations provide a challenge to assumptions because they provide information, which might otherwise be missed.

One team thought Maria (3 years and 6 months) was a well-adjusted, independent child who was able to occupy herself. Through a series of focused time-sampling observations (involving listing which children and adults were involved in each area of learning at 15-minute intervals) to find out how the various areas of learning were being used, it was noticed that Maria was always on the edges of activity and never seemed to be involved. Focused observation of Maria over the next few days confirmed that she was having difficulty making contact with other children and adults and, therefore, remained alongside them. With this information the team were all made aware of Maria's needs and were able to discuss strategies to help her. All teachers know that quiet children are at risk of being overlooked in the busy class situation. Focused observation is the only way of preventing this from happening. Fawcett (1996, ch. 4) describes and evaluates a number of useful methods of focused observation, which teams may wish to build into the daily routine.

The discipline involved in writing down what they see and hear happening opens adults' eyes and ears, and enables them to see and hear more, even when they are not particularly looking or listening. Teachers, who have been asked to make focused written observations as part of a course, often report how much more they are now noticing incidentally about that child and many others. Focused observation strengthens teachers' skills in informally noticing and in making participant observations.

This is why observation and discussion of observations should form a vital part of initial training courses. Many teachers have not been helped to see the purpose of observation and do not realize that everything (particularly their record-keeping) depends on it. Initial and in-service training courses should therefore re-emphasize the importance of observation as an essential, integral part of early years education. The successful implementation of the Foundation Stage Profile depends on this training.

Some points to support discussion: observation as an integral part of record-keeping

How do you currently make observations? How do you ensure that all team members regularly make time to observe? What do you feel it is important to observe? Make a list of the kinds of situations you want to observe objectively. (For example, a new child during his or her first few days, a new piece of equipment in use, a child working in a group, a new or reorganized area of experience.) Ask yourself:

- How can you make relatively uninterrupted time for observation? (Think about those things which prevent you from observing and consider how you could overcome these difficulties.)

- Which methods of recording will you use? (Lindon, 1997, and Fawcett, 1996, suggest a number of alternative methods.)

- How and when will you share and make use of the observations made by all team members?

The record-keeping process

The record-keeping process cannot be seen as a simple step-by-step model. It is more appropriate to see it as a complex meandering activity, integrating curriculum planning and assessment, with stages having to be revisited as necessary. Even though they cannot be placed in a fixed, sequential order, it is possible to identify the component parts of the process.

Teachers and their teams are required to:

- find out about children – both as typical 3, 4 and 5-year-olds and as unique individuals;
- make plans which reflect their intentions for learning – for the group as a whole and for individuals;
- implement and adapt the plans;
- monitor and note what actually happens – how children respond to the provision which has been made for them;
- identify and record children's achievements and regularly review each child's progress;
- share perceptions with others and, on the basis of all information, evaluate what has taken place or what an individual child needs; and
- plan again to find out more about children and to improve provision.

Record-keeping in action

Finding out about children – a general view

Teachers should, during their initial training course, be encouraged to develop their understanding of young children through their study of child development, and through their own observations on teaching practice. However, for some years child development and observation was marginalized. More recently, and particularly since early childhood studies became a legitimate subject for entry onto Postgraduate Certificate of Education (PGCE) courses, the supply of teachers with sound knowledge of child development and how children learn has increased. There are still, however, too many teachers working in the Foundation Stage who were trained to teach, and only have experience of, Key Stage 1 and 2. One-day in-service courses cannot fill the gaps in their understanding. Teachers need to recognize the expertise of qualified nursery nurses who usually have a sound knowledge of child development and can make effective observations.

However intensive their study of children during initial training, teachers still have a great deal to learn. Early years teaching is quite simply about studying and learning about children. There are two related parts to this study. First, teachers need to understand about children in general – ideally from birth until at least 7 or 8. They need to know the kinds of things 0–7-year-olds typically do, say and think, and the kinds of behaviour patterns which can be expected. They need to understand environmental, sociological and psychological theories in order that their view of society is broadened, and is taken beyond their own limited life experience. They also need to know that individual children develop uniquely, and a wide range of behaviour and actions can be considered 'normal'. Throughout their career, teachers need to develop further their general view of children through the study of individuals.

The most committed teachers are addicted to child study. In addition to studying the children in their class, they read about children (in novels, newspapers and magazines), they find themselves compulsively watching children in the neighbourhood (on buses, in the park, etc.) and on television, and they talk with other teachers about children (even after in-service courses which finish after 6.00 p.m.!). In this way, they build up their knowledge of children in general and are better equipped to understand the individuals in their class.

This general knowledge and understanding are essential for the development of a set of principles and beliefs, which underpins effective work with young children. If teachers do not know about children how can they make appropriate provision for them? Theoretical study of child development, backed up by experience with, and observation of, young children is the only way to provide a firm foundation for the teacher (see Lindon, 1993, and Meggitt and Sunderland, 2000, for a practical overview of development from birth to 8).

If we consider Natalie (introduced in Chapter 4) and think about her excited 'babbling' on the telephone, and her temper tantrums when she could not make herself understood, we see that the two aspects of her behaviour are linked. Her language development was at a level usually associated with a much younger child – a 2-year-old. It is no coincidence that we sometimes refer to the 'terrible 2s' since this is the stage when temper tantrums are common. This is because the 2-year-old is at a very early stage of language development and wants to express much more than he or she can say. Natalie's tantrums were consistent with her language development and with her frustration at not being able to communicate effectively with others. She needed help in this area, and, as her communication skills developed, the temper tantrums decreased. Attempting to tackle the tantrums without understanding the cause would have been futile. Knowledge of how 2-year-olds are helped to acquire speech gave the nursery team clues for their involvement – in particular, it helped them to understand the kinds of experiences Natalie might have missed.

Theory without practice is as inadequate as practice without theory. The first may place too much emphasis on norms at the expense of the individual, while the second provides no base from which to assess individual behaviour and development. Reception teachers working with 4-year-olds who have previously only encountered children of 5 and over are particularly at risk if they judge the younger children against the same standards as they judged the older ones. On courses they often express more negative views, and lower expectations of 4-year-olds than their nursery colleagues (e.g. they are more likely to think that 4-year-olds have short concentration spans) and do not always realize that children need a particular kind of environment in which to flourish and show their full potential (EYCG, 1995).

Finding out about children – as unique individuals

Early years staff regard the information they collect from parents (and others) before a child is admitted, as the beginning of the school record. They use it to help them adapt the curriculum they offer to the needs and experience of each child. This information usually includes basic details such as date of birth, names of carers, number of siblings, language(s) spoken at home, religion, pre-school experience, and health details such as allergies, chronic illnesses (e.g. asthma) and contact with specialists and their names. This information may be recorded on the form completed by the parents when they apply for a nursery place.

More detailed information is also considered useful and is often collected during a home visit or when the child and parent make an initial visit to the nursery class or toddler group (if there is one). This may include the following details about the child:

1 Life history:
    (a) What the child was like as a baby/toddler.
    (b) His or her relationships with other children and other adults.
    (c) Any stressful experiences such as hospitalization, new baby, death in the family, house move, etc.
    (d) Details of previous preschool group experience or childcare – how the child settled, how often he or she attended, what he or she liked/disliked about the group and so on.
    (e) The child's eating habits including what he or she likes and dislikes, foods which disagree with him or her (or which s/he is allergic to), what cutlery he or she uses, etc.?
    (f) The child's involvement in religious and cultural activities.
2 Development:
    (a) Physical skills, and physical activities, e.g. can he or she ride a bike, does he or she use the toilet unaided, can he or she dress him or herself, what opportunities has he or she had to play in a large space, to go to the park or swimming pool, etc.?
    (b) Language competence both in English and the language(s) spoken at home, any family words used, e.g. for going to the toilet.
    (c) What the child likes to play with and how he or she spends his or her time, and any special interests or skills.
    (d) Social skills including how the parents think he or she will relate to children and adults at the nursery, and any children he or she already knows.

(e) The child's emotional development including any fears and anxieties, what frustrates or angers the child and how the parent deals with the child when he or she is angry; any special toys or comfort objects.

The aim is to enable parents to talk freely about their child, so open-ended questions are most appropriate. It is more informative to ask 'what kinds of things do you enjoy doing together?' than 'do you read him stories?' – parents will expect teachers to want a 'yes' to the second question and will give the answer they think teachers want to hear. Teachers negotiate with the parent which information is written down, and the parent is often asked to sign it to ensure accuracy. In the case of bilingual parents and children, teachers try to ensure that an interpreter is available to give these families an equal opportunity to share information.

A consistent approach to the collection of information is vital, particularly if both teachers and nursery nurses are involved in the process. Parents need to feel confident that their views are respected, and that value judgements about them as parents, about their home (in the case of home visits) or about their child will be avoided. A structured approach where all members of staff work from the same set of questions or headings, which parents are shown in advance, helps to allay any fears a parent may have.

Teachers also need to make contact with any pre-school group or day nursery the child has attended to gain the staff's perceptions of the child's experience in these settings, to see for themselves how the child operates there and to identify any areas of discontinuity which may make transfer confusing or stressful for the child.

In this way, teachers and their teams begin to find out about children as unique individuals who have a wealth of experience. Without this information the team would be unable to claim to be aiming for a match between each child's needs and the curriculum offered. When children transfer to the reception class, the reception teacher needs to liaise with parents and the nursery team in similar ways. Transfer records from pre-schools and nurseries should be used to inform initial planning for the reception class. It is totally unacceptable that some reception teachers still ignore the records offered by their nursery colleagues saying they want to make their own mind up. This arrogant approach inevitably leads to an underestimation of the full extent of children's abilities. Foundation Stage practitioners are required to assess children's progress using the stepping stones and early learning goals. This information alongside written comments forms the transfer record and should provide the starting points which reception teachers need to build on.

Some discussion questions: improving record-keeping

The questions addressed in this chapter are ones which all teachers need to consider in relation to their own practice. It is essential to ask:

- Why keep records? What are my purposes? What kind of records would match my purposes?
- What information should records contain? What information do I and others need? What information is it most useful to collect?
- Who should contribute to the records and for what purpose? How can various contributions be co-ordinated?
- Which are the best ways of recording different kinds of information?
- What use is to be made of the information which has been collected?
- How will I review my record-keeping system to ensure that it is manageable, relevant and useful?

Planning the early years curriculum

As discussed in chapter 5, early years staff need an understanding of

- child development (so that they can identify and plan for the wide range of developmental needs of the individuals in their group);
- how young children learn most effectively (so they can introduce curriculum content in meaningful and motivating ways); and
- curriculum content (so that they can identify appropriate learning priorities for the children they are working with).

Planning at every stage should involve adults in working through the following process:

1   Identifying their intentions for children's learning – addressing the question: what do we hope the children will learn?
2   Identifying the resources, equipment and experiences they will need to offer to give children access to their learning intentions.
3   Identifying the role of the adult in supporting and extending children's learning.

Careful planning is required if all children are to:

- operate as self-motivated, independent learners;
- gain relevant, meaningful experiences;
- be offered equal opportunities;
- gain access to a broad, balanced, differentiated curriculum; and
- have access to adult time.

Planning is also necessary to ensure that adult time is used productively, and to enable all members of the team to work effectively with the children.

These complex reasons for planning necessitate a varied approach, and teachers will probably always struggle to develop planning methods which are meaningful, manageable, and useful. Many (particularly those working in nursery classes attached to primary schools and in reception classes) believe that the focus on whole-school planning, and the emphasis in Key Stages 1 and 2 on planning to account for National Curriculum coverage, have added further complications. The crucial questions for all teachers (including those working in Key Stages 1 and 2) to address honestly are: are we planning for delivery or for learning? Are we more concerned with our intentions or about children's responses? There is, of course, no clear-cut answer to these questions, since teachers need to plan and be concerned about both sides of the teaching and learning equation – but one side should not dominate at the expense of the other.

One way of clarifying the problem has been to think about the relationship between long-, medium- and short-term planning, and between learning intentions – which can be planned – and learning outcomes – which need to be assessed. Early years trained teachers rightly argue that there needs to be sufficient flexibility within planning, to enable them to grasp the moment at the point when children have made a discovery, or have shown an interest. It is at these times that learning is most likely to happen. Evidence from, amongst others, Tizard and Hughes (1984), Hughes (1986), Wells (1986), Athey (1990) and POST (2000) supports their argument that, if meaningful contexts (ones which are relevant and interesting to the child) are essential to motivate children, they must adopt a flexible approach to curriculum planning and cannot be expected to predict up to a year in advance what will generate enthusiasm.

Since the introduction of the Foundation Stage in 2000, teachers in England have been required to show how their curriculum is broad and balanced and helps most children achieve a set of early learning goals by the end of the reception year. This has required them to review their approach to planning the curriculum yet again. The following overview of early years approaches to long-, medium- and short-term planning emphasizes that effective planning requires knowledgeable, reflective practitioners who are aware of the need for greater accountability but also of the needs and interests of the children they work with.

Long-term planning

Long-term planning should provide the framework which underpins and informs all other aspects of an early years establishment's work and includes the following.

Developing, through policy development, a strong philosophy and ethos to underpin all aspects of their work with the children

Practitioners need to work together to clarify the overall aims for their setting and to develop policies to inform their approach to all aspects of their work. Policies, which are understood by the whole team, are essential if a consistent, rigorous approach is to be achieved.

In Chapter 3 the range of policies for the early years was discussed and examples given. In this section, the emphasis is placed on the early years curriculum policy. It is essential that nursery and reception staff work together to document a distinctive curriculum for the nursery/reception years. This curriculum must highlight what it is developmentally appropriate for children to learn and experience. It should not be governed exclusively by the stepping stones and early learning goals, which were never intended to be a curriculum in themselves (QCA/DfES 2000 p. 26). It is clear that some children will need further experience of the Foundation Stage curriculum in Year 1 and that others, who have achieved the early learning goals in the reception class, need to be stretched. Foundation Stage staff therefore need to plan an early years curriculum, which takes account of progression into the National Curriculum for those children for whom it is appropriate. Year 1 teachers need to take account of some children's need for additional Foundation Stage experience.

Curriculum policies should set out the team's beliefs about young children as learners and should identify the learning which staff intend to introduce – this should be an overview of children's entitlement during their time in the nursery/reception classes.

Teams in England are now required to plan around the following six headings:

- Personal, Social and Emotional Development;
- Communication, Language and Literacy;
- Mathematical Development;
- Knowledge and Understanding of the World;
- Physical Development; and
- Creative Development.

A framework for a curriculum policy is offered in Figure 6.1.

Clarifying overall learning intentions – identifying what they hope the children will learn during their time in the setting

The stepping stones and early learning goals set out in *Curriculum Guidance for the Foundation Stage* should be used as a broad framework for identifying in more detail the knowledge, understanding, skills and attitudes it is hoped children will acquire as they progress through the Foundation Stage.

Practitioners need to take account of the length of time children spend in their setting, their knowledge of their catchment area and the typical starting points of the children they admit, in order to develop a realistic and challenging curriculum framework. For example, a setting, which admits large numbers of children learning English as an additional language or children whose language development is immature or delayed, will need to give more detailed attention to the early stages of speaking and listening than a setting where most children are fluent and articulate communicators when admitted. Where children spend their entire Foundation Stage in the same setting, practitioners should work as a team to plan for progression through the whole stage.

Foundation Stage staff may find the chart given in Figure 6.2 provides a useful structure for this work. Teams should think about different aspects of learning, i.e.:

- *Knowledge and understanding.* What it is hoped children will begin to know and understand, e.g. facts such as names of things, concepts such as size, weight, position, fairness, etc.
- *Skills.* What it is hoped children will be able to do, e.g. co-operate, count, cut with scissors, observe and notice detail, negotiate with each other, etc.
- *Attitudes.* The ways in which it is hoped children will approach their learning, e.g. with persistence, curiosity, enthusiasm, confidence.

Attitudes towards learning are particularly important in the early years. Early years staff need to ensure that in their planning they consider the attitudes they wish to develop in the children as well as the knowledge and skills they would like them to acquire (see Chapter 7). They need to consider how content can be introduced in a range of interesting and challenging ways which do not 'separate cognitive development from those associated motivational, social and affective aspects' of the child's development (Swann and Gammage, 1993, p. 40). Published LEA documents such as LEARN 2000, Tower Hamlets Early Years Service and Newham Early Years Unit, 2000a, and Wandsworth Borough Council 2002 can support teachers in developing this long term plan.

Some learning intentions are ongoing and need regular consistent planned and spontaneous reinforcement (e.g. many of those in Personal, Social and Emotional development, Communication and Language

Rationale

Why do we need a policy on the curriculum for children in the Foundation Stage? What do we believe about

- young children as learners?
- planning and developing the early years curriculum?

Purposes/outcomes

- Which learning processes should the children be engaged with?
- What curriculum content do we want the children to have the opportunity to access? (Highlight areas of learning and a brief overview of learning intentions for each.)
- What evidence should there be of responsiveness to individual needs?

Broad guidelines

- How are our purposes reflected in our planning and approach to assessment?
- How do/will we ensure it is possible for children to gain access to the learning intentions we identified?:
  - what provision do we make?
  - how do adults get involved in both adult-directed and child-initiated learning?
  - how do we monitor children's access to the curriculum?

The following gives some idea of the kind of statements, which might be included in each section of an early years curriculum policy NB: It is not a complete policy

Rationale

We believe that

- Young children are individuals and progress at different rates.
- All aspects of their learning and development are equally important and are interdependent.
- Young children learn best if they are offered access to the curriculum through first-hand experience, play and talk with sensitive adults and their peers.
- All children should be enabled to have equal access to a broad curriculum which enables them to reach their full potential.
- The contexts in which children learn need to be relevant, meaningful, motivating and interesting to them.
- Early years staff need to enable parents to understand the Foundation Stage curriculum so that they can support their child's learning.

The statutory Foundation Stage is the first part of the national curriculum and is important in its own right.

Purposes/outcomes
We want to encourage children to be active, independent learners (both physically and mentally) who

- are curious and explore using their senses;
- make informed choices, represent their ideas in a range of ways and take responsibility.
- talk about their experiences, raise questions and seek reasons – want to try new things and are willing to learn from mistakes; and
- persist until they have completed an activity to their own satisfaction.

The Foundation Stage team offers a broad curriculum using the 6 areas of learning and ————————— LEA curriculum guidelines as a planning framework (see attached overview of our learning intentions in each area). We want early years staff who

- develop a meaningful curriculum in response to observation and assessment of the children's developmental needs and interests,
- enable children to initiate their own learning as well as take part in adult-initiated experiences;
- intervene sensitively in children's learning using language to support and extend children's thinking;
- monitor children's access to the curriculum to ensure that they are making progress in all areas of learning, and
- explain the early years curriculum to parents and encourage them to support their child's learning.

Broad guidelines
(NB: Examples of planning and more detailed guidelines may be added to an appendix.)

- The learning environment in and out of doors is planned carefully to ensure that all areas of provision offer children access to the areas of learning and so that children can independently access resources and materials
- Learning intentions for medium and short-term planning are drawn and developed from the long-term curriculum overview, but weekly and daily planning are informed by observation, assessment and evaluation. Ideas are taken forward from one week/day to the next – see examples of planning sheets. Staff monitor what has been covered each half-term and ensure that any gaps or needs are addressed in future planning.
- Developmental records are kept for all children. These are reviewed by class teachers on a half-termly basis, progress is noted and learning priorities are identified for each child.

Figure 6.1 Framework for developing an early years curriculum policy

PERSONAL, SOCIAL AND EMOTIONAL DEVELOPMENT	KNOWLEDGE AND UNDERSTANDING OF THE WORLD		
	SCIENCE (exploring and investigating)	TECHNOLOGY/ICT) designing and making/ICT	HISTORY AND GEOGRAPHY (sense of time, sense of place, culture and beliefs)
COMMUNICATION, LANGUAGE AND LITERACY	MATHEMATICAL DEVELOPMENT	CREATIVE DEVELOPMENT	PHYSICAL DEVELOPMENT

Figure 6.2 *Chart for planning overall learning intentions*

development and Physical development). It is useful for teams to identify which of their long term learning intentions they need to remember to focus on every day and to record the situations and times of day when they can work with children on these. This forward planning can be permanently displayed (avoiding unnecessary repetition in medium- and short-term planning) and helps to maximise spontaneous opportunities for learning in everyday events and routines such as meal/snack times, story sessions, etc.

Considering how children will be given access to curriculum content

Once broad curriculum content has been identified, teams could record some of the many ways they introduce children to this learning. Blenkin and Whitehead (1996, p. 32) point out that the 'most neglected and misunderstood dimension of the planned curriculum is the creation of an environment or setting in which education is to take place'. The environment indoors and outside must be organized and resourced to enable children to engage with all areas of learning. Practitioners need to identify and record the cross-curricular learning potential within each area of provision indoors and out (i.e. sand, role-play area, construction, etc.) and make sure that resources are available to promote this learning (see LEARN, 2000).

Copies of this planning can be displayed above each area so that everyone can see and value what children learn from basic early years provision. Resources to be provided in each area are also identified, e.g. literacy will only be encouraged in the home corner through the addition of telephone directories, message pads, diaries and pens, empty food packets, recipe books, catalogues, magazines, etc.

Another approach to linking long-term learning intentions to provision is that adopted by Tower Hamlets Early Years Service and Newham Early Years Unit (2002). Learning intentions for all curriculum areas were identified and organized into a broad developmental sequence. It was then possible to identify:

- areas and resources inside and out which would enable children to learn spontaneously;
- planned activities and experiences which would be led by an adult; and
- the adult support and specific language support which would be needed.

(See Figure 6.3 for an example of this approach.)

For staff trying to ensure continuity and progression across the Foundation Stage (particularly those working in the growing number of large Foundation Stage units which integrate nursery and reception classes), this work provides a supportive framework which can be dipped into, and developed to meet the needs of any group of children – like all other published materials, it should not be followed slavishly.

In developing guidelines of these kinds, teams seek to ensure that opportunities for progression in learning are made available through:

- careful resourcing of areas to allow for children to interact at their own developmental level; and
- ensuring that adults are aware of how they can stretch more experienced children by introducing practical or verbal challenges.

Long-term planning should *not* indicate *when* staff should introduce curriculum content. Published schemes which set out to tell workers what they should be doing week by week over the year, or one or two-year topic cycles for Foundation Stage children, are inappropriate because they take no account of developmental needs or interests and also reduce the creativity and motivation of trained staff. Adults need to be free to choose when and how they will introduce content.

Teams, which have documented their curriculum in a detailed way, have set themselves a standard, and are usually well equipped to monitor and evaluate their provision. They realize that children can access the same learning in a wide range of contexts indoors and out, and will be more likely to observe and note achievement in the full variety of situations rather than setting up sterile assessment tasks. Parents can be given access to this planning, for example, in workshop sessions.

In the absence of clear intentions and expectations, provision can become static, and standards may slip without anyone realizing the significance for children's learning. If staff do not clarify that children need a full set of plates, mugs and cutlery to enable them to set the table and develop mathematical concepts, such as one-to-one correspondence (one plate, mug, cutlery set for each child), and addition and subtraction ('I've got two plates. How many more do I need for the four dolls?'), they may not see the importance of replacing broken or missing items.

A settling-in curriculum Settling young children into a group setting is a major priority. It is useful to establish 'a curriculum for settling in' by identifying what children need to know and understand about being in the new setting, the skills they need to function in the group and the attitudes towards learning it is hoped they will begin to develop (see Figure 6.3). In their early weeks in the setting personal, social and emotional development, physical development and communication and language development are the most important areas of learning and should take priority in planning. Children, who are not well settled, are unlikely to be able to access the more academic areas of learning. This kind of planning can be used at the beginning of new terms when larger numbers of children are admitted or for individuals joining the group. Children can be observed and their progress can be assessed after about half a term using these learning intentions. Staff

Strand A - Settling Children into the Setting 2 - dispositions and attitudes

(Practitioners need to continue to work on the settling in learning objectives throughout the Foundation Stage to ensure children retain a positive attitude to themselves, to others and to learning)

Learning intention: knowledge/skills/attitude	Well-planned provision in and out of doors to provide opportunities for child-initiated learning	Planned adult-led activities/experiences in and out of doors	Adult input and specific language input
To feel good about themselves as a person and learner To develop positive attitudes towards learning To be: motivated enthusiastic persistent confident *To show curiosity* To feel: secure good about self successful competent a sense of enjoyment To trust others *To have a positive approach to new experiences* *To be able to ask for help from adults and other children*	● Opportunities to choose from a wide range of well presented areas of provision in and out of doors, with time to sustain interest and develop ideas ● Resources within the setting which connect with children's home and community experiences and interests e.g. the railway set for the child who has travelled by train to visit relatives at the weekend ● Experiences to cater for a range of learning styles - all areas of learning need to be offered indoors and out	✓ Ensure planned adult-focused activities are meaningful, motivating and give all children a chance of feeling successful/competent. ✓ Evaluate child-initiated and adult-focused activities with a view to finding out about the attitudes children are developing. ✓ Plan a range of ways of giving children access to the same learning objective - to cater for different interests and learning styles. ✓ Plan activities which build on children's interests and which emphasise practical experience. ✓ Ensure that the adult-focused time is planned for play provision in and out of doors e.g. sand, water, role play, construction as well as for table-based activities. ✓ Ensure that any recording required of children relates to a practical first hand experience. ✓ Avoid worksheets - they do not motivate children and can lead to some children feeling a sense of bewilderment and failure.	■ Explain purpose of activities - what it is hoped children will learn/find out and how it links with prior experience. ■ Take an interest in child-initiated learning making comments if appropriate. ■ Observe children to discover what motivates them and what they are finding difficult/boring. ■ Praise children's efforts saying why praise is being given. ■ Encourage children to review what they have learnt within child-initiated experiences. ■ Encourage children to persist e.g. *'Have you thought about trying ...'* and to ask for help.

Figure 6.3 *Developing guidelines for the development of positive dispositions and attitudes*
Source: reproduced from Tower Hamlets Early Years Service and Newham Early Years Unit (2000) with permission from Learning Design

can identify specific needs arising from assessment to incorporate into the next half-term's planning. This kind of sensitive monitoring of the settling-in process is essential

Planning to respond to spontaneous interests   Many of the things which Foundation Stage staff see as spontaneous happenings or interests are absolutely predictable. Using their knowledge of children in general, they know that during a typical year children's interest will at some point be captured by events, such as a windy or a snowy day, someone's new baby, a weekend visit to the park or zoo, a long journey or holiday to visit a relative, an interesting object someone has brought to school, a 'plague' of creatures (ants, or worms after rain), a bird building a nest in the school guttering, the building site or hole in the road visible from the school playground – the list is endless.

If teachers are to respond in depth to these interests when they happen, they need to have organized their thoughts and resources in advance. It is futile to teach young children about the properties of snow when there is no snow in sight, and yet how often are children asked to represent snow with cotton wool just because it is December or January? This is the classic example of activity planning taking precedence over learning intentions or even sense! After all, what does the use of cotton wool teach children about snow? By the time snow comes in April, the books have been returned to the library!

It is essential to take advantage of the day when it snows. Unless this eventuality has been considered and prepared for, the snow will have melted by the time teachers have gone to the library for books, or sorted out the outdoor spades, or decided what possibilities there are for exploring snow. Young children's interests will not always wait for us to catch up with them. Through their response, teachers have the power to capture and develop interest, or to turn children's attention to something else. As role models they encourage (or discourage) nursery nurses and the children's parents to be more aware of the value of following up events in this way.

Although it is not possible to say in advance if or when it will snow, or when exactly a new baby will be born, it is possible to say what could be done about these happenings if they occur. Teachers, rather than feeling they have to come up with plans for a topic or theme for a whole year or even a term (which is often peripheral to the children's real interests), could instead think about the everyday things they know are likely to generate interest, and plan for extending these interests. These plans could take the form of web diagrams (stored in a loose-leaf folder for easy reference), which demonstrate the cross-curricular learning potential for each starting point or interest, and the resources which would be needed to support each learning possibility. Staff could highlight on a copy of their curriculum overview what learning has been covered by developing the interest. These plans could be drawn on and implemented when an interest is shown.

Staff could collect relevant resources and store them so that they are easily accessible when the need arises. For example, books about different kinds of weather could be bought and stored together to be introduced when appropriate, and boxes or drawers containing resources relevant to particular interests could be collected and labelled, e.g. a box relevant to babies could contain feeding equipment, a selection of baby clothes, pictures or photographs (perhaps of the staff as babies); a windy-day box could include flags, streamers, windmills, a windsock, bubble pipes and wands, a kite, etc. This is not to say that resources of this kind should not regularly be available to the children – obviously, young children have a general (as well as a specific) interest in babies, and will want to pursue this during their home corner play, where baby dolls, clothes and feeding equipment should be available. However, it is also important to have some special resources available to stimulate and extend specific interests.

Planning from a range of starting points in this way is time-consuming but, once accomplished, only needs occasional updating in the light of experience. Teachers and nursery nurses could be encouraged to work together on in-service courses to develop and share plans.

Considering how the daily routine and staffing rota can be organized to maximize opportunities for learning

The organization of the daily routine and the ways in which staff are deployed have a profound effect on children's learning. Practitioners need to ensure that the pattern of the session ensures that children make a positive start to the day, offers children uninterrupted time to work in depth and is not fragmented by rigid routines such as carpet time, snack time, etc. (see Chapter 5). Children need time during the session, when there is free access to an outside play area so they can integrate in and outdoor learning. Staffing rotas need to be drawn up to maximize the time adults spend working directly with the children. This should include regularly planned adult-led experiences and also time when adults can observe and join in with child-initiated learning.

Long-term planning is time-consuming but once completed will need only occasional review and development. If done well, it provides practitioners with a secure, efficient framework from which they can develop medium- and short-term plans. It can also save time at the medium- and short-term planning levels as much thinking has been done in advance.

Medium-term planning

Whilst long-term planning provides a *permanent* framework, which only needs to be reviewed and updated from time to time, medium-term planning helps staff focus on how they will develop the curriculum during the next few weeks. Medium-term planning must be informed by observations staff have made of children's interests and enthusiasms during the previous weeks, and by community and seasonal events (e.g. the building site which has just been set up, festivals, etc.). Many staff also review children's progress on a termly or half-termly basis and identify a number of learning priorities for the next few weeks (see Figure 6.4).

Date:			
Child's name	Learning priorities	Provision/experiences	Adult support
Jason B.	To develop interest in written word. To be able to use knowledge of numbers 1–5 in real-life situation	Garage outside with signs & pens & pads. Market stall role play – prices up to 5p, only 1p coins. Display fruit names & pictures	Get involved in role play. Talk about signs – 'what does that say?' 'Is the garage open or closed?' Encourage counting out coins and produce 'How many more do you need to buy the pear? Which is more expensive the apple or the banana?'
Samantha	To develop confidence to use all areas of nursery		Key worker to encourage S to move to new areas with her. Ask mum to stay to encourage her

This planning would be continued to include the rest of the group (it is not unusual to find that several children have the same or similar needs) and progress would be reviewed after a few weeks.

Figure 6.4 *Medium-term planning: identifying individual learning priorities*

When developing a medium-term plan, adults need to identify what they hope children will learn and what they will give priority to during the next few weeks, focusing the learning intentions on the starting points/interests they hope to develop. If the children are interested in babies, because a number have new babies at home, some of their learning intentions will be related to this starting point. Other learning intentions will be related to the learning priorities that have been identified for groups of individuals, or to seasonal events or festivals. When new children are to be settled many of the learning intentions will be concerned with adjustment to the new setting. When an existing group are continuing their early education practitioners should use their knowledge of the general needs of this group to identify key learning priorities – for example, in one setting, the team identified that a substantial group of children needed to develop confidence to express their ideas in language and planned a half-term focus around the re-enactment of familiar stories. Learning intentions are drawn and developed from long-term planning and recorded under the same curriculum headings. The next step is to think about and list the resources, equipment and experiences which might be offered to support this learning.

Forward planning enables staff to collect the resources they need and arrange any special experiences (e.g. visits, visitors). Medium-term planning should be seen as a means of generating ideas, not all of which will be implemented in practice – it should not become a straitjacket which has to be slavishly worked through. It is not necessary or helpful to set out in advance week by week what will be covered over the half-term. It is far more effective to develop the curriculum in response to the children's needs and highlight what has been covered each week on the medium-term plan.

Short-term planning

If staff have developed long- and medium-term plans as outlined above, short-term planning can be more focused and should be less time-consuming. Long- and medium-term plans act as a guide to remind teachers of the range and depth of curricular experiences they need to offer. Short-term plans, made on a weekly basis, and evaluated and amended daily, encourage a more responsive approach to the curriculum, and provide a more accurate record of learning and teaching.

A responsive approach to curriculum planning involves:

- helping new children settle into the nursery class;
- enabling all children to operate confidently within the learning environment and to develop attitudes and skills described in Chapters 4 and 5;
- enabling children to extend their personal interests or schemas (see Athey, 1990; Nutbrown, 1994) and to introduce them to new experiences;
- providing challenges for experienced or particularly able children;
- supporting the development of children with special educational needs;
- supporting children who are experiencing emotional difficulties; and
- enabling children to take part in group activities.

Observation is central to this process. Focused observations ensure that each child is regularly the centre of staff attention, while informal observations highlight daily incidents which are worthy of extension.

Many teams meet together formally each week to evaluate how the previous week has gone, share some of their observations of children (i.e. those which they feel need to inform future planning), and make plans for the week ahead – this weekly meeting is often supplemented by informal evaluation and planning sessions at the end of each day.

There are many ways of recording short-term plans and what works for one setting rarely works for another. There is not one definitive format – much as some teachers say they would like to be given one! However, the elements within the most effective planning are the same, and include the following:

Specific learning intentions which will be focused on/given priority by adults during the week or day

At the beginning of each week, a small range of learning intentions for each curriculum area will be identified – these are often added to as the week develops. Some of these will be for individual children (e.g. C needs to develop his understanding of what it means to take turns) and some will be drawn from medium-term planning to develop ongoing interests (e.g. learning about how to care for babies). These intentions may be recorded on a chart similar to that in Figure 6.2. This does not mean that this is all the learning which will be on offer – the well-planned learning environment offers much more than is contained in a weekly plan – rather it highlights what adults intend to give priority to. The planned intentions provide a focus for staff when they decide on the additional provision they need to make, the activities or experiences they need to offer and the ways in which they could be involved with the children. It also helps them decide which children they particularly need to observe or spend time with.

Special or additional provision which will be made to support the identified learning intentions

These may be offered to encourage child-initiated learning, or could be developed as an adult-initiated experience. For example, set up a baby clinic; add baby-bath foam, flannels and towels to water tray to encourage baby bathing; introduce hand forks and trowels to digging area, etc.

Specific activities or experiences which will be initiated and led by adults (including when these will take place)

Sometimes any child can opt for the activity or experience, and several small groups may be involved during the course of a session, while on other occasions adults will decide which children can take part to ensure that equality of access is achieved. These experiences may be led by parent helpers and students as well as by basic team members, and might include the following:

- cooking;
- outings into the local neighbourhood;
- setting up an interesting display based on a recent experience or event;
- activities to introduce or reinforce specific concepts, such as floating and sinking, turn-taking, size, magnetism;
- a woodwork project, such as making a run for the class rabbit;
- a demonstration which provides first-hand experience to feed into other experiences such as role-play, e.g. father coming in to demonstrate baby bathing and feeding;
- the introduction of a new piece of equipment or a new area such as the newly set-up baby clinic;
- an introduction to a new set of expectations, e.g. staff working outside helping children understand how to park their wheeled toys in the newly painted parking bays when they have finished riding;
- planting some bulbs in tubs in the outside area;
- sewing;
- music and movement sessions; and
- planned story sessions.

Teachers are responsible for helping untrained staff and visitors understand the purpose of their involvement. In planning adult-initiated experiences, teachers need to consider with their team:

- why they are being offered – how they relate to the children's needs and interests;
- what their intentions are for children's learning – which attitudes, skills and knowledge it is intended that the children might develop through their involvement in this experience;
- which children would benefit most from being involved and how the activity could be differentiated;
- what resources will be needed; and
- what language the adult might need to introduce to help children verbalize and extend their learning.

It is useful for staff to identify key words, which they could introduce during an activity, and a few open-ended questions to encourage children to think more deeply and express their ideas. This helps adults respond to the ideas and interpretations children bring to an experience. Adults need to be responsive, sensitive and flexible. For this reason short-term plans should be seen as working documents to be adapted as the week or day develops. An example of planning for adult-initiated activities is given in Figure 6.5.

Learning intentions have to incorporate the range of needs within the class so that the experience offers an opportunity for learning to all children who take part. If a gardening activity is planned, it should be possible for some children to handle and dig in the earth and discuss their discoveries, alongside others who are keen to learn more about planting and growing vegetables. Similarly, during a cooking activity teachers will intend that some children will benefit most from the sensory experiences involved in mixing ingredients, while for other more experienced children an intention might be to encourage them to put the changes they observe during the mixing and cooking process into words.

This does not mean that the teacher has rigid intentions for particular children. She uses her knowledge of children and her awareness of the next challenge for them to predict possible learning outcomes. However, through having a variety of possibilities in mind she is able to respond to the unexpected – the experienced child who is gaining comfort from stirring his ingredients as he tells her of a distressing experience which is worrying him (the learning outcome is still language related but not in the way the teacher expected), or the new child who exclaims as she mixes margarine and sugar: 'Look! My mixture's gone lighter.'

Teachers must ensure that plans are made for adult involvement in all areas of provision, and that the adults involved are aware of the possibilities for crosscurricular learning in every experience (this awareness comes from developing long-term plans in the way described earlier). Children are given powerful messages about male and female roles when observing adults in the setting. Foundation Stage staff are predominantly female, and it is easy for them to reinforce stereotypes through their own involvement in traditionally female activities such as art, cooking and sewing, and through their encouragement of male visitors to undertake activities such as woodwork or outdoor activity.

Many teachers have confronted these stereotypes by involving themselves in the full range of experiences, and by specifically asking fathers to bath their baby or cook in the nursery, and mothers to garden or mend wooden toys. They have had to encourage some parents to involve themselves in this way since attitudes about what men and women should do are still entrenched.

Where adults will be working at different times of the day

Adults need to think about how they could get involved in children's self-initiated activity. As well as setting up and leading experiences for the children, early years staff also need to involve themselves in the activities children have initiated for themselves. Often adults respond on the spur of

Learning intentions	Activity/resources	Adult involvement	Language/challenges
Knowledge and Understanding of the World – Science To develop observation skills To describe similarities and differences	Comparing three different kinds of apple – resources Cox, Golden Delicious and Braeburn apples, chopping boards, knives, paper towels	Encourage sensory exploration – observing, touching, smelling, tasting. Encourage children to describe texture, appearance, taste, smell. Examine outside of apples carefully before cutting. Focus on similarities as well as differences	Possible questions: what does it look/feel/taste/smell like? What do you notice about this apple? How are the apples the same/different? Which one do you like the best – why? Which one is the sweetest? What do you think we would see if we cut the apples in half? etc. Possible vocabulary: colour names, shiny, dull, smooth, peel, core, pip, sweet, sour, smoother, shinier, softer, harder, etc.

Figure 6.5 *An example of planning for an adult-initiated experience*

the moment, but their involvement may be fleeting and lack depth. Another problem with a reactive approach is that it has a tendency to involve some children and some areas of experience at the expense of others.

These problems may be overcome through planning loosely how adult time will be spent. Team members usually work to a rota showing which area they will be working in at different times of the day. Each day they will spend some time out of doors and some time indoors. When involving additional adults, such as parents and students, staff need to decide where this extra help is most needed and communicate this to the person concerned.

Careful planning of the deployment of adults is essential for effective time management. If in-depth interactions and observations are to be undertaken and sustained, staff need to know that at certain times of the day they will be free from the day-to-day management tasks, such as intervening in quarrels or changing wet pants, which often cause interruptions. It is only possible to minimize disruption if staffing ratios are favourable. In classes with one teacher and one nursery nurse (one working inside and one outside), other adults need to be added to the team on a regular basis to provide the required flexibility, while in classes with three or more members of staff it is possible for one member to take responsibility for all interruptions, while another involves herself in-depth with the children. These roles must be interchangeable, so that everyone gains experience of both equally important kinds of work.

When planning for their involvement in children's self-initiated activity, adults need to take into account their recent observations. One member of staff may have been observing a small group using some planks, milk crates and tyres to make themselves an obstacle course, when time ran out and the equipment had to be packed away. She may decide to see if they continue this play and, if so, may plan to involve herself and help them set themselves even greater challenges. Similarly, a member of staff may have observed that the brick area is being dominated by a particular group of boys and may decide to place herself in this area to encourage the boys to allow others to join in and to encourage some of the girls, who like to be near her, to take part in brick play. Or a member of staff may have observed a worrying change in one child's behaviour and may plan to observe the child again and perhaps involve herself in the child's activity with a view to finding out what is wrong.

If staff and helpers are to work as a team, it is essential that they share their intentions with each other so that priorities can be identified and appropriate support offered. There is nothing more frustrating than to find that you are just gaining a child's confidence, when an incident across the room takes away your attention. Sometimes this is the reality, but it need not always be – particularly if extra adult support is encouraged.

The key to successful intervention in children's activities is observation. Without it adults run the risk of interrupting children and destroying their activity. If we want to be involved in child-initiated activity, we must watch, listen and, on the basis of what we have seen and heard, find a role for ourselves which is consistent with the child's purposes and allows him/her to retain ownership (see Chapter 7).

Children to be targeted for specific support or for focused observation

Examples of this kind of planning, which is aimed at particular children, might include notes such as:

- Spend time at beginning of session with new children (particularly Jodie and Darren) to help them select resources more confidently.
- Suggest to Adam that he finds books on spiders to develop the interest he was showing in webs yesterday.
- Work with Elena and Matthew at tidying-up time to encourage them to see this as fun rather than as something to be avoided.
- Introduce bottles with holes pierced at different levels to extend bottle-filling activity which Sam and Claudette have been interested in for the past few days. Encourage talk about the rate at which different bottles empty and why.
- Add first-aid kit to home corner in response to Gemma's play yesterday (seen using wooden spoon as stethoscope). Join in play if appropriate to help her explore her feelings about her sister being in hospital.
- Observe Tariq to see how he is negotiating for a turn – support him in this.
- Read one-to-one stories with Raj and Karen who find group story time difficult.

Obviously, it is not possible for plans to be made for every child every day. Teachers need to prioritize and decide which children need specific adult support, and which children will be able to extend their own activity if additional resources are made available. Notes such as those above serve to focus attention on specific learning needs, and to remind all staff of particular interests. Members of staff involved in implementing the above plans would be responsible for noting what happened. Some teams record the names of children for whom a learning intention is especially relevant on their weekly overview.

Special events

Plans need to take into account all out-of-the ordinary occurrences. These include events such as the admission of new children, a new member of staff, a parent coming to do a baby-bathing session, an informal visit by the school dentist or the fire engine, an outing by a small group of children, parents and staff to a local place of interest, a visiting theatre or puppet group or a visit by school governors.

Careful planning of special events is essential if they are not to be stressful or a complete waste of time.

A space for evaluation

This is essential to enable staff to reflect on the extent to which children received the intended curriculum and to take forward ideas into the next day or week.

Planning involves a process of informed guesswork. Teams use their knowledge of young children and their curricular knowledge to help them work through this process. Plans need to be flexible and sometimes (as we will see later in this chapter) have to be abandoned.

Weekly or daily planning records are the working documents of the early years team. It is unfortunate, therefore, that some teachers seem to believe that they have to be neat and tidy – that they are there more for the scrutiny of others than to inform their own practice. This attitude is changing and it is increasingly common to see tentative, weekly forecasts being added to or amended as the week progresses. Planning records should demonstrate that teams are thinking about children, and about their work.

Recording plans for outdoor learning can seem more difficult because much depends on weather conditions. However, when teams are identifying their learning intentions for the week, many think of the possible experiences which could be offered out of doors to complement indoor provision. Staff setting up outside could include these experiences when appropriate, and also resource collections to explore particular weather conditions. Outdoor learning needs to be observed, evaluated and extended in the same way as indoor learning and staff will often find that some children can access aspects of the curriculum better out doors than in.

Each stage of planning informs the next, and those teams who have taken time to record detailed long- and medium-term plans, are best supported when they need to develop plans for the week. If the first two stages are not in place, the planning process becomes bottom heavy and repetitive because teams are working in a vacuum – unable to prioritize and feeling that they need to write down everything they can think of every week. Above all approaches to planning should reflect the distinctive features of the Foundation Stage rather than constraints imposed by the rest of the school. Rather than giving in to top-down pressure to work in inappropriate ways, Foundation Stage teachers need to help Key Stage 1 and 2 colleagues to see how their approach has relevance for work with older learners.

Some points for discussion:
Evaluating the early years curriculum

In order to evaluate the effectiveness of the early years curriculum, teams need to use their planning and observe practice to address the following questions:

- Is there a clearly defined and documented Foundation Stage curriculum?
- How is medium-term planning influenced by the needs of the group?
- Is short-term planning informed by observation and assessment and are adults able to differentiate provision and experiences to cater for different developmental and cultural needs?
- Are children given access to the curriculum through first-hand experience, play and talk, and are they encouraged to be active, independent learners?
- Is there a balance of child-initiated and adult-initiated activity/experience? How are adults given time to become involved in both types of experience?
- Are all areas of provision (in and out of doors) well planned to give children access to a broad curriculum? Do adults plan time to work with the children in all areas of provision?
- Do adults have strategies for monitoring children's access to the curriculum?
- Are adults flexible enough to respond to children's interests/needs and is this flexibility reflected in the planning/evaluation?
- Do adults use a range of language strategies to support and extend children's learning? Is there evidence in planning that language is planned for?

Implementing plans and monitoring and evaluating what actually happens

Throughout the last section the need to see plans as tentative documents has been emphasized. Sometimes the experiences we provide for young children capture their interest and develop in the ways we had predicted. Sometimes they even learn what we intended them to learn. On other occasions, however, children surprise us and respond unexpectedly. It is essential that we monitor how the children actually respond to the provision we make, and to our interactions with them.

It is futile for a teacher to continue to pursue her exploration of the capacity of different containers when the learner she is working with is preoccupied with her weekend visit to granny, which involved travelling by train for the first time. Better to talk about the visit first and then see if interest in the capacity activity develops. Even if it does not, the teacher will still have involved the child in an important learning experience. In describing to her teacher an event, which only she knows about, the child is involved in a complex intellectual and linguistic exercise. She will be motivated to persist because she wants to communicate.

Young children let adults know when they have been switched off, or when they are interested in something else. Reception teachers in particular need to be able to resist feeling pressured to persist with their intentions even when it is obvious the children are not learning. Teachers encourage children to give feedback on the curriculum verbally or through their actions. By listening carefully to their responses to experiences, and observing how they use materials or behave in the presence of adults or other children, teachers gain insight into their interests and needs.

Teams need to monitor the following:

- The use of the learning environment. Has the space been organized effectively? Are all children gaining access to all areas of provision – or are some areas being dominated? Are the learning experiences offered out of doors as varied and as richly planned as those on offer in the classroom? What is working well/not so well? What is missing?
- The use of equipment and materials, particularly noticing unexpected uses (the plastic pegs being stirred in the home corner saucepan indicating a need for some materials to represent food); any gaps in provision (the child searching in vain for a piece of 'fur' to make a collage cat); and any creative combinations of equipment (the small group using some woodshavings and twigs from the art workshop to complete the 'fire' in the fireplace they have built out of large, hollow blocks).
- The responses of individual children:
  - to the same adult-initiated experience – highlighting what each child did, said and was interested in; considering whether the children learnt what was intended; and
  - to adult involvement in their play or behaviour. How did the child respond? Did adult involvement enhance or destroy play/ reinforce or change behaviour? Why?

The answers to these questions, although sometimes painful to accept, broaden the team's thinking about the provision they are making and about their own role in children's learning. It is very important to know that a child's aggressive behaviour is being reinforced by the staff's handling of him or her. Evaluation should be a challenging, rather than a cosy, affirming process.

Monitoring and evaluating the curriculum

In order to be able to evaluate (i.e. make judgements about) the quality of the education they are offering the children, teachers need to monitor (i.e. gather evidence). As we saw in Chapter 3, staff should base judgements about their practice on the criteria set out in the *Currciulum Guidance for the Foundation*

Stage, their own policies and other written guidelines. They may gather evidence by recording for a day (or over several days) on a grid which children and adults are working in each area of provision at 15 or 30-minute intervals, in order to highlight which areas of provision might be being dominated, which are not being used, or are being neglected by the adults, which are overcrowded and so on. This general view might be followed up by team discussion, and more focused observations to gain a more detailed view.

Observations made by staff are discussed informally at the end of each day or before school starts in the morning, and used to initiate observations (to find out more about particular children) or to inform future planning.

Teachers also ask regular visitors to the class, such as the headteacher, adviser, governors and, of course, parents, for their perceptions of how the class is actually working (see Chapter 3). They may also call in specialists, such as educational psychologists, to help them gain an outsider's view of what is happening – particularly in relation to behavioural difficulties.

These more objective views are important because often staff are too closely involved to see clearly what is at the root of a situation.

At times when external demands are being made, early years staff must remain clear about what is valuable for their children. They need to ask whether the experiences they offer are really engaging the children or merely occupying them (Lally, 1995) and whether they show respect for children's innate curiosity and enthusiasm for learning – too many activities for 3–5-year-olds in nursery and reception classes still involve colouring-in, handwriting practice or tracing sheets, which keep children busy for a few moments, but may damage children's attitudes to learning.

Identifying achievements and reviewing progress

'What children can do, not what they cannot do, is the starting point in children's education' (EYCG, 1989, p. 3).

Teachers of young children must find ways of establishing what each child knows and can do, and use this information to identify starting points, which offer each child a chance of success. In order to make these kinds of judgements, teachers must develop a system which regularly makes all children the focus of attention, and reviews the progress of all children from time to time. In this section, we focus on the kinds of information teachers record.

Most of the information collected by team members should take the form of observations. Records should be positive, and should provide evidence of what children have achieved. This does not mean that teachers are not interested in identifying where a child needs support – this is usually obvious from what is not included in a positively written record. However, many teams have a section for 'next steps' or 'further support needed' so that they can highlight implications for planning. In this way achievement to date is celebrated whilst the child's developing state is also acknowledged.

The kinds of information teams might record include the following:

- *Attendance record* – the regularity of attendance, punctuality and the effects of these on school achievement.
- *Attitude to learning* – motivation; curiosity; use of imagination; ability to cope with and learn from problems or failure; persistence; ability to respond to new experiences.
- *Preferred activities/interests* – how a child chooses to spend time, i.e. which activities and how they are used.

Achievements are also recorded within areas of learning. (It is important to recognize that the points below are offered as a guide to what observational evidence should be collected – they are not meant to be ticked off!)

- *Personal, social and emotional development* – commenting on the child's:
  - confidence and self-esteem (as exhibited in school) – situations in which the child is most/least confident; ability to be assertive and stand up for own rights or ask an adult for support;
  - relationships – with peers and adults including particular friendships; sharing, turn-taking and negotiating ability; understanding of rules; ability to care for and empathize with others, and to show an understanding of and respect for cultural, religious and linguistic difference, etc.;
  - feelings – ability to express feelings (controlling them when appropriate) or anxieties;
  - dispositions and attitudes – how the child approaches learning; and
  - independence – self-help skills, e.g. toileting, feeding and dressing; ability to use the whole environment, select resources, plan own time, initiate ideas, ask for support when required; ability to take responsibility for clearing up, for younger children, taking messages, etc.
- *Physical development* – the child's ability to:
  - use outdoor equipment (climbing frames, bats and balls, seesaws, bikes, etc.);
  - control and co-ordinate his or her body (running, jumping, hopping, skipping, kicking, throwing, etc.);
  - use tools (for drawing, painting, cutting, woodwork, sewing, cooking, etc.), and other equipment (for building, threading, doll dressing, etc.); and

- care for own body and show an understanding of what constitutes a healthy, hygienic lifestyle.
- *Communication, language and literacy* – speaking and listening: the child's ability to:
  - express needs;
  - describe present and past experiences;
  - ask questions;
  - describe a sequence of events;
  - reason and supply logical explanations;
  - talk imaginatively;
  - retell or make up stories in his or her own words;
  - explain a process;
  - take a message;
  - negotiate verbally;
  - listen and contribute in one-to-one, small and large group situations;
  - listen and respond to stories, poems, songs and rhymes; and
  - use language to take part in role play.

It is important that bilingual children are assessed in the language used at home as well as English to give a full view of a child's linguistic competence.

- *Communication, language and literacy* – reading and writing:
  - response to story times;
  - interest in books (story and reference);
  - ability to handle books appropriately showing an understanding of book conventions;
  - ability to recognize that words tell stories;
  - interest in written words including environmental print;
  - interest in his or her own talk written down by an adult;
  - interest in reading his or her own talk written down;
  - ability to read names or words in books;
  - interest in and knowledge of letters and sounds;
  - ability to play with sounds and words and to show humour;
  - interest in writing and willingness to have a go; and
  - ability to write name or other words.
- *Mathematical development* – his or her ability to:
  - sort objects or materials in the course of play or tidying up and explain reasons for groupings;
  - make comparisons, e.g. height, weight, size, texture, etc.;
  - use the language of position – between, over, under, inside, outside, on, behind, in front, etc.;
  - put graded objects into order, e.g. graded saucepans, beakers,

cubes, etc., in the course of play and use the language of size, e.g. big, bigger, biggest;
- construct with two-dimensional and three-dimensional shapes and name and describe properties of some regular shapes;
- use numbers – count in one-to-one correspondence in the course of play, e.g. one plate for each doll; carry out simple addition and subtraction, e.g. if you take one cake there will be two left;
- recognize numbers in the environment;
- put events into time sequence knowing what happens next during the day;
- make patterns in a variety of situations and discuss patterns in the environment; and
- describe mathematical experiences using appropriate language.

● *Knowledge and understanding of the world – exploration and investigation (science)* – his or her ability to:
- make and discuss observations of everyday objects, materials, living creatures and plantlife;
- discuss similarities and differences;
- question his or her experiences and plan and set up his or her own explorations and investigations;
- communicate discoveries to others;
- make predictions to suggest what would happen if ...;
- interpret and give reasons for the results of explorations, e.g. this boat floats because it's made of wood; and
- tackle and find a solution to problems.

In addition to achievements under the above headings, which are concerned with the scientific process, early years teachers increasingly need to record experiences children have gained which are relevant to specific scientific content, e.g. types and uses of materials and how materials can be changed, forces, energy, living things, etc.

● *Knowledge and understanding of the world – designing and making and information, communication teachnology* – his or her experience of:
- the use and effects of tools;
- the exploration of properties and use of materials;
- the exploration of design features;
- the uses of technology in the environment;
- the use of tools and materials to design and make models, including his or her planning and problem-solving ability;
- design features, e.g. when examining component parts of a clock or telephone which has been taken apart, or when looking at buildings in the local environment;

- the use of information and other technology such as computer, tape recorder, programmable toys and simple camera.
- *Knowledge and understanding of the world – sense of time, sense of place, cultures and beliefs* – his or her ability to
  - talk about personal life history – about family and past and present events in his or her life;
  - understand that life is different now from the past;
  - talk about and recognize features of the local environment and understand the purpose of some of these; and
  - recognize the jobs which people carry out within the community
  - recognize, talk about and respect different cultural traditions.
- *Creative development – his or her*
  - interest in activities such as drawing, painting, woodwork, modelling, clay, music, movement and drama/role-play;
  - ability to represent and communicate ideas using a variety of media and in a variety of ways (music, drama, role-play, movement, dance);
  - use of imagination;
  - use of tools and materials to carry out own creative ideas;
  - awareness of and eagerness to explore sound, colour, texture shape, form and space in two dimensions and three dimensions; and
  - response to the creativity of others, e.g. move to music, talk about a painting.

When reviewing the child's achievements, areas where encouragement or specific help are needed – either because of an exceptional aptitude or because of a lack of confidence or developmental delay – are noted.

Gathering this information should not require early years staff to set up special assessment tasks. They should be able to identify the kinds of contexts in their everyday provision, which will offer children the chance to demonstrate their competence within particular areas of learning. If a teacher wants to discover if children can name and recognize the properties of shapes she could observe children when they are building with or tidying up wooden unit blocks, or when they are using mosaic pieces or Logi-blocks to make patterns. Lally and Hurst (1992, p. 56) emphasize the need 'to recognize the impact which an unfamiliar setting has on achievement' and argue that 'we gain a much clearer view of what children know and can do when we observe them setting their own challenges and taking responsibility for their own learning'. This is particularly important if we wish to avoid perpetuating inequality and low expectations through our record-keeping.

It is particularly valuable to observe children taking part in self-chosen play. This may seem a random way of gathering information, but it is reassuring to discover that one short observation can often provide evidence of achievement within a number of areas of learning (see below). It can also challenge a teacher's view of a child. Reception teachers need to bear these points in mind when gathering evidence for the Foundation Stage Profile. Assessment is not a precise art. We can never know exactly where a child is at a specific point in time. Because children are learning and developing at such a rapid rate, they will be constantly changing and it will therefore be difficult to pinpoint accurately their level of achievement (Harlen, 1992). The more evidence we have, which has been collected over time in a range of contexts, the more confident we can be about our judgements. When summarizing a child's achievements teachers have to consider how to extract the specific information they need from their collection of observations. Some now code observations (particularly the more detailed focused observations) and the dated work samples they collect to highlight the kinds of evidence they contain.

Consider the following observation:

Samantha (4 years 1 month) sat down at the dough table and asked Ahmed if she could have a piece of dough. He gave her a small piece and she said: 'That's not much. You've got a big lot and I've only got this tiny bit. Can I have some more, please?' She helped Ahmed to share out the dough so they had roughly pieces of equal size. She then selected from the shelves a cake tin with spaces for nine cakes, a rolling pin and a cutter. She matched the cutters against the holes in the cake tin and chose the one closest in size to the holes. She then rolled out the dough and began to cut out the cakes placing them into the tin one at a time. She commented to the nursery teacher: 'The tin's nearly full.' The nursery teacher replied: 'Yes it is. How many more cakes do you think you need to cut?' She glanced at the tray and answered correctly: 'Three more.' She finished filling the tray and placed it into the toy cooker next to the dough table, turning the control knobs as she did so. She then said to the nursery nurse: 'I'm going shopping now. Can you look after my cakes, please?'

We can see that it provides evidence on which to make assessments relevant to the following headings: *attitude to learning* – persistence in seeing her activity through to its conclusion; *personal, social and emotional development* – negotiating skills with Ahmed, confidence (in use of resources), independence (planning her own activity and selecting from a range of equipment); *physical development* (use of tools); communication, *language and literacy: speaking and listening* – when reasoning with Ahmed; and *mathematics* – when choosing the right-size cutter and when working out how many more cakes she needed to cut. This is true of most observations.

By devising a coding system, based on the first letters of the areas of learning, teachers can mark their observations so that they can see at a glance where they will find specific evidence. When they review the information they have collected for a child, they can see more easily what kinds of evidence are missing, and can plan with their team how to gain additional information.

Developing a system for reviewing children's progress

So far the emphasis has been on gathering information about children's development and learning over time, and using this to inform planning – formative assessment. Foundation Stage teachers also need to devise a system which focuses their attention on, and sums up, each child's achievements at particular points in time – summative assessment. The initial record completed with parents before children start at nursery provides the team with a starting point. They will want to complete a further summative assessment to show the child's progress during his or her first term, and will complete a transfer record if the child leaves the setting. Reception teachers are required to make summative assessments of children using the Foundation Stage Profile's nine-point scales. It is not enough to make summative assessments at the beginning and end of each child's time in a setting. Teachers also need to complete interim reviews of children's progress. These reviews should highlight the progress children are making through the Foundation Stage stepping stones and early learning goals, but also need to say something about the child as an individual learner – perhaps in the form of some brief comments under each of the six curriculum headings. The frequency with which teachers are able to do this will depend on the numbers of children, the length of time they stay in the class and on the staffing situation. During periods of staff absence it is always difficult to keep systems going.

Some teams now regularly (perhaps once a term) complete a form for each child, summarizing the child's achievements under headings similar to those in the previous section. They highlight the stepping stones/ELGs for each area of learning, which they feel the child has achieved. Learning priorities for each child are identified on the basis of these summative assessments. In this way no child is missed, and children who are not making progress, and may have special educational needs, are identified.

▌ Sharing perceptions with others and identifying needs

Teachers, nursery nurses and parents value the informal discussions they engage in daily. These daily interactions help keep everyone up to date with the most recent developments, and foster a mutual commitment to the children.

Teachers also make time for more focused, in-depth discussions about aspects of policy and practice and about the children, and often organize weekly meetings for this purpose. These meetings are usually set up for specific purposes – either to discuss a practice issue, such as the ordering of new equipment, or to review some of the children. An expected outcome of these meetings will be a collective identification of needs (both in relation to policy and practice and to children's development) based on information supplied by all members of the team. Sometimes the team will involve other professionals working with the child. In this way, a consistent approach is more likely to be achieved.

Parents are also offered opportunities to share their view of their child's experience at home and at school. A natural extension of the pre-admission record has been the regular involvement of parents in record-keeping, with some now regularly contributing their observations of their child learning at home. In addition to their informal daily chats, both staff and parents benefit greatly from meeting together more formally to discuss children's progress.

Using summative assessments, teachers invite parents (with an interpreter if necessary) to add their views about their child's achievements, particularly the developments and interests they have noticed at home. These discussions also provide an opportunity for parents to question what happens in school, and for teachers to learn about the child in the home situation. Often plans for supporting the child's progress are made at the meeting and parents are helped to see how they could use everyday activities at home to complement school-based activities.

When children move from one Foundation Stage setting to another, it is essential that teachers make time to meet colleagues to discuss how best to support children in making the transition.

Making more plans

The record-keeping process has now come full circle. Information is collected, plans are made and implemented, more information is collected, and plans are reviewed in the light of evidence contributed by all team members. It is now time to plan again.

Through sharing their perceptions the team can decide what further action they need to take. This process of finding out, using information to make plans, monitoring plans in action and sharing perceptions, lies at the heart of the responsive early years curriculum. In trying to develop methods of recording which match their principles and purposes, teachers have been intensely challenged. They freely admit there is much more to be done, and yet the most effective teachers have a great deal to be proud of. Early years staff need recognition for the quality of their work in this area and time to meet together as a team. Reception teachers often say that their teaching assistants are not paid to attend meetings with them, making teamwork impossible to achieve. Headteachers and governors need to be helped to recognize the cost-effectiveness of paying an extra hour's salary to these staff members.

Some points for discussion: Evaluating existing records

Collect all the written documents you have produced for the Foundation Stage (for example, policy statements, guidelines, school booklets, curriculum planning). To what extent do they communicate to the team and to others:

- Your aims for all aspects of your work?
- How you intend to put these aims into practice?

How consistent are these with the *Curriculum Guidance for the Foundation Stage?*
   Think about the records you keep to provide evidence of children's achievements in your class. Consider the oldest group in your present class, i.e. those transferring shortly to the next class: which of these children do you know most/least well? (Make a list from memory of the children in your class – which ones came to mind first/last or not at all?) Identify one or two children you feel you know well, and one or two you feel you know less well. Collect all the recorded information you have on these children, examine it carefully and ask yourself: what does this tell you about the strengths and weaknesses of your current approach to assessment?
   Which parts of the record-keeping process described in this chapter do you feel you need/would like to develop? What support will you need to develop your work in the ways you have identified? How will you make a case to get this support? Which parts of the record-keeping process described in this chapter do you feel you need/would like to develop? What support will you need to develop your work in the ways you have identified? How will you make a case to get this support?

▪ Further reading

Fawcett, M. (1996) *Learning through Child Observation*, Jessica Kingsley, London.
Hutchin, V. (2000) *Tracking Significant Achievement: The Early Years*, 2nd edn. Hodder and Stoughton, London.
Hutchin, V. (2003) *Observing and Assessing for the Foundation Stage Profile*, Hodder and Stoughton, London.
London Borough of Wandsworth (2001) *Planning for Foundation Stage Learning*, Wandsworth Council, London.
London Borough of Wandsworth (2002) *Ideas for Foundation Stage Learning*, Wandsworth Council, London.

Nutbrown, C. (1994) *Threads of Thinking: Young Children Learning and the Role of Early Education*, Paul Chapman Publishing, London.

Tower Hamlets Early Years Service and Newham Early Years Unit (2000) *Planning for Progress 2: An Early Years Curriculum Framework*, Learning Design, London.

7

Learning with children

'There is potential in all children which emerges powerfully under favourable conditions' (EYCG, 1989, p. 3), In the last chapter, we saw how detailed records can help identify the most favourable learning conditions for each child. Teachers of young children regularly face demands from those who wish to see children being 'made to' sit down and do some 'real work'. In particular, recent initiatives such as the literacy and numeracy strategies have challenged Foundation Stage teachers, who do not believe that whole-class teaching and the structured hour format is an effective way of working with the youngest learners. Holt (1989, p. 152) defines learning as 'making sense of things'. This definition is useful because it reminds teachers that their role is to help children to reach deeper understandings – not simply to enable them to regurgitate by rote.

Young children, because they want to please adults, can be persuaded to do what is asked, however little it means to them (Katz and Chard, 1989). Donaldson (1978) points out that many children, as they grow older, become dispirited through being given tasks which are beyond their capability, or which do not interest them, and that many have given up, or become helpless (Dweck and Leggett, 1988) by the time they reach adolescence. In a review of research Sharp (2002) draws attention to the possible negative effects of the UK's early admission policies on children's attitudes towards learning. Teachers must ensure that children 'continue to be interested, excited and motivated to learn' (QCA/DfES, 2000, p. 32). This goal is appropriate for learners of all ages.

The teacher's aims for children's learning

Some visitors to Foundation Stage classes – particularly those who believe learning only takes place as a result of formal instruction – may get the impression that the children can do as they like, and learn only what they choose to learn. It is therefore important to explain the role of the teacher in influencing the content of the curriculum for individual children.

Katz and Chard (1989) provide a helpful overview of the kinds of goals teachers need to have for children's learning. They identify (ibid., p. 20) four major types of learning goal: 'knowledge, skills, dispositions, and feelings'. Early years teachers need to help children acquire new knowledge and skills but it is not their only concern. Young children will be more likely to acquire knowledge and skills if they are also encouraged to develop positive dispositions and feelings. Katz and Chard (ibid., pp. 20–1) define dispositions as 'habits of mind, or tendencies to respond to situations in characteristic ways'. Persistence, curiosity, initiative and interest are all examples of dispositions. There is evidence that an overconcentration on skills and knowledge acquisition at the expense of dispositions is counterproductive in the long term (Schweinhart, Weikart and Larner, 1986; Schweinhart and Weikart, 1997) – after all, what is the point in having skills if you do not have the disposition to make use of them? Many adults never read for pleasure even though they can read. This is because they learned the skills involved in reading, but were not helped to acquire the disposition to read. Foundation Stage teachers aim to build on the children's natural curiosity and zest for life and encourage an enthusiasm for learning. They want children to feel good about themselves and as learners. They hope that the dispositions and feelings which children have acquired in their class will stay with them through life, and will help them to cope with the less favourable conditions they might meet in the future.

They do not make children sit down to learn a particular skill – they know that this would be likely to lead to resentment and, possibly, to feelings of incompetence. There are many opportunities for introducing skills and knowledge during activities the children have chosen for themselves from the carefully structured provision. Sensitive adult intervention in these activities is more likely to result in the desired learning outcome. They also know that they have a role in enthusing children to try new experiences.

Responsive teaching – what is involved?

Responsive teaching of the kind outlined in the previous chapters is only possible if the adults involved have developed a range of personal qualities. Teachers act as role models for the children and their colleagues – it is no coincidence that teachers with loud voices produce classes of noisy children, and that teachers who use negotiating strategies produce children who can negotiate with each other! It is not just behaviour which is imitated. If teachers wish to encourage the acquisition of knowledge, skills, dispositions and feelings, they need to have acquired these themselves.

Foundation Stage teachers need:

- *knowledge*: of child development, of the backgrounds and experience of individual children, and of curriculum content (in order to be able to recognize opportunities for extending learning);
- *skills*: including communication skills, some practical skills (which develop through the pursuit of personal interests in art, gardening, music, woodwork, pottery, cookery, scientific exploration, writing, etc.) and organizational skills;
- *dispositions*: similar to those they expect children to develop such as an inquiring mind, curiosity, interest, warmth, persistence and a willingness to have a go; and
- *feelings*: such as confidence, enthusiasm and pleasure in the achievements of others.

Learning how to learn

Many teachers talk about the joy of learning how to learn when they start to observe and work alongside young children. Teachers, who have not been supported by appropriate training are unlikely to feel this joy. They are usually unable to make sense of what they see and hear young children doing and saying, and are not expecting children to teach them anything. This is why so many teachers who have transferred to the Foundation Stage from Key Stages 1 and 2 have found 3–5-year-olds difficult to work with.

A secondary-trained teacher, who had returned to teaching after a career break and had been placed in a nursery school without the benefit of any retraining, commented to her colleagues that she thought the nursery must be very boring for the children. She felt that, because the staff had created a learning environment where everything had a definite place and where children could operate autonomously, children would get bored because the rooms always looked essentially the same. This view took no account of the fact that the experienced staff adapted the learning environment in subtle ways in response to their observations, or of the fact that children were using this environment very confidently and with ever-developing competence. A colleague asked her: 'Do you think the children look bored?' After thinking for a moment she said: 'No, they always look very busy and involved. But I would be bored if I was them.' This was what was at the root of her comment – she was bored because she did not know how to relate to children who were operating so independently.

This example highlights a dilemma, which many staff are facing when translating Foundation Stage principles, and messages from research, into practice. Many adults, particularly those who have been used to directing activities, have found that giving children more power and control over their learning has involved them in rethinking their whole approach. Some have found it difficult to relinquish power over children and others have felt they no longer have a role to play. With the benefit of experience, teams are learning from children that adult support is still necessary, and that a less didactic model of support actually has more potential in terms of lasting learning.

Case study: the team at Adamsrill Primary School in Lewisham describe how they developed provision for writing in their reception class (see Chapter 5 for further information about this Foundation Stage setting)

During nine years in Reception each child had a writing book and every week we did a drawing or a piece of topic-based work on a one-to-one basis giving lots of encouragement and support on letter sound, letter formation and punctuation. On our return to Reception (after three years in the nursery class), we found that the work books were a chore for us so how must the children feel! We decided to concentrate on the physicality of fine skills and offered activities that encouraged children to be dextrous and use the pincer grip in all areas, e.g. in the art area – fine brushes, cotton buds, malleable table – rice and tweezers for putting grains in containers, water tray – turkey basters, sponges, syringes for squeezing to develop hand muscles. We aimed to put writing into every area: construction – large sheets of paper on the floor, magnetic wedge always available with pens. In the writing area we wanted them to experiment and gave each a book that they could work in any time that they wanted to with a free choice of what they did. We found that as they experimented they became more adventurous without prompting. The total transformation came from a course we attended about 'Writing for a Purpose'. This opened our eyes to wonderful opportunities, e.g. our meal supervisor was unwell and it was suggested that they made get well cards for her. This transformed the children into writers wanting desperately to communicate how much they missed her. We found the 'Dear Zoo' book a wonderful example of a child writing for a reason. We made our own page format for the children to write for an animal – the children loved this idea. We made sandwiches and they made their own recipes. These activities produced an enthusiastic response turning them into writers rather than coaxing them into being writers.

As a unit we treat each term differently and have developed our own settling policy, part of which states that during the first term the children do not have to sit on the carpet first thing but go to an activity of their choice. At the beginning of the second term when they were confident and settled we then began to sit on the carpet in the morning to do the register and have a focus time for new ideas. During this term they became interested in the register so we gave them their own large register on the wall for them to mark. We also copied blank registers which they used with a clipboard and used their wonderful knowledge of the format – PL for packed lunch, M for absence with a reason, / if present and O if absent without a reason and L for late. We also did the weather and date and, as always, I would forget and have to look in my own diary, a yearly one with a ribbon marker. A child in the class decided to make her own diary with folded paper stapled together with wool for the marker. This started a surge of diary making and writing. They asked if they could take their diaries home. We were amazed how many children took to taking them home to record what they did. We had always encouraged parents with reading but I felt that this was the first real home/school provision for writing. Some books were full of marks, others letters and others sentences and drawings, recording at their own level. The highlight of this was a whole A4 page of emergent writing and a comment from his mum saying 'I hope this is alright, he insisted on doing it all on his own'. By the final term we felt the children were confident and always willing to have a go. All the experimenting and freedom had paid off.

This case study shows how adult-initiated experiences support and inspire child-initiated learning and how, by using observation, adults are guided to plan for future learning. It also highlights the importance of inspiring professional development opportunities.

Above all it shows the progress children can make in a less restricted setting where creativity and resourcefulness are promoted. A transmission model of teaching can feel relatively safe for the teacher as she is in control, and can initiate or put a stop to activities as the mood takes her. This approach also very quickly becomes boring because it closes the teacher off from the learners' ideas.

A responsive approach to children feels much less safe, because children share control and have an equal right to initiate or end activities. Teachers cannot be sure where the learners will lead them, or that they will follow the leads the teacher introduces. This approach is never boring though. It offers both teachers and pupils the chance to learn from each other and requires teachers to make countless judgements and adjustments during the course of each day – an intellectually demanding process.

In order to adopt this complex approach, Foundation Stage staff have to accept the role of learner, and have to replace the role of director of learning (which implies a hierarchical structure) with the role of enabler and extender (which emphasizes a partnership approach to learning).

Building relationships with children

When teachers are asked on courses to explore materials and equipment to be found in the early years classroom, it is fascinating to observe how they respond. Three main responses can usually be observed. First there are the writers. These teachers have arrived with notebooks and are determined to use them. They spend the entire session noting book titles, listing equipment and asking about stockists. They do not use any of the equipment, they merely pick up some items to look at them more closely. Second are the embarrassed watchers. These teachers stop at each activity or piece of equipment, and handle something in an embarrassed way. While doing this they watch (out of the corner of their eye) what others are doing. Third are the enthusiastic players. They have a good look round to begin with (often with a friend) and then decide what they will do. They spend the whole session playing at one or two activities, finding out how things work, setting themselves problems to solve and sometimes being naughty – often with water!

These descriptions are obviously stereotypical (and possibly unkind, although they are not intended to be). They remind us how our response to situations can give us insight into our own attitude to learning. Most teachers can probably relate to all three types, since all of us find it easier to get involved with some activities than others. It is obvious which of the three types of teacher would be most likely to inspire and respond effectively to young children.

Sadly many adults have suppressed the playful side of their personality. Without it they are unlikely to be able to empathize with young children's playful responses. If, for example, we have forgotten how much fun it can be to be naughty or to play a trick on someone, we may deal much too harshly with children's experiments with the boundaries of acceptable behaviour. After all, blowing water through a tube is irresistible, so how can you be expected to stop just because it is landing on someone's head? If we want children to take responsibility, we must allow them to consider and discuss calmly the consequences of their actions.

An ability to enjoy, and to share in the enjoyment of others, is an essential characteristic for the early years teacher. So is an ability to see the world through a child's eyes. Without these abilities adults are unlikely to be invited to share in children's adventures. Children can help teachers to let go of their inhibitions. There is no need to worry about looking foolish – in the eyes of the children we do not look foolish, even if we are wearing a hat from the dressing-up box!

Of course, enjoyment is not the only aim of early education, although it is a 'side effect or by-product of being engaged in worthwhile activity, effort and learning' (Katz and Chard, 1989, p. 5). Teachers also need to know when to be solemn and to take their pupils' concerns seriously. Many of the young child's perceptions of the world seem funny to the adult. We have to remember that they are not so to the child and, that if we wish to encourage the expression of developing ideas, concepts and feelings we must treat children with respect.

Adrian (aged 4 years 6 months), who had just been baptized, was re-enacting the church service with a group of friends. He invited his teacher to join in. He had taken the role of the priest and organized his friends and the teacher to sit on chairs in a semicircle in the book corner. He gave them each a 'prayer book' and then told them to 'sing this after me'. He began to chant solemnly 'come by liver us, come by liver us, come by liver us Lord'. As the play continued, Adrian was stretched to the limit of his intellectual and linguistic abilities to explain how he wanted his non-Catholic friends and teacher to behave. The teacher's role was to enable him to take the lead in reconstructing an important personal experience. She entered into the solemn nature of this activity, and gave no hint that there were times when she was amused. In common with the other children, she acted the part of a member of his congregation asking for explanation when necessary. She made a point of sharing her observations of Adrian with his mother at the end of the session, to enable his family to support his growing understanding of his religion.

This sensitivity to children's moods is vital. Teachers need to be able to match their own interactions to the mood of the children's activity. The teacher who responds earnestly to a playful interlude, or laughs at a child's serious remark will soon find children avoiding her.

All children need to know that the teacher notices and values them as individuals. The sincere smile, the interested question or comment, the encouraging glance or remark, the meaningful words of praise, the sympathetic arm round the shoulder or the firm but understanding reprimand, all demonstrate that the teacher has noticed and cares. Those of us who can remember from our early schooldays how lonely it felt to feel invisible within the group, or to be continually out of favour with the teacher, will understand the importance of these signs of positive recognition. The children need to see that their parents are also responded to warmly. The most skilled teachers can adapt their approach to reach even those children and parents who seem unreachable.

Young children deserve teachers who care, are interested and interesting (ESAC, 1989), join in, and are able to share in both fun and solemn pursuits. Teachers who exhibit these qualities attract children. The children want to do things with them and want to share their experiences with them. From this sound relationship teachers are in a strong position to respond to children and help them develop and learn.

Enabling children to learn

Teachers enable each child to learn and develop by helping them to sustain their current interests; and also by interesting them in new things. This involves a number of teaching roles and strategies. Whichever approach she uses, the teacher keeps the needs of the children in mind to help her determine the optimum moment for learning – the moment when the child wants to, or needs to, learn. Moyles, Adams and Musgrove (2002, pp. 168–9) worked with practitioners to highlight a range of teaching strategies under the following headings:

- Teaching skills and knowledge directly.
- Teaching through modelling behaviour.
- Teaching through interacting with children.
- Teaching through scaffolding.
- Teaching through communicating.
- Teaching through giving children feedback.

- Teaching through questioning.
- Teaching through intervening.
- Teaching through responding to children.
- Motivating children and fostering their interests.
- Encouraging children's enquiry.
- Encouraging children to think about their learning.

These highlight the complexity and subtlety involved in teaching young children. They are explored explicitly or implicitly in the outline of strategies below.

Stimulating, sustaining and extending interest

The first task for any teacher is to capture the children's interest and offer starting points for learning. It is then equally important to sustain and extend it. Strategies used by teachers to stimulate the curiosity of individual children and groups include the following.

Adding equipment to particular areas

Assuming that the environment has been well resourced with permanently available provision as described in Chapter 5, the teacher then needs to consider how she can add to areas to support and extend the children's learning. This may be done as follows:

- *In response to observed behaviour.* Children had been observed making police and fire service vehicles with the large, hollow, wooden blocks, and had been using these in dramatic play. They were using small, rectangular blocks as 'walkie talkie' radios. The teacher, remembering that she had two unwanted, broken pocket radios at home, brought these into school the next day and added them to the block play area. These added a further dimension to the play as the children developed their knowledge and understanding of technology by learning where the on/off switch was, how to change the frequency and how to put the aerial up and down. The teacher planned to be involved in the block area for the first part of the session so that she could support the children in learning how to share and take turns with the radios (any new item of equipment has novelty value and will be wanted by everyone), and in learning about two-way radios. She noted that a further extension would be to ask the local beat officers to call and show their radio to the children and talk about how they used it.
- *To arouse curiosity.* Teachers also need to judge the kinds of additions which will fascinate the children. One nursery school team had been on a technology course. They had been asked to make boats from

junk materials, and were able to keep their creations. It was decided to put these boats on a plank across the top of the water tray the next day and to observe how the children reacted. Several children were struck by the odd sight in their water tray. One child exclaimed 'What's all this?' – the cue for the teacher to explain what the staff had been involved in, to answer the children's questions about which boat belonged to which member of staff, and to ask the children, who were interested, to find out which boat stayed afloat longest.

When they had made their decision she asked them to explain why they thought this boat stayed afloat longest, helping them to express their discoveries in words by prompting them with questions like 'Do you think it was because this boat is small?', to which one child replied, 'No, this one's smaller and it broke'. The children themselves decided to tell each member of staff what had happened to their boat and took great delight in telling one teacher 'Your boat's no good – it's all broken'. Lucy (aged 4 years) decided she wanted to make a boat and several others joined her in the creative workshop area where they spent the remainder of the morning making and testing boats.

The teacher cannot always follow up in this way, but she can make sure resources are available which would enable all children to develop their interests. She can ensure that the books on flight are displayed prominently to inspire the children who were trying to make paper aeroplanes this morning; she can put buckets of water and large decorating brushes near the play house so that the children can go beyond pretending to paint the walls; she can put old order forms in the graphics area to enable those children, who watched her order some equipment, to imitate what they saw her doing; she can hang long scarves in the dressing-up area to enable the little girl, who wishes to imitate her mother with the new baby, to carry a doll on her back; and so on.

Setting up a display or area of interest

Displays in the early years should be interactive – they should be for touching and talking about – and situated where children can see and use them easily. Sometimes they develop into a role-play area or inspire a specific activity.

Displays set up to inspire interest might include the following:

- Photographs taken on a teacher's or nursery nurse's holiday plus items collected such as shells, rocks, fossils and souvenirs, to inspire holiday talk – in one class a small tray of sand with play people was placed on a table next to such a display to inspire small-scale re-enactment of holiday experiences.

- A collection of objects which can be taken apart, such as interlocking wooden puzzles, an old radio, graded, nesting dolls or barrels and pieces from different types of construction kit, to encourage discussion of design features and experience of taking apart and putting together.
- Pictures and examples of different kinds of fruit to encourage discussion and tasting, and to provide the focus for cooking sessions.

Often the teacher will start a display and encourage children to contribute to it, e.g. children may bring photos and items collected on their holiday for the holiday display. Displays focusing on one colour or one letter of the alphabet (which have made a comeback) are rarely inspiring for young children – far better to set up an interactive display involving the range of colours in kaleidoscopes, colour paddles and prisms or a display of writing for many different purposes, e.g. letter, lists, greeting cards, order forms with opportunities to 'have a go'.

Displays may also be set up in response to an already developing interest, or to serve as a reminder of an interesting activity. Responsive displays of this kind might be set up:

- after a visit by the school dentist. Books, posters and items left by the dentist, such as mirrors and plastic teeth, would enable staff and children to discuss the visit and any fears the children may have and would almost certainly inspire role play;
- around an item brought to school by a child. Andrew (aged 3 years 6 months) had been to visit relatives in Canada and had brought a hat he had worn there to show his teacher. The hat was a balaclava helmet complete with face cover with slits for eyes and nose. This item generated much interest and discussion, and led to the setting up of a collection of headwear worn in different climates and for different purposes and also books, photographs and posters; and
- after an activity, such as cooking or after an outing, to serve as a reminder of the experience, and to enable those children who took part to relive their experience in words and share it with other children.

In setting up displays, teachers are aware of the need to monitor their use and relevance to the children's interests. Displays can quickly become stale and uninspiring, and then either need to be taken down or regenerated by the addition of other items. The most successful displays provide a powerful link between the children's home and school experience.

Organizing outings

Further links between school and the children's community are encouraged by outings within the local area to broaden children's life experience. These include everyday activities such as shopping, going to the post office or bank, or taking a pet to the vet, as well as trips to the fire station, a local museum, the park or local workshops. Occasional outings to places further afield, such as the seaside, a wildlife park or a theatre performance, involving the whole class and their parents may also be arranged.

Outings must be well-planned and followed up (Ironbridge Gorge Museum, 1989). A small group of children had been 'writing' letters to each other and pretending to post them. Their teacher arranged a visit to the local sorting office so that they could see what happened to letters once they were posted. Whilst there they posted a letter addressed to the school and watched as it was sorted – there was great excitement the next day when the letter was delivered.

The teacher explained to the staff in the sorting office (as well as to all adults involved in the visit) why she wanted the children to come, and what she hoped they would learn. She also provided opportunities for follow-up work so that the children could consolidate their learning – she, and the children involved in the visit set up a sorting office in the classroom using some of the resources they had been given. They also made photos taken during the outing into a book for the whole class to share. In these ways, the interest of the children involved in the visit was sustained and other children, who had not been able to go, were also drawn into the experience. Parents were told about the experience, and several of them followed it up at home by encouraging their children to send letters to relatives.

Outings of this kind validate the child's home and community experience, and encourage parents to see the value of many of the routine tasks which they and their children undertake. If it is not possible for staff to take all children on an outing within the locality (e.g. to a particular shop), teachers sometimes suggest that parents take their own child at the weekend – it is helpful to provide a list of things to notice.

At Wingate Community Nursery School, County Durham, outings are often inspired by one child's interest and are used as a starting point for medium-term planning. Children at this school develop a high degree of confidence and independence because staff have high expectations of them and give them many opportunities to take responsibility for their own learning. In the following case study an outing was inspired by Abigayle, a confident 4-year-old, whose behaviour had improved to such an extent, that she had been rewarded by her parents with a trip to Metroland an indoor funfair in Newcastle upon Tyne.

Case study written by Becky Wood

Her keyworker, Becky, invited Abigayle to tell her friends about it at group time.

She talked to the group of six other 3 and 4-year-olds for 30 minutes about her experiences, explaining in detail about the choice of tickets/wristbands, how each ride worked, the cost, safety issues, the technicalities of the scanning process and turnstiles. She described the event in such a way that the whole group listened with interest, fascination and intrigue, the children asking her to elaborate on the more interesting details.

Following this session, and acknowledging the interest and enthusiasm for Metroland for several children, the staff team discussed how they could offer the next step for these children and take their learning forward. It was decided that the children should be offered the chance to plan their own visit to Metroland the following week. There were many opportunities when the group worked together to make plans – look at the Metroland website, talk ideas through, study maps, book a minibus, etc. Becky met with the parents of the seven children to inform them of the plans and to explain why the visit was worthwhile educationally. In particular she stressed how the staff felt the visit would extend the children's language, social skills and knowledge and understanding of the world, and perhaps more importantly their self-confidence and independence.

The children were offered the chance to discuss, plan and negotiate with the wider community, with the minimum amount of adult input. After discussing the possibility of travelling to Metroland by train they agreed to use a bus 'like the one we went on to buy our guinea pigs' said Olivia. They searched for the telephone number in the directory and independently rang the (pre-warned) minibus company asking for a bus for 'three adults … and seven kids'. They gave details about their school and the time they needed to be picked up in the morning and returned at the end of the day. The visit was a huge success with both children and adults recording it on camera and camcorder, to enable them to share the experience with the rest of the children and staff. The images were dropped into PowerPoint and shown on a large screen and a 15-minute edited version of the video was shown to all children the next day. The seven children who had been to Metroland were given the opportunity to take control and present their day to the others – talking and answering questions as they arose. These children were then invited to represent in a variety of ways their memory of 'the shows' (rides) encouraging them to display their understanding of the connections and workings of each one. The results were stunning (see Figures 7.1 and 7.2). The children worked with rigour, talking through their sketches with each other and with the adults observing, often drawing more than one picture.

The staff team discussed how all the children might benefit from the experience of the original group. After close observation of the children immediately after the visit there appeared to be two possibilities for extending and developing their learning:

1   Imaginative play – children were talking about giving their wristbands to the dolls in nursery.
2   Problem-solving and creative thinking – as most of the rides went round and round, the team decided to explore the concept of circular movement with the children.

And so Metroland was created on a small scale, using the construction kit Bauplay, for the dolls to enjoy. A pulley and cog system, using recycled bicycle wheels mounted on a large

Olivia drew
The aeroplane and helicopter
rides
- the arms have got 'flashy lights on them'
- all the arms are connected to a central hub
- at the end of each arm, there is an aeroplane or a helicopter

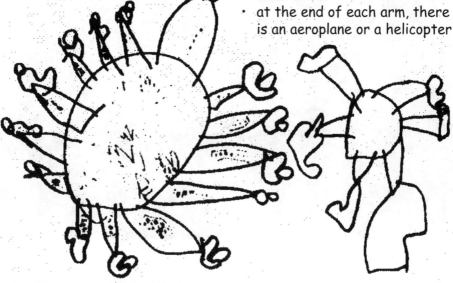

Figure 7.1 *Olivia's metro drawing*

Abigayle drew:
An ice cream
factory
- cones
- hosepipe to get the ice cream in cones
- a machine
- open and closed signs
- wire to plug it in

Figure 7.2 *Abigayle's metro drawing*

Figure 7.3 *Metroland*

wooden board in both horizontal and vertical planes was created for exploration and investigation. (See Figure 7.3 showing the big wheel for the dolls to use.)

The Metroland project lasted approximately four weeks, involving and motivating almost every child in the nursery. The project appealed to all interests and levels of development and covered all areas of the curriculum in a real and meaningful way for the children.

This case study demonstrates clearly the role of the adult in valuing, supporting, facilitating and extending children's interests and ideas. It also shows how medium-term planning can evolve organically and effectively from children's own starting points rather than from a set topic or theme.

Acting as a role model

Teachers can help children to see the purpose of, and become interested in, a wide range of activities if they are prepared to demonstrate their skills, and encourage other adults to use their talents in meaningful contexts. Too often adults keep their own activities hidden from children forgetting that children learn from imitating a more experienced person. This imitation is not merely copying. Through watching others with more experience and expertise the child 'makes use of and reconstructs an event after the event' (Bruce, 1997, p. 73).

Modelling literacy

The teacher inspires an interest in reading and writing through her own involvement in these activities (Whitehead, 1997). She reads recipes, labels, timetables and instruction leaflets in the children's presence, she responds to their request to tell them 'What does this say?', and she encourages others to read those scripts and languages she cannot read herself (thereby emphasizing that Britain is a multilingual society and that others have skills which she does not). Similarly, she demonstrates the ways in which she needs to write. The children when seeing her writing observations, reminder messages to herself, notices and labels, or recording captions on their work (i.e. scribing their talk) will inevitably ask 'What are you writing?' or 'What does that say?' or 'That letter's in my name'. These questions and comments provide the teacher with many opportunities for emphasizing the nature and uses of literacy skills and offer considerably more meaningful starting points for learning than the isolated (and often meaningless) handwriting drills, phonics sessions and alphabet recitation which have become common in some early years classes.

Modelling numeracy

Teachers also respond to daily events to demonstrate how they make use of mathematics: counting to see if they have enough money to buy the cooking ingredients, counting and dividing to see how many fish fingers each child can have at lunchtime, using a calculator, measuring a space to see if a new piece of equipment will fit, weighing the bag of flour to see if there is enough for a recipe, cutting the fruit into pieces so there is enough for everyone and so on. These are real-life experiences concerned with seeing mathematics as a tool (Metz, 1996; Montague-Smith, 1997).

Modelling scientific and technological processes

Some Foundation Stage teachers may feel more nervous about acting as a role model in the areas of science and technology (Johnston, 1996). They are reassured when they realize that it is not necessary for them to know all the answers. Their role is primarily to give children experience, and some understanding of scientific and technological processes. Above all they need to encourage children to explore, investigate and make their own discoveries (Richards, 1996).

Everyday opportunities for exploration and investigation arise. Through their own awareness, interest and willingness to respond to events, teachers encourage children to ask questions such as 'Why has this container gone rusty?' and 'How could we stop the boat sinking?', and to explore problems such as 'Why does the bridge keep collapsing?' and 'How do you think you could make the boat move?' Children will gain inspiration from seeing their teachers ask open-ended questions and attempt to solve problems, as well as from adult demonstrations of skills. Many teachers mend and make equipment with the children, involving them fully in the process. Children's woodwork skills develop noticeably after they have worked with their teacher or another adult to make an item of equipment. The teacher does not need to be an expert. Through the use of reference books and plans, children can see again how literacy skills are applied, and any mistakes or problems can be worked on collaboratively. It may even be necessary to ask advice from someone with more experience.

If adults act as if they know everything, the children do not have the benefit of seeing an adult learner at work, and are given the impression that there comes a point in life when you stop learning. This is clearly not the case, and learning alongside adults is an important experience for young children.

Modelling creativity

Many Foundation Stage staff and parents have creative talents, which they share with the children. Seeing a talented artist or musician at work is undoubtedly inspiring for children. The children, whose teacher regularly played the piano to them, learnt a great deal about the use of this instrument. They could be observed imitating her use of the foot pedals, her hand and body movements, the way she played softly and loudly, and the way she turned the pages of the music she was using.

Similarly, seeing an adult paint, draw or use clay can also develop children's awareness of the possibilities for using these media. However, this should not be confused with adults drawing outlines for children to fill in, or pictures for children to copy. The talented artist who illustrates a poster for the school jumble sale in the children's presence is offering children the chance to see a more experienced person use his or her skill. On the other hand, the adult who draws or make pots for children to copy is undermining the children's skill, imposing ideas on them and limiting their imagination. From the first adult the children may take away those aspects of the experience which have personally inspired them – they are free to respond in their own way. The second adult expects all children to respond in the same way, and shows no respect for individual creativity. The first adult offers a stimulating role model, the second a stultifying template. Adults foster children's personal, social and emotional development, and provide the foundation for literacy when they sing, dance, tell (as opposed to read) stories, use puppets and take on dramatic roles.

Modelling anti-sexist behaviour

Teachers have not always been seen as positive role models out of doors. Their negative attitude can result in all members of the team adopting a passive supervisory role out of doors. It is essential that adults get involved in physical activity both to prevent boys from dominating certain equipment and to encourage girls to develop the physical skills they need. This involvement includes joining in with throwing, climbing, hopping, etc., and making use of physical skills during gardening, building a low wall and when retrieving a ball from the nursery roof. Seeing women engaged in vigorous, sometimes dirty, physical activity challenges the stereotyped views which even very young children hold.

Boys and girls need to see both men and women involving themselves in the full range of activities.

Parents as role models

The Foundation Stage teacher also needs to encourage parents to share their skills with the children – particularly those parents who have developed interests and skills not usually associated with their gender. Adults involved with the Foundation Stage class can enable each other to tackle tasks they have not tried before. Those with specific skills can involve other adults as well as children. The rabbit run, which was referred to earlier, was an example of this kind of collaboration. The nursery teacher in this case was the skilled carpenter, but through using a detailed plan containing instructions, and by offering verbal support she involved nursery nurses, parents and children in the project, which took several days to complete.

This kind of apprenticeship model, where skills are demonstrated and shared, offers adults and children the chance to develop confidence as well as expertise. Enabling parents to work alongside their children in this way helps them to understand the teacher's approach and encourages them sometimes to take on the role of enabler in relation to staff, e.g. parents who work with computers are often able to offer advice to inexperienced workers. Parents can also take a lead in helping children and staff understand more about their religion, e.g. in one class Rheena (aged 4) was delighted to help her mother show a group of children, parents and staff how to make a rangoli pattern on the floor during Diwali.

Seeing their parents and the nursery staff working together in this way contributes to the children's self-esteem and security. Teachers must ensure that all parents can be involved. Some parents may not be able to spend time in school. However, they may be willing to arrange for a small group of children to visit them at work, or may be able to contribute items from work such as old forms, X-ray plates and card. Those who speak languages other than English may be involved in supporting children who speak their language and, perhaps, teaching the staff a few words. One teacher asked parents who spoke languages other than English if they would sing a song they had learnt in childhood onto a tape. The final collection included songs from France, Bangladesh, Vietnam, Jamaica, Iran, Italy and Pakistan. The parents involved, although shy at first, were encouraged by the teacher's enthusiasm and the interpreters' explanations, and enjoyed trying to remember the words to songs from their past. The tape became a valuable and unique school resource.

It is the teacher's job to enable all parents to be involved positively in their child's school experience. This requires her to take a broad view of involvement, which goes way beyond expecting parents to stay in the classroom. She needs to interest each parent in some aspect of school life and build on that. The skilled teacher does not say things like 'the parents are not interested'. She knows that all parents are interested in their child in their own way, and that many of them wish to be more involved in their child's education (Smith, 1980; Tizard, Mortimore and Burchell, 1981; Hughes, Wikeley and Nash, 1994; Whalley and the Pen Green Centre Team, 2001).

Acting as a role model: discussion points

Ask yourself honestly:

- What kind of person am I? For example, am I gregarious or shy, confident or timid, open or afraid of discussing feelings, eager to try new things and meet new people or nervous about new experiences, positive or negative, and so on?
- Do I enjoy playing with young children or do I feel uncomfortable in this role?
- What kind of an example am I and other members of the team setting the children in our class? For example, are we encouraging them by our example to be kind, calm, excitable, enthusiastic, noisy, adventurous, etc.?
- Are they learning to have a go, to believe that girls cannot do some things, to behave inappropriately to gain attention, to listen or ignore?
- What kind of role model do you want to be? How can you make sure you all achieve this?

Initiating activities and experiences

There is often a difference between what is planned and offered, and what the children receive. The following example demonstrates how a planned activity is spontaneously adapted and developed to take account of the responses of individual children.

Natalie (3 years 7 months) and Terri (3 years 11 months) were close friends at school and nearly always played together. Both were receiving speech therapy for articulation difficulties, and the nursery staff had worked closely with both the children's therapists with a view to supporting the children's language development. The teacher had noticed that they were currently interested in water play, and her planned involvement for one morning was to be focused on the water tray. She intended to pursue their interest in transferring water from one container to another through the addition of equipment – sieves with different-size holes, funnels, waterwheels, guttering, tubing, spoons, different types of cloth, etc. – through posing challenges such as 'Can you find a way of getting the water from that container into that one without pouring it in?', and through a discussion of their discoveries. This could, of course, involve other children as well as Terri and Natalie.

However, on the morning of the activity snow had fallen (the first for over a year), and the teacher knew that this would be the major interest of the day. She also knew that, as the snow was not likely to settle for long, it was important to use this rare opportunity for learning from first-hand experience. This is the reality of 'following children's interests'. If we truly believe that enthusiasm and motivation are important factors in learning, we must not waste the opportunities which arise.

The teacher, therefore, met with the team before school started and together they planned and set up ways of exploring snow. Clean shovels and pattern-making objects were placed in the snow-covered garden, books (both fiction and reference) and relevant posters were prominently displayed, the tape and book of *The Snowman* (Briggs, 1978) were available to listen to on headphones and during a movement session. The nursery nurse planned to focus on feeding the birds and offered to make bird cake during the afternoon session to encourage the children to think about the effects of winter weather on other living creatures. The written plans were revised to take account of these changes.

The teacher decided to postpone her planned activity. She knew that some children would prefer to stay indoors so she decided to fill the water tray with snow instead of water. Before the children arrived she jotted down some of the discoveries, which might be encouraged:

- The appearance of snow – the colour and shape of snowflakes (seen through a magnifying glass). What other substances does it look like?
- What does it feel like and what happens when we hold it in our hand? The concept of melting – in which conditions does snow melt quickly/slowly? Why has the snow in the water tray melted while the snow in the garden has not?
- What can you do with it? What effect do different tools (spades, rakes) have on it? Can it be used in a water wheel? Will it go through a funnel, etc.? Can we build with it?

The usual selection of water-play equipment was available plus magnifying glasses and some transparent containers for use in melting experiments. However, the teacher intended to encourage sensory exploration before the use of equipment.

At the beginning of the morning session the teacher filled the tray with snow with the help of some of the children who had arrived early. She positioned herself near it. As expected, the majority of children wanted to play out of doors. However, Natalie and Terri, following the pattern of the last few days, headed immediately for the water tray. The unusual sight which greeted them stopped them in their tracks and Natalie exclaimed: 'Look Terri, there's snow!' The teacher responded, 'Yes, come and find out what it feels like'. Natalie walked on past the tray to the shelves of equipment and called back over her shoulder to the teacher 'It's cold', and proceeded to collect a jug. She went to the classroom sink and filled it with water. Terri copied her. They returned to the water tray and started to pour the water over the snow. As they did so, they noticed that, as the water landed on the surface of the snow, holes appeared. Almost simultaneously they shouted, 'Look, I've made a hole'.

This did not feature in the teacher's plans! She had a choice – either to attempt to focus the children on her plans (and run the risk of losing the children's interest), or to respond to the children's enthusiasm. The latter choice requires quick and flexible thinking. In this case, she responded enthusiastically to the children's discovery, even though she was aware that the snow would soon be water. After sharing their initial excitement, she helped them sustain their interest and extend their understanding of what was happening by offering a set of challenges, such as:

- I wonder what would happen if we pour the water very slowly or drip it through a pipette or syringe?
- How else could we make holes in the snow?
- What would happen if we used hot water?

By valuing the children's discovery and helping them to explore it further through the investigations she suggested, she sustained their interest and created a positive – enjoyable but demanding – environment for learning. She took some photographs of their experience both to remind them and to share with other children.

What the children actually learnt is more difficult to determine but the teacher is given clues by their comments. They may not yet understand why, but they undoubtedly knew that hot water had a different effect on the snow than cold water. They learnt the word for steam. Later that morning Terri and Natalie could be seen making connections in their learning by showing the nursery nurse how drips of melting snow from the roof of the playhouse were making holes in the snow on the grass below. Above all, they had been encouraged through this experience to express their discoveries in spoken language – which was one of the teacher's original intentions – and they had been encouraged to set up investigations.

Surely this is how everyone learns. From first-hand experiences and explorations we gradually gain a clearer picture of the world, and make connections between one experience and another. Communicating our experiences to others takes our learning a stage further as we struggle to describe what happened to someone else. The skill of the teacher lies in offering inspiring experiences, sustaining interest and helping children to find some possible explanations for their own discoveries. As they gain in experience so their ability to reason and predict is enhanced.

Merely offering experiences and activities is relatively simple. What distinguishes the skilled Foundation Stage teacher from other practitioners is her ability to take her lead from the children, to see ways of maximizing the interest they are showing and to enable them to relate one experience to another. There is also skill involved in knowing when to stop – recognizing the point at which the question you have posed is outside the interest or understanding of the child.

At the end of each observation or interaction, the teacher records the significant knowledge, skills, dispositions and feelings each child demonstrated. It was just as important to record that Natalie and Terri had the confidence to pursue their own intentions and responded enthusiastically to the teacher's challenges, as it was to record that they were able to describe some of the properties of snow, and could skilfully pour water quickly and slowly. It was also important to record how they were able to refer back to their discoveries later that morning, and how they were able to remember enough to dictate captions for the teacher to write next to the photographs when they were developed a week later.

Siraj-Blatchford et al. (2002, p. 11) found that the most highly qualified staff 'were the most effective in their interactions with the children, using the most sustained shared thinking'. Sustained shared thinking is defined as: 'an episode in which two or more individuals "work together" in an intellectual way to solve a problem, clarify a concept, evaluate activities, extend a narrative etc. Both parties must contribute to the thinking and it must develop and extend' (ibid., p. 8).

The researchers found that, even in the excellent settings in their study, episodes of sustained shared thinking were rare. This may be because the open-ended nature of such episodes worries some teachers. These teachers may be afraid to deviate from their planned learning intention, not having the confidence to follow the children's lead and account for their learning afterwards. It may also be because teachers lack confidence and skills in open-ended questioning. The same research found that only 5.1 per cent of questions asked in the 'effective' settings studied were open-ended, whilst 34.1 per cent were closed and 60.8 per cent were of a 'socially related caring' nature such as 'are you alright?' (ibid., p. 55) Professional development opportunities focusing on these interactive strategies clearly need to be given high priority.

Demonstrating skills and imparting knowledge

There are occasions when the teacher needs to teach more directly. There are times when it is appropriate to show children how to do something or tell them the information they need. It is still essential that the teacher carefully selects the moment for intervention of this kind. Sometimes a child will ask directly for help. Young children learning to use scissors will often ask an adult to hold the paper or fabric they wish to cut, knowing that they can achieve this task with help. They may also ask 'What is this?' or 'What's that called?' in relation to new equipment, giving the teacher a clue that they are ready for this knowledge. Children love naming things, particularly things with unusual names – of all the new musical instruments in one class, the guiro and the cabasa were the names most quickly learnt.

Teachers will also use opportunities when children make a mistake to develop understanding. The child who rushes up to the teacher holding a beetle and says 'Look, I've found a spider', will be helped to understand the similarities and differences between a beetle and a spider, perhaps with the help of a book. The teacher who replies 'It's not a spider, it's a beetle', would not take the child's knowledge further because she would not have helped the child to understand why it was not a spider. She may also have inhibited the child from sharing ideas with her in the future. By acknowledging the similarities the child has seen and then helping him to identify some of the differences, the teacher encourages the child's own ideas and shows him ways of investigating them – this enables children to engage with the scientific process.

Young children often have ideas which they do not have the skills or knowledge to execute. They often become frustrated as their attempts end in failure. They may ask adults for help, or may accept the help of an adult who has observed their difficulty. In both cases, the teacher has the opportunity to teach new skills and knowledge. Lynne (3 years 7 months) wanted to stick a cardboard tube onto a box. She had been applying the glue to the sides of the tube rather than to the part she actually wanted to stick. She called to her teacher 'Glue won't stick'. The teacher was able to explain to her that the glue had to be applied to the surface you want to stick. With this information Lynne was able to continue her project.

Anita (4 years 8 months) had spent most of the morning building herself a house from milk crates. She wanted to make a roof and had selected a blanket to place over the top. However, the house was too wide and the blanket kept sagging into the house. Each time it sagged she put it back on again. After three attempts she was visibly upset. The teacher noticed this and approached her as she started to put the blanket back for the fourth time. She asked, 'Have you got a problem?' Anita replied tearfully: 'The blanket keeps falling down.' The teacher suggested she weighted the blanket down at the edges. This was enough support to enable Anita to solve her problem. She got some solid wooden bricks and was able to continue her game successfully.

Observation helps teachers select the most receptive times for this kind of help. The moment to help a child form letters correctly is when she is attempting to write her name, just as tidying up time is the moment to show a child how to use the brush and dustpan effectively. These moments can also be planned for. Teachers can suggest that a child writes his name on his painting or drawing in order to be able to help with letter formation, or she can ask a small group of children to help her put away the bricks in order to check which shapes they know, and to introduce new names. The teacher exploits these meaningful, pleasurable contexts for learning to the full.

Group times provide another opportunity for demonstrating skills and imparting knowledge. At these times teachers may show children how letters or numbers are formed by writing their ideas on a whiteboard. They may demonstrate how books work and share new vocabulary such as author and illustrator. They may also use these times to introduce new equipment and concepts. The success of group times depends on:

- the size of the group – smaller groups where children have similar developmental needs are most effective;
- the length of time spent on direct teaching – too long and children begin to switch off or become disruptive; and
- the opportunities for active involvement of all the children – teachers need to cater for the different learning styles outlined in Chapter 5.

Playing with children

In order to respond to individual needs, teachers also need to make time for spontaneous observation of and involvement in children's play. Siraj-Blatchford et al. (2002, p. 11) stress the importance of adult involvement in child-initiated activity: 'In the most effective (excellent) settings the importance of staff members extending child-initiated interactions is also clearly identified. In fact, almost half of all the child-initiated episodes which contained intellectual challenge, included interventions from a staff member to extend the child's thinking.' Teachers with the personal qualities described earlier in this chapter will find that they are often asked by children to join in – through requests to come and have 'dinner' in the home corner, or to come shopping on the 'bus', or to be the patient in the 'hospital' or to have a story 'read' to them. These are some of the most valuable opportunities for gaining more insight into children's thoughts and feelings.

Sometimes the teacher is not invited by the children, and has to find her own way of being involved. If she wishes to avoid rejection, she needs to listen and observe in order to find a natural role for herself. The teacher who walks into a situation where children are doing each other's hair and asks 'What are you doing?' is less likely to be enthusiastically received than the teacher who asks 'Can I make an appointment to have my hair washed and cut, please?' This is because the first teacher is remaining aloof from the situation, while the second shows value for the activity and involves herself directly in it. The first is being the 'teacher' while the second is offering herself as a play partner.

Teachers use their observations to give them clues about where they need to involve themselves spontaneously, and what the purpose of this involvement should be. They also draw on their knowledge of individual children to help them decide how they should approach a particular situation. The following examples are provided to give some insight into different approaches to involvement in play.

Playing to encourage imitation

Possibly because they spend so much time watching television or videos, teachers report that some young children arrive in school apparently unable to play. Role-play in particular depends on children having had some first-hand experience of the context they are playing in – you cannot pretend to be the firefighter or market stallholder unless you know what the job involves. Teachers engage with children to offer them a play role model, or to introduce the language needed to enable them to relate to, or join in, the play of others. This scaffolding enables the child to achieve something, which he would be unable to manage alone. Early years educators in the Netherlands, working with children acquiring Dutch as an additional language, have been encouraged to identify and list (in Dutch and the children's home language) the words and phrases children would need to learn to enable them to take part confidently in a role-play setting (Pompert, 1994). Monolingual and bilingual staff can then consistently use this vocabulary when they play with the children.

Children whose language development is delayed may also need help in order to put their actions into words. Fergus (3 years 4 months) was playing alone in the home corner. The teacher, who was concerned about his speech, which even his parents found difficult to understand, observed him put a doll to bed. She went into the home corner with a doll and said:

'My baby's tired. I'm going to put her to bed.'
Fergus: 'Baby bed.'
Teacher: 'There. My baby's in bed like yours.'
She tucked in the blankets. Fergus copied.
Teacher: 'My baby's asleep now. Is yours?'
Fergus: 'Baby see.' (Asleep.)
Teacher: 'Shh. We'd better be quiet now.'
Fergus: 'Ssss' putting his finger on his lips.

This gave Fergus the opportunity to play with someone else. Although he was unable to take a lead he was able to respond to the teacher in a meaningful way. He was being offered some words to describe his actions in a relaxed, meaningful context. The next day he approached the teacher again holding a doll and said 'Ssss. Baby see'.

Teachers also join in play to demonstrate more appropriate use of equipment. Dinosaurs had been placed outside on a patch of earth decorated with twigs to encourage imaginative play, but one child was digging with the neck end of the Tyrannosaurus rex. By playing alongside, the teacher can decide whether the child needs to be offered a trowel or whether he or she needs support to develop imaginative play.

Playing to broaden knowledge

Teachers sometimes join in play to broaden the children's knowledge.

A 'dentist's surgery' had been set up following the visit of the school dentist, but it was clear that the children seemed to think that you went to the dentist only to have teeth out. The teacher made an appointment to see the 'dentist' for a check-up, asking the child at 'reception' to write down the details for her. When receiving her treatment, she was able to extend the children's limited knowledge by suggesting things to them such as 'I'm a bit worried about my filling. Can you look with your mirror to see if it's come loose?' (When the child said it had to come out she said 'No, I don't want it taken out yet, I'd like you to put another filling in it please'); 'Has your nurse written down that my teeth are alright?'; and 'Have you got a glass of water I can rinse my mouth out with, please?'

Playing in this way the teacher broadens the children's knowledge of what is involved in a variety of roles. She also uses play to extend children's access to the curriculum. In one class a health clinic had been set up and record cards made for each child and staff member. Part of the play involved using the alphabet to find the relevant record in the index box – a meaningful and motivating way of introducing children to letter names and sounds and to the sequence of the alphabet.

Challenging and extending thinking during play

Through involvement in play the teacher presents challenges, which the children had not anticipated.

One teacher had been invited on a 'journey' with a group of three children, who were being led by Emily and Elisabetta (both 4 years of age). Both children had recently returned from holidays abroad and both had vivid imaginations. The 'journey' involved making full use of the outdoor play equipment to travel around the world. The playhouse became the aeroplane, some milk crates a train and the playbox a bus. After using each of these modes of transport and visiting all the countries the children could name, the travellers finally came to what Emily described as 'A very dangerous river. It's got crocodiles and snakes in it so you'd better be very careful'. She instructed the group to get across the river by straddling a plank which made a bridge between two metal supports. The children went

Figure 7.4 *Playing to broaden knowledge*

first followed by the teacher, who quickly discovered that she could not sit straddling the plank without her feet touching the ground (going in the water). She called out 'Help! My legs are too long. I can't keep them out of the water'. This captured the children's imagination and they quickly came to her aid. They all returned to the 'shore' to tackle the problem. After much discussion they decided the teacher would have to crawl across the plank on her tummy! Many of the problems, which arise when adults join in play are concerned with size, and solving them provides valuable mathematical experience as well as opportunities to work co-operatively. It is worth noting that many companies spend vast amounts of money sending their staff on 'team-building' courses which involve very similar problem-solving activities.

Teachers also intervene in play to help children think in more depth about the way they represent their experiences. Following a visit by a police horse and rider Adrian (4 years 6 months) and David (4 years 8 months) were reliving the experience. Adrian was moving around the playground on his hands and knees, and David was walking beside him pretending to beat him with the inner tube from a kitchen roll (they had not observed the police officer doing this). David said to his teacher: 'Look at my horse.' Knowing that these children benefited from being encouraged to think in more depth she replied 'Is he like the police horse?' David looked at Adrian for a moment, giggled and said: 'No, he hasn't got a tail.' The teacher asked if there were any other differences and Adrian said 'No tongue'. (The tongue had been an important feature of the police horse because it was large and produced a lot of dribble as it ate an apple.) Without any further prompting, the children rushed inside and when they came out later Adrian had a paper tail, a card tongue (which they had stuck to his tongue with Sellotape!) and two, pointed card ears. They continued to play – but this time included eating episodes. As Bruce (1996) points out, children will use their representations as props within their play and often move comfortably from playing to making a representation and then back to playing.

Intervention of this kind must be informed by the teacher's knowledge of individual children, since it is just as easy for adults to bring play to an end as it is to move it forward. Children are most effectively supported in their play if they are given suggestions but are not made to take them up (Bruce, 1996).

Teachers may extend children's thinking within role-play by broadening their experience of a particular role. Kitson (1994, pp. 95–6) describes how the adult can introduce an unexpected or incongruous element into the role to encourage children to engage at a higher level of thinking:

> The children meet a police officer (the teacher in that role) but the police officer is crying (the element of incongruity, as police officers are not supposed to cry). The police officer is frightened of the dark and now has to work at night. The children have to talk, discuss, persuade and draw upon their own experiences of the dark in order to help the police officer.

If they take the role of the baby or the pupil, teachers also have the chance to stretch children to take on a more dominant role.

Challenging stereotyped ideas

Children need to develop a broad view of society. Teachers need to listen when playing and intervene if stereotyped ideas are being put forward.

Tamsin (aged 3 years 6 months) announced loudly to Luke and Clare 'Girls can't be the doctor'. The teacher asked her why not and, when she replied 'They can't', reminded her that the school doctor (whom she saw the previous week) was a woman. She also made a point of reading a book involving a female doctor at story time.

Teachers have to monitor carefully the kinds of play they involve themselves in to be sure that they are not reinforcing gender stereotypes. For example, too much involvement in domestic play at the expense of construction and vigorous outdoor play gives powerful messages to all children about female roles. Similar stereotyping occurs if male staff are seen to be the ones who are always involved in rough and tumble play.

Involvement in play can alert teachers to other prejudices children may hold, and enables them to tackle this with the children concerned. Negative attitudes towards black dolls, images in posters or towards other children in the class will often be expressed innocently at this stage and teachers are given many opportunities to encourage children to reconsider.

Andrew (3 years 6 months) was playing with a small group and the teacher at the dough table. A display nearby showed photographs of a cooking session, which had been led by a Vietnamese parent. Looking at the pictures Andrew announced 'I don't like that food. It's yukky'. His teacher checked whether he had tried the food in the picture and when he said no, told him that she had, and that it had been delicious. She told him that he would only know if he liked it if he had tried it. She also pointed out to him that other children could be seen enjoying the food in the picture. It was therefore not true to say the food was 'yukky'. She told him about some food she disliked, but made the point that just because she disliked it did not mean she called it 'yukky'. Other children were present during this discussion and the teacher was interested to overhear one of them telling another child at lunchtime not to call something 'yukky' just 'cos you don't like it'.

These are the kinds of discussions referred to in Chapter 4 and are essential if we are serious about confronting racism and sexism.

Moving on repetitive play

Sometimes teachers will want to involve themselves because they have observed that some children's play has become repetitive and is limiting their ability to try other activities. This can be because a child lacks confidence and has found security in one activity.

Amy (3 years 4 months) had attended nursery for half a term and rarely ventured out of the art and craft workshop. She enjoyed using the range of painting, collage and recycled materials to construct and create and then playing with her creations, but the nursery team felt she was using the enclosed area as a shelter from the rest of the nursery class. The teacher worked alongside her and was able to draw her out of the area briefly to find other materials for her creation. Gradually Amy gained enough confidence to venture out alone.

In other cases, groups of children establish a pattern of behaviour in school which they cannot break. Often these group games are inspired by television programmes and more often than not involve boys chasing each other (on foot or wheeled toys) and/or 'shooting' each other. This type of play often seems to motivate the children more than anything else. Many teachers observe to try to discover what it is that the children enjoy – is it the chasing, the shooting, the shouting or ...? If they understand what is motivating the children they are better placed to extend the activity, or offer an equally exciting alternative. Setting up a space station in one class transformed what had been largely aggressive space play into a more varied, technological learning experience. As the children's interest developed so the aggressive incidents decreased.

Abruptly stopping them from doing the things they want to do is usually counter-productive as anyone who has ever told children they are not to make guns in the nursery will know! It merely results in them keeping their concerns hidden from adults. A more effective way is to show interest in what they are doing and offer them exciting, related alternatives. Holland (2003) suggests that adults should consider working with boys' play interests to promote their imaginative development, rather than against them by enforcing zero tolerance.

Making time to play

Nursery schools centres and classes generally offer more opportunities for child-initiated play than reception classes (Siraj-Blatchford et al., 2002; Adams et al., 2004). The continuing division between work and play in many reception classes continues to be unhelpful, if not damaging. It results in adults who have little understanding of young children's true potential, and children who learn that their most important interests and concerns are not valued in school. All 3, 4 and 5-year-olds (and also 6 and 7-years-olds) need to learn through play and teachers of this age group are responsible for giving play high priority, planning and resourcing rich provision, and making time to involve themselves in it. How teachers manage time within a day is at least to some extent their personal choice – they need to recognize that they make time for what they value. They also need to be able to persuade the rest of their colleagues in school that Foundation Stage children need a fluid, flexible daily routine and that this is difficult to achieve within the context of interruptions such as assembly and playtime and rigid structures such as literacy and numeracy lessons. (See Chapter 5 on organizing time.) Legh Vale Community Primary School and Early Years and Childcare Centre is a large school in St Helens Merseyside. It was designated an Early Excellence Centre in 1999. The reception team have developed three formally organized reception classes into a 70-place reception unit. Joy Potter, the Foundation Stage Manager, describes how they have transformed their planning and practice.

Case study

The changes that have been made have been firmly rooted in the Foundation Stage Guidance and its key values. At the outset of the implementation of the Foundation Stage Guidance we wrote down as a team what we wanted for the children. These included values such as 'Children having the skills to be independent learners; strong feelings of self-esteem and self-respect being fostered; and children *wanting* to learn.'

This document has been the driving force behind any decisions made and the Literacy and Numeracy Strategy documents used as additional tools. This has ensured that the content of the strategies serve the values of the Foundation Stage Guidance rather than the other way round.

What has it meant for our planning? Planning is very thorough. Individuals and groups are targeted specifically and opportunities to visit, revisit and reinforce objectives are numerous.

Long-term continuous provision plans support both the play-based provision and the regular daily routines. The plans include routines such as 'Rhymes and Sounds' with daily learning opportunities like 'hearing and saying initial sounds', 'identifying families of rhyming words' and 'naming and sounding the letters of the alphabet'. The plans include examples of what children might do such as 'Learn and invent new rhymes'. Similarly there are continuous provision plans for 'Story time' 'Oral and Mental Maths' and 'Guided and Shared Reading'. These plans for the regular routines are delivered within the activities of the day, in focused activity groups, through everyday events and as the children's play is supported.

In the medium term, the provision is carefully enhanced in order to use every opportunity to promote the key objectives for that period. For example, in order to meet the numeracy objectives related to money and coins we introduced a supermarket. Practitioners observed and supported the play.

A snack café emerged (often with a spontaneous crèche). Real food and drink was served with the opportunity to have snack continuously through the session. A daily menu with prices was written by the children. Waiters with order books to serve and add up the prices in the café were needed. We also incorporated tables with numbers, signs, notices, directions to show people which way to go, where to queue, even a place to clear the dishes and wash up. So every day in a whole variety of ways the objectives were being accessed:

- to distinguish coins;
- to choose the appropriate number operation to solve a problem;
- to work out what to buy and how to pay; and
- to begin to read and write prices.

During the same medium-term block other key objectives were recognizing the relationship between letter sounds and letter shapes; working with an adult to scribe and reread writing; and to think and discuss what to write ahead of writing it.

The café needed a kitchen, the kitchen needed chefs. The chefs need recipe books, the recipes needed ingredients bought at the supermarket with the right coins and the appropriate use of vocabulary.

There were guided and shared writing opportunities in abundance. A shopping list, a menu, a favourite food survey, a 'try something new' day – all real-life experiences during which children can learn and practise their skills.

Both in medium- and short-term planning, practitioners use their observations and subsequent knowledge of their children to plan. This ensures that what is provided not only achieves the objectives set but is also based on children's interests and previous achievements.

A group of children were not choosing to write independently. Their main interests were pirates and treasure. Their interest was captured by a 'writing cave'; a 'name the pirate competition'; a set of instructions and a map to follow. These were followed up by guided and shared writing sessions recording their ideas for the adventures of Parrot Patch Pete, Big Bad Billy and Treasure Trove Tim. (At the same time everyone got a chance to consolidate their alliteration skills.)

What are the implications for organization?   Decisions about the changes made in our organization were again based on values. We begin the academic year with a flexible day very similar to an average nursery day. Children are organized into small pastoral groups prior to entry and parents bring them in and settle them in to activities. Each group has a home base and key worker. The group meets together for a short group time during the sessions with a story at the end of the day. Practitioners focus on building relationships and supporting the children's play.

Once the children are settled, we introduce a focused activity, then a later group time. Eventually we will introduce a 'teaching time' during which there may be a variety of different activities going on at once. These may include shared reading or writing, maths games, rhymes or word games. Flexibility is the key, alongside our knowledge of the children, which enables us to plan for and provide appropriate and targeted activities. As the year continues we move to two teaching time sessions each day, one at the beginning of the morning session and one at the beginning of the afternoon so as to avoid interrupting the children's indoor and outdoor play. This also gives practitioners time to observe, support and respond to the children's choices. At this stage of the year guided reading and writing are delivered as a focused activity during the sessions, again with activities matched clearly to children's interests and levels of achievement.

As part of our induction process we ask parents what they want for their children during their first year at school. The overwhelming concern is that children are cared for, happy and confident. As a result of the developments described above we have seen children exceeding the expected national standard by the end of the reception year in an area that falls within the top 15 per cent of social deprivation.

Understanding children

Responsive teaching requires teachers to value the children's concerns, and to acknowledge the potential for learning within activities the children have chosen themselves. Teachers who work in the sensitive ways described above demonstrate that they value the children's ideas. They are usually able to offer suggestions and ask questions in ways which children want to respond to. When children do not respond, they know they have got their approach wrong and need to learn from their mistake. As Wood and Attfield (1996, p. 112) point out: 'Children quickly learn that educators who value their play and are interested in what they do are good players and will be invited to play in a variety of contexts.'

The idea that children as young as 3 and 4 have anything to teach adults is difficult for some people to grasp, and yet we only have to listen to a 3-year-old for a short while to realize that an adult view of the world can be narrow, and hardened by experience. Teachers need to allow children to help them recapture some of the wonder and innocence they have lost and to gain insight into their struggles to make sense of their world. Teaching is not about imposing our views, concerns or values on others. It is about enabling children to carry out their own investigations and draw their own conclusions. They have already begun to do this before they come to school. The Foundation Stage teacher should make it possible for them to continue in the school situation.

Some points for discussion: involvement in learning experiences

How do you enable learning to take place in your class? Make a list of some of the things you do/say and provide to stimulate interest, and to support and extend learning. Think about your recent involvement with the children and remember actual incidents – identify the different kinds of support you offered. What was successful/unsuccessful? Why? How do you make sure that all children are supported?

What is the balance of time you spend involved with activities you have initiated, compared with the time you spend observing and joining in with child-initiated activity? To what extent do you observe and involve yourself with children's play?

From your own observations, can you identify features of the kinds of learning contexts and adult interactions which most effectively stimulate and sustain the children's interest? What conclusions can you draw from this about:

- how children learn; and
- the role of the adult in children's learning?

How could you share this understanding with colleagues, governors and parents? How do you show that you value play? Do you observe children playing? Are you comfortable about being a play partner? Do you help children to reflect on their play experiences?

Further reading

Holland, P. (2003) *We Don't Play with Guns Here*, Open University Press, Buckingham.

Hurst, V. (1997) *Planning for Early Learning*, 2nd edn, Paul Chapman Publishing, London.

Lindon, J. (2001) *Understanding Children's Play*, Hodder and Stoughton, London.

Moyles, J., Adams, S. and Musgrove, A. (2002) *SPEEL Study of Pedagogical Effectiveness in Early Learning*, DfES, London.

Siraj-Blatchford, I., Sylva, K., Muttock, S. Gilden, R. and Bell, D. (2002) *Researching Effective Pedagogy in the Early Years*, DfES, London.

Wood, E. and Attfield, J. (1996) *Play, Learning and the Early Childhood Curriculum*, Paul Chapman Publishing, London.

8

Managing complexity: looking outwards, looking inwards

In this book the complexity involved in educating young children, and the expertise of the specialist teacher has been highlighted. It is difficult to understand why this work is still so undervalued. One reason may be the general lack of respect given to those who are involved with young children. However, part of the answer rests with the teacher herself.

The most effective early years teachers seem to be the most critical of themselves and of their work. They are conscious that they will never be able to do the job as well as they would like. They know, for example, that responsiveness to individuals is only as possible as staffing ratios allow. In spite of this they generally do not become disillusioned. They constantly strive to improve their practice because they are commited to offering young children the best possible education.

Knowing that there is always room for improvement tends to make teachers too modest about their achievements. If they can be persuaded to talk about their strengths they tend to counter these immediately with a list of weaknesses! In this chapter some of the broader issues that challenge the Foundation Stage teacher are highlighted.

Teaching as personal development: looking outwards, looking inwards

Effective education of young children requires the teacher to evaluate and adapt her practice in response to her own observations, to statutory requirements and to the growing body of research evidence. Teachers need to develop their knowledge and understanding of the social context within which they are educating, in particular, how developments in society influence the lives of the families they work with.

Teaching is still a predominantly white, middle-class profession – although this is changing gradually, as the introduction of access courses and more varied routes into teaching, enable a wider cross-section of the community to become involved (for information on teacher training see www.tta.gov.uk). However, figures collected by Ross (GTC, 2003) reveal that approximately 2.4 per cent of all teachers are from a minority ethnic group (compared with a minority ethnic population of 9.1 per cent). It is, therefore, not unusual for a young teacher from a sheltered middle-class background to find herself working in an inner-city school with children from social and cultural backgrounds outside her personal experience.

Initial training courses must, therefore, help student teachers to begin the, often painful, self-evaluation process. Students need to be helped to see that they have formed a set of attitudes and values based on their own life experience, and that these are not necessarily shared by others. They also need to recognize that attitudes and values are not fixed – teachers must be prepared to question themselves in the light of new experiences and alternative points of view. Attitudes and values associated with childrearing, discipline, cleanliness, the roles of men and women, living in a multicultural society, etc., are acquired consciously and unconsciously from birth. They are expressed in our work 'not explicitly for the most part, but implicitly, in the thousands of judgements and decisions that we make in the course of a single day' (Drummond, Lally and Pugh, 1989, p. 42).

Unless teachers make themselves aware of their own beliefs and the reasons they acquired them, they run the risk of communicating 'values and attitudes which may not only be unfamiliar to many children but may also seem to reject their own experiences' (Hazareesingh, Simms and Anderson, 1989, p. 24). The process of understanding the nature and origins of our own attitudes can be a painful one – it is disturbing to realize that some of the attitudes we hold are racist or sexist. Discussing attitudes and values with others is also difficult and can feel threatening, and yet it is often through discussion with someone who holds a conflicting point of view, that we clarify our thinking and reach new insights.

Foundation Stage teachers will be confronted with a range of views held by their colleagues, by parents and by members of the school community. Their own attitudes will equally be laid open to question. The broader their own view of possible viewpoints, the more sensitive they will be to others. A collaborative approach to early education requires teachers to respond in full to the questions of others. It is not appropriate for them to say 'this is how we do things here' (or words to that effect) without giving any reasons. The more successfully teachers involve parents and community members in the life of the setting, the more questions will be asked – in the same way that the more teachers encourage children to negotiate with others, the more they will negotiate with adults. It is essential that teachers do not become defensive and are able to respond to these approaches confidently.

Tutors on initial and in-service courses have a responsibility to help teachers to face up to the 'why' questions which will be asked of them. They need to see that these questions represent a genuine and legitimate interest, and that the content of the inquiries will change over time. Within an achievement-oriented, outcome-led culture it is inevitable that Foundation Stage teachers are asked for more detail on their curriculum by parents seeking to ensure their children are given the best possible start. They have welcomed the support given by statutory documents and nationally produced materials for parents (Sure Start, 2003b).

Teachers need to review and sometimes change their attitudes – not so that they unthinkingly take on board every other attitude they are exposed to, but in a thoughtful way to show respect for the concerns of others even when attitudes cannot be shared. An ability to respect others depends on self-awareness (see Chapter 4). This is as true for the teacher as it is for a child. The more they confront themselves, the less likely teachers are to be afraid of the questions of others. If they allow themselves to learn from the children and parents they come into contact with, they will have many opportunities to reflect on their own assumptions, and will be offered many different, and often equally valid, ways of looking at the world.

Personal development: some points for discussion

- How has your understanding of and attitudes towards society and people changed since you became an early years teacher?
- Has your view of the role of the teacher changed?
- What do you think caused these changes?
- How has your thinking and practice been affected?

Teaching in a developing society

Teachers who have been involved in early childhood education for 10 years or more talk enthusiastically about the ways in which they have developed as people, and the ways in which their practice has changed. It is the dynamic nature of teaching young children, and the relationships teachers develop with families, which help teachers to maintain their commitment to this work in spite of the low status. In fact, some teachers are committed to early years teaching precisely because it offers the opportunity for personal development via community involvement.

Educational, political and sociological factors have influenced the way in which the Foundation Stage teacher approaches her work. Curriculum-related changes have already been described. Many teachers believe that they have also developed personally through becoming more aware of social issues affecting the families they work with.

Disadvantage and discrimination in British society

Through their involvement with families from a variety of social and cultural backgrounds, teachers have been confronted with the inequalities based on class, culture, gender and disability which exist in British society. Seeing for themselves how families cope with situations, which they themselves would find impossible, is a powerful learning experience for teachers.

How can you expect a child to be in bed early when he is living with his parents and sister in one small room in bed-and-breakfast accommodation? Or, how can you expect a lone mother to arrive on time to collect her child every day when she is trying to hold down a low-paid job within the few hours her child is able to attend nursery class? With increasing numbers of children living in poverty (Piachaud and Sutherland, 2000; Trudell, 2002), many teachers have become vocal advocates of extended day provision. They are aware of the difficulties involved in finding jobs which fit in with the school day or, even worse, half-day. They have also recognized that support for parents and carers is necessary, if the cycle of disadvantage is to be broken for some children. Penn and Lloyd (2001) found that, with no additional funding, a majority of nursery schools had found creative ways of supporting the most vulnerable families in their communities. They provided a focal point for some of the most disadvantaged groups in society. Staff in these schools recognized that working with the children in isolation from their families was ineffective. They adopted a more holistic, em-powering approach – even though this stretched their resources to the limit.

Teachers have had to consider whether they, through their actions, interactions or practice are adding to the discrimination experienced by some families. Many are concerned about the inequalities experienced by those families who speak a language other than English at home. How is it possible to make sure that these families gain equal access to information and have the same opportunities to share their feelings with staff when the support of translators and interpreters for all the required languages is often impossible to come by? Many teams try to ensure that speakers of community languages are recruited because children and parents 'need to see a teaching workforce that reflects the diversity of society as a whole' (GTC, 2003, p. 12).

Foundation Stage teachers, in collaboration with other professionals, are at the forefront of government social inclusion initiatives. Early Excellence Centres, Sure Start projects, Children's Centres and Extended Schools all have a role to play in tackling inequality. They all offer family support and adult education opportunities alongside the educational provision for children. However, Trudell (2002) and Toynbee (2004) highlight the danger of repeating history and ghettoizing the most vulnerable. Toynbee (2004, p. 14) asserts that 'if we really want to change class destiny, it can be done. But it takes good teachers in high quality children's centres where children of all classes mix, not bundling all the deprived together'.

Family composition

The traditional idea of the family as two parents and an average of two children with an extended family network living nearby for support has become a myth. Many children currently live in one-parent families (usually with their mother), and many have been involved in family breakdown and in subsequently formed stepfamilies. Britain has one of the highest divorce rates in Europe (2.6 divorces per 1000 people compared with a European Union (EU) average of 1.9 divorces), and the number of children born outside marriage is increasing – 40 per cent of births in 2001 occurred outside marriage in Britain compared with 12 per cent in 1980 and 6 per cent in 1960). However, many of these children are registered and brought up by both parents (up to date statistical information can be found on www.statistics.gov.uk). Families are less likely (particularly in the south-east of England) to live as part of an extended family.

Teachers must take account of these trends and must not make assumptions or value judgements about family structure. Through contact with actual families they see for themselves that many different kinds of family structure can work well.

Childrearing practices

Traditional attitudes to childrearing have been challenged by changes in family composition, and by the traditions of the many ethnic groups living in Britain. Teachers, through discussion with parents, can make themselves aware of differences in childrearing practice, and about pressures on parents, and avoid judging some practices negatively. 'There is no single "best" way to bring up a child, and there are as many differences in childrearing practices among white and among black families as there are between them' (CRE, 1990). Lindon (2003, p. 92) points out that:

> It would not be justified to assume that the way you were brought up, or the way that you and your colleagues deal with the children is the only right way. You need to be open to other possibilities and this should be your approach, whatever your own cultural or religious background.

Teachers need to respect and value these differences, and to understand the importance of gaining concrete information about each child's background and experiences (Hazareesingh, Simms and Anderson, 1989).

Attitudes to childrearing are influenced by the political priorities of the day. During the Second World War, when women were needed in the workforce, it was considered acceptable for children to be cared for in nurseries. After the war with the men returned and wanting their jobs back, the nurseries were closed and women encouraged to see their role back in the home (Riley, 1983). A similar but, perhaps, more ambivalent pattern is currently emerging. Women are needed in, and being urged to join, the workforce (e.g. through government initiatives such as the Childcare Tax Credit), and yet there is still the prevailing view that they are responsible for childcare and must make their own arrangements with the help of employers and the private and voluntary sector. The decline in publicly funded services is a matter of great concern. As Grenier (2004, pp. 10–11) explains:

> there are many good places where the resourceful and the affluent can find
> high quality education and care for their children. This satisfies the
> individual family's pursuit of good quality services, but it does nothing to
> promote these as public services. The whole point of public services is that
> they should be a public good, for everyone.

Teachers who see for themselves the stress caused to many young families by this shortage of provision are more likely to campaign for the high-quality full and extended day provision families need.

The role of women in society

The Foundation Stage teacher is as much a victim of discrimination as many of the women she works with. Work with young children is still seen as 'women's work', even though the numbers of male teachers and nursery nurses are increasing steadily. Parents often consider early years teachers to be less able than teachers of older children. Many teachers report that a move into Key Stage 1 is seen as promotion, whilst those moving into the Foundation Stage from Key Stages 1 and 2 may have to face the suggestion that they were unable to cope with older learners and have been demoted! In order to raise the status of women, the effort and skills involved in caring for and educating young children must be recognized and valued. It should no longer be the norm for women to devalue themselves with phrases like 'I'm just a housewife' or 'I'm only a nursery teacher'. Second, women need to be helped to believe that they are capable of achieving outside the home, if that is what they want to do.

Clearly, the Foundation Stage teacher, because of her involvement with mothers of young children, has a role to play in both these areas. Her attitude to herself as a woman will determine how much she is able to support the women she comes into contact with. She needs to believe in herself, and value her own achievements in order to be confident enough to encourage others to value themselves and try new things. In response to this challenge and to parents' requests, teachers have organized adult education classes to enable women to develop new skills. Alternatively, or alongside these classes, support groups for parents focusing on the parenting role have also been set up, to offer participants the chance to discuss with others (with and without professional involvement) the pleasures and problems involved in bringing up children. Family literacy and numeracy projects have been particularly successful in empowering parents to support their children's development and learning.

Teachers have made a strong case for the extra space and resources required to respond to parents needs. Spare classrooms, Portacabins in playgrounds and even staffrooms are all being used to facilitate support of these kinds (Pugh and De'Ath, 1989). This work has been extended within Early Excellence Centres, which have been funded to facilitate greater community involvement and interagency working. Some of the most vulnerable families are benefiting from this support and it is projected that this early intervention will be cost-effective in the long term (Bertram and Pascal, 2000).

Child abuse

Child abuse is certainly not a new development in society. However, it was not until the second half of the twentieth century that there were moves to introduce effective child protection procedures (through the Children Act 1989 for England and Wales, the Children (Scotland) Act 1995 and the Children (Northern Ireland) Order 1996). This legislation was supported by national guidance documents. Lindon (2003, p. 8) explains that the decline in the numbers of children on child protection registers in recent years:

> does not necessarily suggest that less children are at risk. It is more likely
> that, in response to new guidelines in the mid- and late 1990s, professionals
> in the child protection system are more alert to protection through bringing
> in family support services, which may avoid use of the register.

Nevertheless around 30,000 children from birth to 18 years will be placed on child protection registers with a similar number being taken off the registers each year. Around 80 children are killed every year, mostly by parents and carers (see www.nspcc.org.uk for more information from the National Society for the Prevention of Cruelty to Children).

Children under the age of 4 are vulnerable and some start nursery with their names already on the child protection register. Others rely on Foundation Stage staff to pick up the signs. Local authorities have organized training courses to help practitioners to identify signs of abuse and to inform them of the procedures they need to follow if abuse is suspected. These courses bring professionals from different statutory and voluntary services together, and all local authorities have published procedures and guidelines for their staff to follow. Foundation Stage staff need to be fully aware of national legislation and both national and local guidelines.

Acknowledging the fact that young children suffer physical, emotional and sexual abuse has been difficult for many Foundation Stage staff. Most would prefer to believe that such things could never happen. However, teachers realize that they are in a key position to offer support to a child. It is their responsibility to monitor behaviour, to notice any suspicious injuries and to listen carefully to what the children say. If there is any reason to suspect that a child may have been abused then this must be reported. Being aware that this action must be taken makes it virtually impossible knowingly to turn away from the issue.

Nevertheless, this is probably one of the most stressful responsibilities any teacher can hold. If she (and her team) fail to notice the signs, the child risks further abuse, and yet if she gets it wrong her relationship with a family is put at risk. Some teachers honestly admit to the anguish they feel when trying to decide whether or not to report something they have seen or heard. Some cases are clear cut – the child with the very obvious cigarette burns – while others are less so – the rather sad, pale and withdrawn child. Teachers know that if they report a suspicion, they will set in motion a chain of social work, and probably police inquiries, which will irrevocably change their relationship with a family. Those who have reported their suspicions have often felt deeply distressed, even though they know they have acted properly.

Working with children and parents where abuse has been proved also causes anxiety. Continuing to support a parent abuser, when you really want to despise her, is a dilemma all professionals involved in child protection work have to face. Child abuse brings us all in touch with very powerful emotions. Teachers have to cope with their own feelings as well as with helping other members of staff and sometimes other parents cope with theirs. It is also possible that a member of staff was abused herself, and is being reminded of what happened to her. Working with abused children who may talk about, or act out, what has happened to them may leave staff feeling inadequate. Their training does not on the whole equip them to deal with these very difficult and often distressing situations.

Many teachers have been supported by their contacts with other professionals involved in child protection and family support work, such as health visitors, school nurses and doctors, social workers and educational welfare officers. It is easier to discuss suspicions with someone you know who also knows and cares about a family. These interagency links have developed because the teacher knows that she needs to draw on the expertise of others if she is to be able to offer informed support to children and their families. As a teacher, her training is limited and there are times when she needs to refer a parent or child to another professional or agency

(Dowling, 1992). She also needs the support of others to help her cope with her responsibilities and the feelings these generate.

These human issues cause the teacher to reflect on her own attitudes and feelings, and this can be a painful process. Less painful, but equally demanding, are the technological and political issues she has to address in her work.

Working with diversity: some points for discussion

- How much do you know about the backgrounds of the children you teach?
- How are these different from your own background?
- What steps have you taken to make yourself aware of your own stereotyped attitudes towards childrearing practices, cultural backgrounds and religious beliefs, the role of women, etc.?
- How have you tried to see things from the point of view of the families you work with?
    - Which families do you find it difficult to relate to? Why?
    - What could you do to improve your relationship with these families?
- Can you remember anything you have done or said which revealed your own prejudice?

Technological advances

Young children are growing up in an increasingly technological society. A considerable amount of their leisure time is spent watching television or video programmes – some of the programmes not entirely appropriate for children under 5. A growing number of 3–6-year-olds have televisions in their bedrooms and have access to a home computer, video and/or digital camera. This generation of young children is seeing, and needs to continue to see, technology as an everyday part of their lives. However 'the use of IT must be properly integrated with the early years curriculum to be effective' (Wake, 1997, p. 3) and software must be carefully chosen – in too many classes children are merely occupied with programs which provide little intellectual or creative challenge. Siraj-Blatchford and Macleod-Brudenell (1999 p. 116) warn that:

> a lot of adult time will need to be invested in the selection of appropriate software and in developing computer related activities that support a rich experiential preschool curriculum rather than detracting the child away from it. In practice this usually requires the use of content-free software such as word processors, drawing and painting programmes and databases.

Where Internet access is available, even the youngest children can be taught how to access the wealth of information on the World Wide Web and can communicate with children in other parts of the world. Some principles of good practice for developmentally appropriate information and communication technology (ICT) with children have been developed by Siraj-Blatchford and Siraj-Blatchford (2003).

The effects of television and video viewing on young children are apparent on any visit to a Foundation Stage setting . Groups of children may be playing out a scene from their favourite programme, and lunchtime discussions often focus on what was seen the night before. Many programmes are not fully understood and can have a profound, even if temporary, effect on these young viewers. One of the major challenges facing teachers and parents involves finding ways of countering some of the negative effects of television viewing. Many teachers try to watch some of the programmes enjoyed by the children at home so that they can join in discussion and extend the children's understanding of the programmes.

Most teachers have had to learn new skills. They have attended computer literacy courses, and some have learnt to use digital cameras and video equipment, so that they can show the children what is involved in film-making (and also make presentations for parents). It is perhaps in this area of the curriculum more than any other that teachers have needed to learn alongside the children. As we saw earlier, children benefit greatly from working alongside an adult who is demonstrating how to investigate problems, test theories and seek support.

Nursery education and politics

The majority of children in the Foundation Stage have not attained statutory school age. They attend a variety of private, voluntary and maintained settings, all of which are vulnerable if they do not attract sufficient numbers to remain viable. Since the introduction of the nursery education grant for 3 and 4-year-olds, the inevitable competition between providers has increased. As we saw in the introduction, the long-established definition of nursery education has been gradually undermined and in 2003 the numbers of children attending maintained nursery classes and schools decreased (DfES, 2003a).

As one experienced teacher commented to a group of newly qualified colleagues, 'when you become a nursery teacher you also become a campaigner – the two roles go together'. The reality of working in the non-statutory sector, where nothing (not even the continued existence of your class) can be taken for granted, is the inevitable involvement (either conscious or unconscious) of the early years teacher in politics.

This involvement takes the form of working through lobbying organizations, such as the National Campaign for Real Nursery Education (NCRNE) and unions, or through charitable organizations such as Early Education, and includes local as well as national activity. Teachers need to be aware of local and national developments which may affect their employment prospects and the future of the children they teach. Developments such as a change of political control at local or national level, or the need to cut local authority budgets, or to redeploy teachers into the statutory sector to counter teacher shortages, or the decision to admit all 4-year-olds to reception classes, can all have serious implications for nursery education. Teachers have a responsibility to make themselves and others aware of these developments, and to put forward a strong case. Some parents are unaware of the vulnerability of nursery education, particularly if they have always lived in an area with good provision, and often need to be told that it is not their child's automatic right. When faced with the prospect of transferring their child to infant school, at what seems to them a very young age, they also need advice. They need to know that they are not legally obliged to send their child to school until the beginning of the term after his or her fifth birthday. Reception teachers working with 4-year-olds need to remember that a 4-year-old does not 'have to go to assembly' – he or she does not even have to go to school!

Foundation Stage teachers need to take account of national education legislation – even when it does not apply directly to them. If they want to survive, they must be seen to be operating both as part of mainstream education and as part of the network of services for children up to the age of 5. However, operating as part of mainstream has its disadvantages and nursery class teachers complain that their greater involvement in the primary school sometimes leads to unrealistic and inappropriate demands being made on them. It is worth reiterating that, for the sake of the children, teachers must keep sight of the principles which underpin their work.

Teacher as campaigner: some points for discussion

- To what extent have you seen your role as a campaigning one?
- Are the families you work with aware of the discretionary nature of nursery education?
- What can you do both individually, and with other nursery teachers in your area, to help others understand more about nursery education?
- How do you view developments in education? How do you keep up to date with new initiatives?
- Do you feel that your firm principles enable you to interpret new initiatives in ways which are consistent with the needs of the children, or do you feel pressured to work in inappropriate ways?
- How could you and your team (including parents) learn together about new developments?
- Which early years organizations do you belong to and how do you get involved?

Recent developments in education have stretched all teachers to the limit, but nursery teachers, because of their position on the fringes of some of the changes, have been particularly challenged. Experienced teachers have been able to adapt their approach to take account of whole-school developments, and of the need for greater accountability. Being able to offer acceptable, meaningful alternatives to inappropriate requests is a skill increasingly required by nursery teachers working for headteachers who have little or no early years training or experience. Many headteachers are looking to their nursery staff for this kind of guidance – if it is not forthcoming they have little alternative but to insist on an approach, however unsuitable that may be.

Training opportunities

Since the introduction of the Foundation Stage, professional development opportunities for early years practitioners have increased. This has supported teachers as they lead the change and development process. In the most effective local authorities, courses are differentiated to take account of the diverse needs within the workforce. Introductory courses are offered alongside courses for more experienced practitioners. However, it is not uncommon for trainers to be faced with groups where some practitioners have received no initial training and have had little experience, and others who have a wealth of experience and have studied for advanced early childhood diplomas and masters degrees. This situation benefits neither group and is frustrating for the trainer. Neither does it support the development of positive relationships between practitioners from different types of setting. It is not surprising that some teachers stop attending local authority courses and look elsewhere for professional development opportunities or organize these for themselves (e.g. some nursery schools have organized courses to which they have invited neighbouring nursery and reception class colleagues).

Early years courses are usually oversubscribed and teachers particularly value the opportunities provided for discussion with colleagues. Participants continue chatting (about their work) long after the course has officially finished and many teachers exchange phone numbers or e-mail addresses so they can maintain contact. Their enthusiasm for, and commitment to, their work is apparent. So is their concern to do the job better. It is this willingness to analyse themselves which makes work with groups of early years teachers so rewarding.

Early years teachers are their own worst critics – in fact, the most effective find more to worry about than those who really need to examine their practice or attitudes. This is because the more questions we ask in relation to ourselves, and in relation to the society in which we live, the less certain we are that there are any answers let alone definitive ones. This should not cause concern. As Gura (1996, p. 82) points out: 'Certainties lead to inflexibility and reluctance to dare to ask "what if"? It induces a mind-set which gets in the way of change and development.' Those adults who want or need to be involved with certainty are unlikely to make effective teachers of any age group. Very young children need and deserve adults who are prepared to set out on a voyage of discovery with them.

Training for personal responsibility

Courses which emphasize the analysis of attitudes, situations and problems validate teachers' concerns. The old 'tips for teachers' transmission model of training where the tutor offered ideas for activities for teachers to copy in school is inappropriate, although some teachers still say they want to be told what to do. These teachers have not coped well with change.

They have not accepted personal responsibility for their teaching. They have not realized (or do not wish to acknowledge) that they carry ultimate responsibility for what happens in their class. Nor are they recognizing that they have choices to make. They prefer to delude themselves with the idea that others determine what they have to do: 'the headteacher has told me to do this' or 'the parents wouldn't like it if I did that'. There are always some constraints on what we can and cannot do in a particular situation, but there are also choices. Using others as an excuse (or blaming them) is an effective way of avoiding responsibility It is also an effective way of forgetting or ignoring the needs of young children.

Successful Foundation Stage teachers are characterized by their unswerving commitment to young children and their families. They attend courses because they want the chance to analyse in more depth, in the company of colleagues, some of the concerns which are foremost in their minds. They do not expect answers. Instead they hope for greater clarity or, perhaps, a deeper insight into the issue, and expect to gain strength and support from realizing that they are not alone.

Complexity is never easy to explain, but for the sake of the children teachers have a responsibility to try. They know how easy it is to be diverted from their own priorities and feel the need to get together regularly with like-minded practitioners to revitalize themselves and retain the courage of their convictions. Teachers working in classes attached to primary schools particularly need this support.

This does not mean that in-service training should be left to the group. Courses, which involve unstructured group work and offer little in the way of stimuli or ideas for teachers to consider, are nearly always unsatisfactory. (See Chapters 3 and 10 for guidance on effective training.)

Teachers as agents of change

This book has emphasized a number of areas where teachers have been required to change and develop. These include:

1 Developing effective teamwork – to establish effective working practice with a wider range of professionals. This includes working as part of large multidisciplinary teams.
2 Organizing the learning environment into workshop areas (as described in Chapter 5).
3 Developing equal opportunities policies and practices to counter discrimination.
4 Developing partnership with parents.
5 Building links with other agencies to promote the development of the 'whole child'.
6 Developing a distinctive Foundation Stage and supporting developments in the curriculum for children from birth to three.
7 Record-keeping – as described in Chapter 6.
8 Ensuring continuity and progression from home/pre-school or nursery to nursery school/class to reception class and into Key Stage 1.

Many of these are pioneering initiatives. Experienced nursery teachers have taken a strong lead in developing Foundation Stage practice and in whole-school and local authority initiatives.

The introduction of the Primary Strategy in 2003 gave the first signal that the 'bottom-up' model of education that early years teachers have always wanted might become a reality. Key Stage 1 and 2 colleagues will certainly need to take account of what children have learnt in the Foundation Stage if they are to provide continuity as well as progression – particularly in relation to independence skills.

Influencing primary practice

Although teachers need to increase their influence within the primary sector it is not yet easy for them to do so. When asked how they will share ideas discussed on courses with colleagues, Foundation Stage teachers regularly express the view that it is difficult for them to have any influence. How much this is due to a real lack of interest on the part of primary teachers or to a feeling that Foundation Stage practice is different and therefore irrelevant, and how much it is a reflection of a lack of confidence on the part of Foundation Stage teachers, is not entirely clear. What is apparent, though, is the isolation and low status felt by many early years staff – they often feel they are marginalized or even patronized by colleagues.

Time is also an issue. In a climate of unrelenting change it is not surprising that there is no time for sharing of the kind being advocated and that many staff meetings are taken up with (often simplistic) accountability issues. For the sake of the children in their classes, and in the interests of the school as a whole, Foundation Stage teachers must be encouraged by headteachers to share their expertise more widely.

Raising the status of early years teaching

As we saw in Chapter 3 many schools have promoted a teacher to the role of Foundation Stage co-ordinator. Where this teacher has a place on the senior management team of the school, she has the opportunity to raise awareness, and the status, of work with young children. Through demonstrating her skills within the wider school community, whether in relation to community work, shared record-keeping, science, language or maths, she has the opportunity to show her professionalism – to make it clear that teaching young children is not a soft option. If she is able to help others understand her philosophy or use some of her ideas to improve their practice, she can command their respect.

Many of the skills involved in teaching young children are directly transferable to work with adults. Adults respond to warmth and en-thusiasm, patience and interest, just as children do. They also respond best to someone who facilitates their learning and does not tell them what to do. Some teachers lack confidence in their own ability and need support if they are to reach their full potential. Some local education authorities have recognized this need and have offered training in group-work skills to experienced early years teachers. This enables them to contribute more confidently to in-service initiatives, both in their own schools and in the authority as a whole. Training in work with adults is essential for the teachers who have taken on a wider role in training and/or supporting Foundation Stage practitioners in the voluntary, private and social services sectors.

Teachers taking on this role must be sure that they will be given time to take on any extra responsibility, and that the children will not suffer while they are doing other things. Whether or not this kind of encouragement can be given at the present time of scarce resources is debatable. Teachers will not wish to undertake any activity, which negatively affects the experience of the children in their class. Young children are too vulnerable to be passed from person to person, and unless satisfactory cover arrangements can be made, many teachers will wish to remain in their classes. Nursery school headteachers, who have seen their staffing ratios eroded over the years, have been adamant that the quality of education they provide suffers if they or their staff are expected to offer outreach work without additional resources.

Involvement in early years education exposes teachers to children at a very vulnerable stage in their development, and requires them to be concerned about whole families and communities in a way less likely to be required of teachers of older children. Contact with colleagues, parents and children from a variety of professional, social and cultural backgrounds heightens the teacher's awareness and prevents her from becoming complacent. Those teachers who do not make time, physically or emotionally, for this contact are unlikely to develop the sensitivity required of an effective early years specialist.

Influencing others: some points for discussion

- What opportunities have you initiated or accepted to explain your work to primary colleagues? Have you invited them to focus on aspects of practice in your class (e.g. subject co-ordinators could look for evidence of children's learning within their subject area – make sure they have the relevant section of the statutory Foundation Stage guidance)?
- What additional opportunities could you make both in your own school and in the local authority?
- What are your strengths as a teacher?
- What do you feel you particularly have to offer colleagues?
- How could you anticipate and equip yourself to deal with difficult questions or comments such as 'Why don't you sit them down to do some real work?' 'Why are they spending so much time playing/outside/choosing, etc.?'
- How could you gain support and confidence from other Foundation Stage colleagues?

Useful addresses

Early Education (British Association for Early Childhood Education), 136 Cavell Street, London E1 2JA. Website: www.early_education.org.uk.

NCRNE (National Campaign for Real Nursery Education), BCM, Box 6216, London WC1N 3XX. Website: www.ncne.org.uk.

National Children's Bureau, 8 Wakley Street, London EC1V 7QE. Website: www.ncb.org.uk.

OMEP (World Organization for Early Childhood Education), c/o Annabel Lewis, 144 Eltham Road, London SE9 5LW.

TACTYC (Tutors of Advanced Courses for Teachers of Young Children), BCM, Box 5342, London WC1N 3XX.

Further reading

Cox, T. (2000) *Combating Educational Disadvantage: 'Meeting the Needs of Vulnerable Children'*, Falmer Press, London.

Dowling, M. (2002) The impact of stress on early development, in J. Fisher (ed.) *The Foundations of Learning*, Open University Press, Buckingham.

Lindon, J. (2003) *Child Protection*, 2nd edn, Hodder and Stoughton, London.

Siraj-Blatchford, I. and Clarke, P. (2000) *Supporting Identity, Diversity and Language in the Early Years*, Open University Press, Buckingham.

Siraj-Blatchford, I. and Siraj-Blatchford, J. (2003) *More than Computers*, Early Education, London.

Trudell, P. (2002) Meeting the needs of disadvantaged children, in J. Fisher (ed.) *The Foundations of Learning*, Open University Press, Buckingham.

Whalley, M. and the Pen Green Centre Team (2001) *Involving Parents in their Children's Learning*, Paul Chapman Publishing, London.

9

Supporting other practitioners

When the second edition of this book was written, I stressed that, if nursery education was to be of a high quality, specialist teachers must be employed in every setting to work directly with the children and to lead the team in curriculum development. This assertion has since been supported by research (Siraj-Blatchford et al., 2002). However, due to teacher shortages and, maybe, also the government's unwillingness to fund services of this quality, the model of teacher 'involvement' or 'input' in settings has been adopted. Foundation Stage teachers have been recruited to support practitioners in the private and voluntary sectors. Some of these teachers have full- or part-time roles within the local authority's early years service, whilst others (including nursery school headteachers) have been seconded from their teaching posts one or more days a week to work with settings in their locality. They have a variety of job titles such as advisory teacher, early years consultant, mentor or lead teacher. According to Sure Start Guidance 2004–06, local authorities should work towards (and beyond) a ratio of at least one teacher per 10 non-maintained settings, but this figure is proving hard to achieve in some local authorities, particularly those with a high proportion of private and voluntary provision. However many settings they support, it is clear that the time of these teachers is spread thinly, and they rarely work directly with the children.

Advanced Skills Teachers, whose practice has been deemed excellent, provide a model of good practice for teachers and other practitioners in schools in their area. The majority of their time will be spent in their own class (sometimes acting as a role model for other teachers), but they also have a role in leading training, developing resources and supporting other teachers in their schools. In this chapter all these teachers will be referred to as advisory teachers.

Advisory work offers a new range of experiences and challenges for the experienced teacher. Most receive no training to take on this work with adults, which may include running training courses and developing curriculum materials as well as visiting and supporting teams in a variety of settings. The majority of teachers have had no experience of working within the private and voluntary sector. They will therefore not always understand the constraints practitioners in some of these services are facing (shift working, having to share premises with other users, high staff turnover, having to go downstairs to access outside provision, etc.). Great sensitivity is required if the teacher is to build the kind of relationship from which a positive partnership can develop. In this chapter some aspects of this role are explored.

Building relationships with other practitioners

What are the pitfalls?

Many advisory teachers realize too late that they have fallen into a trap with some teams and have not established a productive working relationship based on mutual trust and respect. For the benefit of newly appointed colleagues it is therefore worth highlighting some possible pitfalls This list assumes that early years practitioners err on the side of being too nice and too friendly rather than too aggressive!

Common pitfalls in advisory work include:

- *being too friendly or cosy* (not a professional relationship) - the role of advisory teacher as critical friend, who is visiting to support practice development has not been established;
- *being too prescriptive* (giving people the solutions/quick fix) the advisory teacher gives the impression she has all the answers and that there is only one way of doing things – this may be a result of a lack of confidence on the part of the teacher. This is ineffective in the long term. Practitioners may do what they are told but they are not empowered to make their own choices and decisions;
- *encouraging dependency* – practitioners wait for others to tell them what to do, with a resulting helplessness and loss of ownership of practice. This is the inevitable consequence of a too prescriptive approach;
- *being unclear or dishonest about roles* – advisory teachers inevitably have a role to play in supporting settings where practice is weak. Practitioners in these settings need to understand what is, and what is not, negotiable as far as their relationship with the advisory team is concerned. Advisers also need to set a clear standard and be honest about unacceptable practice, giving reasons;

- *losing (or not establishing) credibility* – teachers working with pre-schools and day nurseries are vulnerable to accusations that 'you don't know what it's like …'. Making the assumption that everyone can practice in the same way, or as the advisory teacher did, is unhelpful and likely to lead to an immediate loss of credibility;
- *breaking the code of confidentiality* – in local authorities gossip can spread. Talking publicly about a setting without that setting's permission, and being found out, can have serious consequences for relationships.

Advisory teachers need to consider their relationships with settings (particularly those they find difficult) and highlight if any of the pitfalls described above apply. It is never too late to improve a situation, and an acknowledgement that the relationship set off on the wrong foot is often enough to enable progress to be made.

Avoiding the pitfalls!

Although each situation is individual and there are no easy answers, the following guidelines are offered to support teachers building relationships with other practitioners:

- *introduce yourself and your role*, being clear about what you can/will and can/will not offer – a written approach prior to a visit helps practitioners to understand your role. It also provides a document to refer to should misunderstandings arise at a later stage;
- *take time to get to know/gather information about the setting and the people in it* – the aim of the first visit should be to find out about the setting. Ask questions to be sure you have understood how the setting operates and the constraints/challenges the team have to cope with;
- *keep records of visits to settings* (including names of staff) – when a number of settings have been visited and time passes between visits it is difficult to remember the detail (at worst, memories of settings begin to blur!) so notes provide an invaluable reminder;
- *maintain a professional relationship at all times* – e.g. by focusing on professional and practice development. Obviously it is important to be friendly but it is important that visits are not simply social;
- *avoid giving mixed messages* – when several members of the same team or from the local authority visit a setting, there is potential for each one to give different advice, e.g. pre-school development workers, advisory teachers and area special educational needs co-ordinators (SENCOs) may all advise on planning and it is essential that they all give the same message about what is appropriate.

Advisory teams need to work together to develop a shared understanding of the quality issues;

● *invite practitioners to identify an area of practice they would like to develop with your support* – this should ensure ownership. Using Foundation Stage guidance, in the ways suggested in earlier chapters, can be helpful. Those settings with OFSTED issues to develop can be encouraged to find their own starting points;

● *offer alternative ways of addressing a practice issue* – it is often useful to identify other settings, working in similar circumstances, which the practitioners could visit to see other ways of approaching an aspect of practice. Video material can also be useful for showing practitioners different ways of working;

● *treat everything you see/hear in a setting as confidential* – ask permission to share practice. Practitioners are generally very willing to share their practice, but it is vital that they are consulted about this and do not hear from others that they or their practice have been used as an example.

Encouraging practitioners to develop their practice

Establishing a set of principles

Advisory staff need to ensure that their approach is founded on a set of principles. This enables them to explain confidently why they operate in a particular way. Some local authority advisory teams have worked together to develop a set of principles and practice guidelines, which guides the work of all team members and this can be very supportive of existing and new staff. When made public, it also enables practitioners being supported to understand more about the team's philosophy and to evaluate their effectiveness. Some starting points, which could be discussed by teams and developed into a set of principles to inform advisory practice, are offered below:

● practitioners are more likely to respond positively if they feel some ownership of the development process;

● an external adviser is a guest in a setting and should show respect for, and interest in, the setting's/practitioner's values and traditions;

● advisory staff are also still learning and developing their practice – they need to be aware of their own strengths and limitations, and be able to admit when they are not sure or have made a mistake;

● what practitioners are doing well/have achieved is the starting point for their future development – achievement should be celebrated;

- what seems insignificant to an external adviser can represent a big step forward for a setting or practitioner (particularly for those who are resistant to change);
- development is more likely if it is facilitated through professional development opportunities and ongoing support.

It is a credit to teachers, who have taken on roles involving the development of Foundation Stage practice across settings, that the majority of practitioners have welcomed, and speak highly of, the support they have been offered. However, some practitioners/settings have been more resistant and it has been impossible or very difficult to encourage them to develop practice. In these cases stronger approaches may be needed! If settings want state funding for their 3 and 4-year-olds, they must be developing practice which complies with statutory requirements. If they will not, or cannot, do this, their continued funding should be at risk. This is easily said, but anecdotal evidence shows that some settings are receiving OFSTED reports which are considerably more positive than the local authority advisers believe they deserve. Until rigorous OFSTED inspection criteria are applied to all settings, by real early education specialists, it will be difficult to ensure that all children receive a high-quality curriculum. In order to work effectively with more resistant practitioners, it can be helpful to identify what is making them unresponsive.

What blocks practitioners from developing their practice?

The following blocks are common to staff working in a rapidly changing field:

- *Fear* – they are afraid they will not be able to manage different/new ways of working.
- *Complacency* – they think they are already doing a good job and therefore cannot see the point of developing their practice.
- *Cosiness* – they have become comfortable with existing ways of working and see no reason to rock the boat – they may be unaware of new statutory requirements.
- *Ignorance/lack of understanding* – they are unable to see the complexity of work with young children and genuinely believe simplistic approaches work. They have often received badly pitched training which has not helped them to develop their understanding – in fact it may have confused them or reinforced inappropriate ideas.
- *Laziness* – they want an easy life and are not prepared to give any more to the job.

- *Pressure from others* – they are most influenced by/fearful of those they see every day (e.g. managers, parents, energy sapping colleagues). Those with limited understanding of early years education are most vulnerable;
- *Inadequate resources* – they lose enthusiasm because of a lack of material and/or human resources.
- *Lack of time* – they are unable to plan for development and to work with the team to make it happen.

If they are to work towards moving practice forward, advisory teachers need to identify what might be blocking a team and use this knowledge to focus their initial approach. Sometimes this will require a discussion with the practitioners' managers.

The role of training in practice development

The overall aim of training courses is to effect 'a change in an individual's knowledge, skills, values or attitudes, which lasts over a period of time' (Daines, Daines and Graham, 2002, p. 3). There should be subject-based learning outcomes for practitioners but also personal and interpersonal learning outcomes. After a training course practitioners should:

- know and understand more about the area covered by the course (how much more will depend on individual starting points and the skill of the trainer in meeting individual needs);
- be able to apply and develop their new knowledge and understanding within their workplace;
- be motivated, enthused or inspired to take the initiative and develop their practice (this will also depend on the practitioners' motives for attending the course and the ability of the trainer to inspire and enthuse); and
- be able to work professionally with, and engage, other team members (e.g. when sharing the course and negotiating developments).

Advisory teachers are likely to have a role in organizing the training programme in their local authority and will also lead some of the courses. Many teachers say they are apprehensive about this aspect of their role. They see working with adults as being more challenging and potentially frightening than working with children. However, the way in-service education is planned and developed is not dissimilar to early education approaches.

Effective in-service courses

These should:

- be directly relevant and responsive to the concerns of those taking part (whenever possible participants should be involved in planning the course content);
- draw directly on and build on the experience of the group;
- provide a supportive environment where all participants are treated with respect and have the chance to contribute and share ideas;
- enable group members to operate at different levels of understanding;
- be enjoyable and reassuring, but also challenging;
- acknowledge and celebrate achievements to date and help group members to identify for themselves the next step in their learning and practice;
- question assumptions and encourage the group members to question themselves;
- offer a framework for thinking through and tackling complex issues or problems;
- encourage participants to write their thoughts down, since the process of writing leads to greater clarity;
- draw together the salient points from all discussions and make connections between them;
- encourage participants to develop their learning further through networking with others, or through seeking out books and other resources; and
- leave participants wanting more or wishing there was more time.

In-service courses should demonstrate recognition of achievements to date, but should also challenge and inspire participants to continue to improve their practice further. There is clearly a delicate balance here. It is easy to demoralize teachers, or to encourage them so much they believe they have found all the answers. On any course some practitioners will feel more insecure than others, and it is the course tutor's responsibility to find out about individuals by observing and listening, and to offer an appropriate balance of reassurance and challenge to each one.

Planning training courses

Training programmes, whether they are to take place for a couple of hours at the end of the day, over a whole day or over a number of weeks, need careful planning. The stages in the planning process are outlined below.

Needs analysis

This involves identifying what practitioners need and their different levels of development. All practitioners need support with Foundation Stage planning, but some need to begin the process whilst others need help with refining their planning. It is essential to decide whether the course can be run for practitioners at all levels or whether it is better to run a number of differentiated courses.

Identifying training skills

Having identified needs, it is important to consider who has the skills to lead the training. Many advisory teams offer courses run by a range of internal and external trainers. External trainers, who sometimes work on a national basis, can bring a wider perspective to a local authority and may offer skills where an internal gap has been identified. However, it is essential that the advisory team participate in courses run by new trainers, so they know what messages have been given to practitioners and can offer follow-up support. It is also important to avoid a situation where mixed messages are given by different trainers offering similar courses. Advisory teams need to select trainers who have a similar philosophy to their own and can complement training offered internally.

Targeting

Identify the levels at which the course will be offered and make it clear who the target group for each level will be. The course needs to be advertised appropriately to attract the relevant participants – by personal invitation if necessary.

Aims and objectives

Record the overall aim for the course (this can be fairly general) and the more detailed objectives (specific action statements highlighting what it is expected the practitioner will know or be able to do as a result of the course).

Pre/post-course thinking

Decide whether participants will need to bring something to the course or do a pre-course task. If the course has a number of sessions, decide whether they will undertake some work between sessions. Participants need to have the course information in good time to enable them to prepare.

Venue

If possible, check the venue so that its strengths and constraints are identified. This is particularly important when advisory teachers have invited external trainers to run courses. It is not acceptable for a visitor to have to deal with problems with a venue. A member of the advisory team should be present (at least at the beginning of the day) to deal with any issues which arise.

Programming

Decide how you will organize the available time (including breaks which may be predetermined by the venue). Participants expect to have a programme for the course showing clearly how time will be allocated. It is essential that courses finish on time, and that the planned content is covered, but otherwise a flexible, responsive approach can be adopted.

Introductions

Decide how the group will get to know each other through a carefully framed question at the start of the day. On one-session courses it is not possible to get to know a group well, but trainers should nevertheless try to tune into, and respond to, their expectations and starting points. Aim to get participants involved in a 'thinking' task as soon as possible so they get to know each other.

Deciding content

Include some theory as well as practical ideas. Practitioners need to be able to say why, as well as how, they do things (see Chapter 3). Leave time at the end of the course to enable participants to reflect, and identify what they will do as a result of the course.

Timings

Work out how much time can be allocated to each part of the day, bearing in mind that courses need to be flexible and responsive. It is useful to plan a little too much content but important to decide which parts are essential and which could be dropped. The ability to manage time develops with practice – for inexperienced trainers it is better to have planned too much rather than too little.

Presentation

Decide how content will be presented and developed, e.g. through input, group tasks, video, PowerPoint, overhead transparencies, books to be recommended, etc. It is important to offer a balance of methods to engage all learning styles. If overhead transparencies are used, they should be clear and offer simply the main points or headlines of the content. These can be developed and discussed with the group – a common complaint of trainers or speakers is that they simply read their overheads!

Handouts

Offer handouts, which cover all the main points of the course, to enable participants to refer to these later and share them with colleagues. If group tasks have been set, it can be useful to provide handouts setting out the process that the group worked through. This enables participants to lead similar tasks with their colleagues who were unable to attend.

Evaluation

Decide on what feedback will be asked for (this may be predetermined by the local authority or venue). Some local authorities have carbon evaluation forms so that one copy can stay with the advisory team and the other can be taken back to the setting. These forms usually have a question asking practitioners to say what they will do as a result of the course, and can be referred to and followed up on advisory visits. This question is best put on a separate sheet (with a space for the name of the practitioner and setting) so that the main evaluation form can be completed anonymously if participants prefer. The most useful evaluation forms offer an equal balance of quantative data such as numerical grading (e.g. 0–5) of aspects of the training, and qualitative data in the form of written answers to open-ended questions. If they are to improve their practice, trainers need to know not just how they were graded but why they were given that grade.

Self-evaluation

It is important for trainers to reflect on how *they* feel their training went. They need to take account of course evaluations, but should not dwell on negative comments made (particularly if these are in the minority). It is impossible to meet everyone's needs all of the time, especially on short courses. Obviously, the longer the course, the more possible it is to get the balance right. However, sometimes courses are attended by practitioners for whom the content is inappropriate, e.g. the baby-room staff member attending a Foundation Stage planning course. Instead of worrying about every individual, trainers need to consider what they could do in the future to address *valid* issues participants have raised. These would include comments such as the trainer talking too much, or poor timekeeping or unclear overheads. It is helpful to make some notes on the course programme as a reminder of what could be done differently next time. The more experienced a trainer is, the more they are able to see for themselves when their course has not been as effective as it could have been. Equally they know when they have trained well and can therefore put into perspective the one or two negative comments on the evaluations.

Following up training to support practice development

The majority of practitioners leave courses with a strong commitment to develop their practice. However, once they return to work, the hectic nature of their jobs, or the lack of interest of colleagues, may dampen their enthusiasm. Advisory visits which follow up training courses can therefore be particularly supportive.

Through working alongside an individual teacher and her team following training, it is possible to match the support offered directly to specific needs. It involves trainers, or advisers, in confronting head-on the very real issues faced by particular teams, and offers an extension of the partnership approach to learning advocated in earlier chapters. Those trainers and advisers who can help practitioners find ways of implementing change in their own setting find their credibility is enhanced.

Advisory teams need to create a culture within their local authority where practitioners know there is an expectation that training will be followed up during advisory visits. This can be achieved by explaining how evaluation forms will be used. Before their visit, advisory teachers should check which courses practitioners have attended recently and note what they said they intended to develop. During the visit they should:

- ask the practitioner to talk about or show what they have done as a result of the course. It is important to celebrate achievement – however small – and share this with the practitioner's manager;
- ask if there have been any blocks or challenges which have made practice development difficult and be prepared to offer support – for example, it may be necessary to speak to senior management in the setting;
- challenge any misunderstandings or misinterpretations of course content – practitioners relate to courses within the context of their existing level of understanding and each one will have taken away unique messages;
- ask what the practitioner intends to develop next and note this for future reference; and
- ensure the practitioner knows how to get further support – from the advisory team, others, professional visits or follow-up training sessions.

In this way professional visits can complement and support the training opportunities offered to practitioners.

Providing resources to support practice development

Through working with groups and individuals, advisory teams can gain a clearer view of what resources might be needed to support their Foundation Stage settings. These might include publications or resource boxes produced by the team, or they might be accessed from external sources. Many advisory teams develop collections of internally and externally produced resources. Some teams have developed libraries to enable practitioners to borrow books and videos. Others have established resource loan libraries, which offer those settings on a limited budget the chance to access good quality resources they would not otherwise be able to afford. These services have been particularly appreciated by private and voluntary providers.

Advisory team networks and support systems

As we have seen in earlier chapters, early years teachers are used to feeling isolated and misunderstood. Advisory teachers may experience similar feelings of loneliness and uncertainty. It is therefore crucial that new team members are offered mentors who can help them to prepare for, and cope with, the role they have undertaken. Regional networks have developed in some parts of the country, where advisers from different local authorities can meet together and learn from each other. These networks offer support and also challenge. It is useful for one team to see how others are managing roles and resources, and to share ideas on how to deal with new government initiatives. Some networks also invite speakers to their meetings. It is essential that all advisory teachers receive support and professional development opportunities of this kind.

Further reading

Daines, J., Daines, C. and Graham, B. (2002) *Adult Learning Adult Teaching*, 3rd edn, Welsh Academic Press, Cardiff.
Race, P. and Smith, B. (1995) *500 Tips for Trainers*, Kogan Page, London.
Thompson, N. (1996) *People Skills: A Guide to Effective Practice in the Human Services*, Macmillan, London.

See also the list of videos in Chapter 3.

10

Developing the Foundation Stage: some issues and priorities

This book is a celebration of the work of the specialist early years teacher. This final chapter, will briefly highlight some of the threats to the future quality of Foundation Stage practice.

Implementing the Foundation Stage curriculum

Although the Foundation Stage has been welcomed, there is considerable work to be done to ensure it is fully embedded in thinking and practice. The House of Commons Education and Employment Committee (2000, p. xxi) recognized this challenge: 'We recognise the scale of the challenge in the Guidance to practitioners, who will need to have imagination and flexibility to enable children to learn in ways appropriate to their developmental stage.'

Edgington (2003) listed a number of blocks to successful implementation. These include:

- lack of specialist training in work with young children;
- inadequate training in using the curriculum guidance;
- the history of separate nursery and reception class provision – reception classes are still being drawn towards Key Stage 1 (Quick et al., 2002, Adams et al., 2004);
- lack of resources, including trained staff, play materials and suitable space (indoors and outside); and
- primary school teams' (including governors and parents) lack of awareness of the implications of the Foundation Stage.

Many Foundation Stage settings need to develop their provision and practice to bring it in line with the expectations set out in the statutory guidance. In particular there is a need to:

- develop learning environments indoors and outside to ensure that they truly support high quality child-initiated learning;
- ensure that all practitioners understand the importance of the outdoor curriculum and reflect this in their planning and practice;
- develop understanding of the role of the adult, particularly in relation to supporting and extending child-initiated play; and
- ensure that assessment is based on observation.

Transition to Key Stage 1

Because the Foundation Stage was introduced last, rather than first, it has had to compete with an overloaded curriculum at Key Stages 1 and 2. Targets set for the end of Key Stage 1 exert pressure on Year 1 and Foundation Stage teachers. Many of these teachers are aware that the curriculum content they are being pressed to cover is unrealistic. The national focus in 2004 on the interface between Foundation Stage and Key Stage 1 is therefore to be welcomed (Hofkins, 2003). In schools where the Foundation Stage has been effectively implemented, there is a growing recognition that Foundation Stage approaches to learning and teaching are equally relevant to Key Stage 1 children, particularly those just turned 5. Some schools also see the relevance for Key Stage 2 children.

In order to give these schools confidence to work more creatively the government needs to:

- remove SATs at the end of Key Stage 1 and replace them with a Key Stage 1 profile;
- review the literacy strategy expectations for reception and Key Stage 1 children putting greater emphasis on speaking and listening skills;
- extend the concept of the Foundation Stage to include Years 1 and 2; and
- reduce ambiguity by giving clear messages about how children should be learning at all Key Stages (through Primary Strategy personnel and OFSTED inspectors).

Protecting nursery schools

Nursery schools, because they have specialized in innovative work with 3–5-year-olds, have unquestionably provided the model of good practice on which the Foundation Stage curriculum is based. They have been at the heart of the government's integration initiatives. For some years though they have been vulnerable, because local authorities needing to save money see them as an expensive resource. Over the last three years around 40 schools have been closed. Others have been threatened with closure or with amalgamation with primary schools. These closures have caused considerable distress to the families using the schools and to staff who have lost their jobs. The DfES-funded Nursery School Forum based at Early Education has provided much support to these schools. It has also provided an indication that the government has belatedly recognized their worth. In order to strengthen the position of nursery schools the government should:

- take steps to prevent local authorities from closing any more nursery schools;
- ensure that all of the new Children's Centres have a strong nursery school core – setting up new, properly resourced nursery schools to form this core in areas where there is no existing provision; and
- encourage and enable nursery schools to become specialist Foundation Stage schools catering for the entire 3–5/6 age range.

It is essential for the future of early years education that nursery schools and their staff continue to provide a model for staff working in the primary, private and voluntary sectors. Nursery school headteachers have a particular role to play in sharing their expertise and leading the development of early years services.

Re-establishing real nursery education

The gradual redefinition of 'nursery education' was explained in earlier chapters. Since the introduction of the Foundation Stage it has become clear that some settings are unable (or struggle) to achieve the statutory curriculum requirements. This may be because of lack of space or resources, but more often it is because staff are not well enough trained. They lack the necessary understanding and skills to do the job. Differing OFSTED inspection regimes make it impossible to make reliable comparisons between settings. However, the EPPE (Effective Provision of Pre-school Education) research has shown that nursery schools, centres and classes achieve the best social and academic outcomes for children (see www.ioe.ac.uk/projects/eppe). These meet the criteria for real nursery education set out in the introduction. It is therefore not acceptable for the government to continue to assert that all types of setting offer high-quality education. If all children are to access good or excellent provision there is an urgent need to:

- ensure that all funded settings for Foundation Stage children conform to the criteria for real nursery education (see page xiii); and
- evaluate all settings according to the same rigorous standards, using inspectors who are experienced in nursery education.

Protecting the Foundation Stage teacher

There is now no doubt that specialist teachers are essential to the future development of services for children within the Foundation Stage as well as for children up to the age of three and in Key Stage 1. There is, however, genuine concern that the role of the teacher could be marginalized. We have seen how teachers may not be employed in some nursery classes. We have also seen how the number of teachers working in the Foundation Stage has been reduced to save money and how there is no requirement for a full-time teacher to be employed in the new Children's Centres. Additionally, early years teachers have been set apart (at least to some extent) from their Key Stage 1 and 2 colleagues by the distinctive nature of the Foundation Stage and by their involvement in integrated work. Separate approaches to training have been developing – including training for leadership and management – to take account of these different professional demands. There are therefore fears that, in the future, early years teachers may have different or lower status than colleagues working with older children. In order to prevent this from happening, and to promote the importance of the Foundation Stage teacher, there is a need to:

- ensure that specialist teachers are employed to work directly with children and to lead curriculum development in all government funded Foundation Stage settings;
- recommend that all schools appoint a Foundation Stage co-ordinator to their senior management team; and
- link Foundation Stage training to primary sector training so that all teachers have common core input before or alongside extension into their specialist area.

The view that every child and every early years team needs day-to-day contact with a specialist teacher is not a fashionable one. Those of us who make this assertion are sometimes accused of being elitist or of having 'baggage'. As a specialist consultant, with wide experience of working with, and on behalf of, young children and their families, I am incensed when I am told that my professional views are my 'baggage'. I do not believe that it is elitist to campaign for the best possible provision for all children. It is surely the role of a campaigner to set sights as high as possible. To do less offers excuses to those willing to accept less.

In 2004 we now have a much clearer idea of what quality should look like – evidence referred to throughout this book. It is deeply disappointing to find the government sidelining its own research evidence and refusing to see the need for a strong teacher presence in the new Children's Centres. If Ministers really believed that early education matters, they would ensure that all children had access to the best provision. They would not be content with anything less.

References

Abbott, L. and Nutbrown, C. (2001) *Experiencing Reggio Emilia: Implications for Pre-school Provision*, Open University Press, London.

Adair, J. (1986) *Effective Teambuilding*, Pan Books, London.

Adams, S. and Moyles, J. (forthcoming) *Visions of Violence*, Featherstone Educational, Lutterworth.

Adams, S., Alexander, E. Drummond, M.J. and Moyles, J. (2004) *Inside the Foundation Stage – Recreating the Reception Year*, Association of Teachers and Lecturers, London.

Athey, C. (1990) *Extending Thought in Young Children: A Parent–Teacher Partnership*, Paul Chapman Publishing, London.

Ball, C. (1994) *Start Right: The Importance of Early Learning*, RSA, London.

Barrett, G. (1986) *Starting School: An Evaluation of the Experience*, AMMA/UEA, Norwich.

Barrett, G. (ed.) (1989) *Disaffection from School? The Early Years*, Falmer Press, Lewes.

Bennett, N. and Kell, J. (1989) *A Good Start? Four Year Olds in Infant Schools*, Blackwell, Oxford.

Berenstain, S. (1981) *Bears in the Night*, Collins, London.

Bertram, T. and Pascal, C. (1999) *Early Excellence Centres: First Findings* DfEE, London.

Bilton, H. (2002) *Outdoor Play in the Early Years*, 2nd edn, David Fulton, London.

Bilton, H (2004) *Playing Outside: Activities, Ideas and Inspiration for the Early Years*, David Fulton, London.

Blatchford, P., Battle, S. and May, J. (1982) *The First Transition: Home to Pre-school*, NFER/Nelson, Windsor.

Blenkin, G. and Kelly, V. (1997) *Principles into Practice in Early Childhood Education*, Paul Chapman Publishing, London.

Blenkin, G.M. and Kelly, A.V. (eds) (1996) *Early Childhood Education: A Developmental Curriculum*, 2nd edn, Paul Chapman Publishing, London.

Blenkin, G.M. and Whitehead, M.R. (1996) Creating a context for development, in G.M. Blenkin and A.V. Kelly (eds) *Early Childhood Education: A Developmental Curriculum*, 2nd edn, Paul Chapman Publishing, London.

Brierley, J. (1984) *A Human Birthright: Giving the Young Brain a Chance*, BAECE, London.

Briggs, R. (1978) *The Snowman*, Hamish Hamilton, London.

Brooker, L. (2002) *Starting School – Young Children Learning Cultures*, Open University Press, Buckingham.

Browne, N. and Ross, C. (1991) 'Girls' stuff, boys' stuff', in N. Browne (ed.) *Science and Technology in the Early Years*, Open University Press, Buckingham.

Bruce, T. (1996) *Helping Young Children to Play*, Hodder and Stoughton, London.

Bruce, T. (1997) *Early Childhood Education*, 2nd edn, Hodder and Stoughton, London.

Carnegie Corporation (1994) *Starting Points: Meeting the Needs of our Youngest Children*, Carnegie Corporation, New York.

Carr, M. (2001) *Assessment in Early Childhood Settings: Learning Stories* Paul Chapman Publishing, London.

City of Salford EYDCP (2002) *The Salford Early Years Toolkit*, City of Salford, Salford.

Clark, A. and Moss, P. (2001) *Listening to Young Children: The Mosaic Approach*, National Children's Bureau, London.

Cleave, S., Jowett, S. and Bate, M. (1982) *And So to School*, NFER/Nelson, Windsor.

Coles, M. (1996) The magnifying glass: what we know of classroom talk in the early years, in N. Hall and J. Martello (eds) *Listening to Children Think: Exploring Talk in the Early Years*, Hodder and Stoughton, London.

Cox, T. (2000) *Combating Educational Disadvantage: Meeting the Needs of Vulnerable Children*, Falmer Press, London.

Crawford, M., Kydd, L. and Riches, C. (1997) *Leadership and Teams in Educational Management*, Open University Press, Buckingham.

CRE (1990) *From Cradle to School. A Practical Guide to Race, Equality and Childcare*, CRE, London.

Daines, J., Daines, C. and Graham, B. (2002) *Adult Learning Adult Teaching*, 3rd edn, Welsh Academic Press, Cardiff.

David, T. (1990) *Under Five – Under Educated?* Open University Press, Milton Keynes.

David, T. (ed.) (1993) *Educational Provision for our Youngest Children: European Perspectives*, Paul Chapman Publishing, London.

David T., Curtis, A. and Siraj-Blatchford, I. (1992) *Effective Teaching in the Early Years: Fostering Children's Learning in Nurseries and in Infant Classes*, Trentham Books, Stoke-on-Trent.

Derman-Sparks, L. and the ABC Task Force (1989) *Anti-Bias Curriculum: Tools for Empowering Young Children*, National Association for the Education of Young Children, Washington, DC.

DES (1990) *Starting with Quality*, HMSO, London.

DfEE (1997a) *Early Years Development Partnerships and Early Years Development Plans for 1998/9: Draft Guidance for Consultation*, DfEE, London.

DfES (2003a) *Provision for Children Under Five Years of Age in England: January 2003 (Provisional)*, DfES, London.

DfES (2003b) *Excellence and Enjoyment: A Strategy for Primary Schools*, DfES, London.

DfES (2001) *Special Educational Needs Code of Practice*, DfES, London.

Donaldson, M. (1978) *Children's Minds*, Fontana, Glasgow.

Dowling, M. (1992) *Education 3 to 5: A Teachers' Handbook*, 2nd edn, Paul Chapman Publishing, London.

Dowling, M. (2000) *Young Children's Personal, Social and Emotional Development*, Paul Chapman Publishing, London.

Dowling, M. (2002) The impact of stress on early development, in J. Fisher (ed.) *The Foundations of Learning*, Open University Press, Buckingham.

Drummond, M.J. (1993) *Assessing Children's Learning*, David Fulton, London.

Drummond, M.J., Lally, M. and Pugh, G. (1989) *Working with Children: Developing a Curriculum for the Early Years*, NCB/Nottingham Educational Supplies, Nottingham.

Drummond, M.J., Rouse, D. and Pugh, G. (1992) *Making Assessment Work*, NES/Arnold/National Children's Bureau, Nottingham.

Dweck, C.S. and Leggett, E. (1988) A social-cognitive approach to motivation and personality, *Psychological Review*, 95 (2), pp. 256–73.

Edgington, M. (2002a) High achievement for young children in, J. Fisher (ed.) *The Foundations of Learning*, Open University Press, Buckingham.

Edgington, M. (2002b) *The Great Outdoors*, Early Education, London.

Edgington, M. (2003) Implementing the Foundation Stage, *Primary Practice*, 33, pp. 17–20.

Education and Employment Committee (2000) *Early Years*, The Stationery Office, Norwich.

EEL (1994) Effective Early Learning project, in EEL, *An Action Plan for Change*, Amber Publishing, Worcester.

ESAC (1989) *Educational Provision for the Under Fives*, HMSO, London.

EYCG (1989) *Early Childhood Education. The Early Years Curriculum and the National Curriculum*, Trentham Books, Stoke-on-Trent.

EYCG (1992) *First Things First*, Madeleine Lindley, Oldham.

EYCG (1995) *Four Year Olds in School: Myths and Realities*, Madeleine Lindley, Oldham.

Fabian, H. (2002) *Children Starting School*, David Fulton, London.

Fawcett, M. (1996) *Learning through Child Observation*, Jessica Kingsley, London.

Featherstone, S. (2001) *The Little Book of Outdoor Play*, Featherstone Education, Lutterworth.

Featherstone, S. (2003) *The Little Book of Outside in All Weathers*, Featherstone Education, Lutterworth.

Featherstone, S. and Bayley, R. (2001) *Foundations for Independence*, Featherstone Education, Lutterworth.

Fisher, J. (2002a) *Starting from the Child?* 2nd edn, Open University Press, Buckingham.

Fisher, J. (ed.) (2002b) *The Foundations of Learning*, Open University Press, Buckingham.

Gaine, B. and van Keulen, A. (1997) *Anti-Bias Training Approaches in the Early Years*, EYTARN, London.

Gregory, E. (1994) The National Curriculum and non-native speakers of English, in G. Blenkin and A.V. Kelly (eds) *The National Curriculum and Early Learning*, Paul Chapman Publishing, London.

Grenier, J. (2004) Shabby treament, *Nursery World*, 8 January, pp. 10–11.

Gura, P. (1996) *Resources for Early Learning*, Hodder and Stoughton, London.

GTC (2003) Minority report, *Teaching*, Autumn, pp. 12–13, General Teaching Council, Birmingham.

Harlen, W. (1992) Matching, in C. Richards (ed.) *New Directions in Primary Education*, Falmer Press, London.

Hazareesingh, S., Simms, K. and Anderson, P. (1989) *Educating the Whole Child: A Holistic Approach to Education in Early Years*, Building Blocks, London.

Hill, E. (1980) *Where's Spot?* Heinemann, London.

Hodges, L. (1997) Summer discount, *Times Educational Supplement*, 26 September.

Hofkins, D. (2003) Roots of a revolution, *Times Educational Supplement*, 10 October.

Holdaway, D. (1979) *The Foundations of Literacy*, Ashton Scholastic, Gosford, NSW.

Holland, P. (2003a) *We Don't Play with Guns Here*, Open University Press, Buckingham.

Holland, P. (2003b) War weapon and superhero play: a challenge to zero tolerance, *Early Years Practice*, 5 (1), pp. 37–49.

Holt, J. (1989) *Learning All the Time*, Education Now, Ticknall.

Hughes, M. (1986) *Children and Number*, Blackwell, Oxford.

Hughes, M., Wikeley, E and Nash, T. (1994) *Parents and their Children's Schools*, Blackwell, Oxford.

Hurst, V. (1996) Parents and professionals: partnership in early childhood education, in G.M. Blenkin and A.V. Kelly (eds) *Early Childhood Education: A Developmental Curriculum*, 2nd edn, Paul Chapman Publishing, London.

Hurst, V. (1997) *Planning for Early Learning*, 2nd edn, Paul Chapman Publishing, London.

Hutchin, V. (1999) *Right from the Start: Effective Planning and Assessment in the Early Years*, Hodder and Stoughton, London.

Hutchin, V. (2000) *Tracking Significant Achievement in the Early Years*, 2nd edn, Hodder and Stoughton, London.

Hutchin (2003) *Observing and Assessing for the Foundation Stage Profile*, Hodder and Stoughton, London.

Industrial Society (1969) *The Manager as Leader*, Industrial Society, London.

Ironbridge Gorge Museum (1989) *Under Fives and Museums: Guidelines for Teachers*, Ironbridge Gorge Museum, Telford.

Islington Education (1999) *Early Years Curriculum Guidelines for Children from Birth to Five Year Olds*, Islington Council, London.

Johnston, J. (1996) *Early Explorations in Science*, Open University Press, Buckingham.

Katz, L. and Chard, S. (1989) *Engaging Children's Minds: The Project Approach*, Ablex, Norwood, NJ.

Kenway, P. (1995) *Working with Parents*, Save the Children, London.

Kitson, N. (1994) 'Please Miss Alexander: will you be the robber?' Fantasy play: a case for adult intervention, in J. Moyles (ed.) *The Excellence of Play*, Open University Press, Buckingham.

Lally, M. (1993) Supporting young bilingual learners, *Early Years News*, Autumn.

Lally, M. (1995) Principles to practice in early years education, in R. Campbell and L. Miller (eds) *Supporting Children in the Early Years*, Trentham Books, Stoke-on-Trent.

Lally, M. and Hurst, V. (1992) Assessment in nursery education: a review of approaches, in G. Blenkin and V. Kelly (eds.) *Assessment in Early Childhood Education*, Paul Chapman Publishing, London.

Lazar, I. and Darlington, R. (1982) Lasting effects of early education: a report from the Consortium for Longitudinal Studies, *Monographs of the Society for Research in Child Development*, serial no. 195, vol. 47.

Learning Through Landscapes (1990) *Using School Grounds as an Educational Resource*, Learning Through Landscapes Trust, Winchester.

LEARN (2000) *Learning for Life*, 2nd edn, London Borough of Lewisham, London.

LEARN (2002) *A Place to Learn*, London Borough of Lewisham, London.

Lindon, J. (1993) *Child Development from Birth to Eight*, National Children's Bureau, London.

Lindon, J. (1997) *Working with Young Children*, 3rd edn, Hodder and Stoughton, London.

Lindon, J. (1999) *Too Safe for their own Good? Helping Children Learn about Risk and Lifeskills*, National Children's Bureau, London.

Lindon, J. (2001) *Understanding Children's Play*, Hodder and Stoughton, London.

Lindon, J. (2003) *Child Protection*, 2nd edn, Hodder and Stoughton, London.

Lockett, A. (2004) If you go down to the woods today …, *Early Education*, 42, Spring, pp. 5–6.

London Borough of Wandsworth (2001) *Planning for Foundation Stage Learning*, Wandsworth Council, London.

London Borough of Wandsworth (2002) *Ideas for Foundation Stage Learning*, Wandsworth Council, London.

MacNaughton, G. (2003) *Shaping Early Childhood: Learners, Curriculum, Context*, Open University, Buckingham.

Maxime, J.E. (1991) Towards a transcultural approach to working with under-sevens, in *The Report of Two Conferences Combating Racism among Students, Staff and Children, Nursery Nurse Trainers*, Early Years Anti-Racist Network and National Children's Bureau, London.

Meggitt, C. and Sunderland, G. (2000) *Child Development: An Illustrated Guide*, Heinemann, Oxford.

Menter, I. (1989) 'They're too young to notice': young children and racism, in G. Barrett (ed.) *Disaffection from School? The Early Years*, Falmer Press, Lewes.

Metz, M. (1996) The development of mathematical understanding, in G.M. Blenkin and A.V. Kelly (eds) *Early Childhood Education: A Developmental Curriculum*, 2nd edn, Paul Chapman Publishing, London.

Miller, J. (1997) *Never Too Young: How Young Children can Take Responsibility and Make Decisions*, National Early Years Network and Save the Children, London.

Milner, D. (1975) *Children and Race*, Penguin, Harmondsworth.

Milner, D. (1983) *Children and Race – Ten Years On*, Ward Lock, London.

Montague-Smith, A. (1997) *Mathematics in Nursery Education*, David Fulton, London.

Moss, P. and Penn, H. (1996) *Transforming Nursery Education*, Paul Chapman Publishing, London.

Moyles, J. (1989) *Just Playing? The Role and Status of Play in Early Childhood Education*, Open University Press, Milton Keynes.

Moyles, J., Adams S. and Musgrove, A. (2002) *SPEEL Study of Pedagogical Effectiveness in Early Learning*, DfES, London.

Nabuco, E. and Sylva, K. (1996) The effects of three early childhood curricula on children's progress at primary school in Portugal, paper presented at ISSBD, Quebec.

National Commission on Education (1993) *Learning to Succeed*, Heinemann, London.

NCNE (1997) *What Do We Mean by Nursery Education?* NCNE, London.

Neugebauer, R. (1985) Are you an effective leader? *Child Care Information Exchange*, 146, pp. 18–26.

NFER/SCDC (1987) *Four Year Olds in School: Policy and Practice, a Seminar Report*, NFER/SCDC, Slough.

Nutbrown, C. (1994) *Threads of Thinking: Young Children Learning and the Role of Early Education*, Paul Chapman Publishing, London.

OFSTED (1997) *The Annual Report of Her Majesty's Chief Inspector of Schools: Standards and Quality in Education, 1995/6*, HMSO, London.

Osborn, A.E and Milbank, J.E. (1987) *The Effects of Early Education*, Clarendon Press, Oxford.

Ouvry, M. (2000) *Exercising Muscles and Minds*, National Early Years Network, London.

Pascal, C. and Bertram, T. (2002) Assessing what matters in the early years, in J. Fisher (ed.) *The Foundations of Learning*, Open University Press, Buckingham.

PAT (2003) *The Role of the Nursery Nurse*, Professional Association of Teachers, Derby.

Pen Green Family Centre (1990) *Learning to be Strong*, Changing Perspectives, Northwich.

Penn, H. and Lloyd, E. (2001) *The Potential for Partnership between Maintained Nursery Schools and the Voluntary and Community Early Years Sector*, UEL and National Early Years Network, London.

Piachaud, D. and Sutherland, H. (2000) *How Effective is the British Government's Attempt to Reduce Child Poverty?* London School of Economics, University of London, London.

Play Safety Forum (2002) *Managing Risk in Play Provision: A Position Statement*, Play Safety Forum, London.

Pompert, B. (1994) Going on the bus … Second language acquisition in meaningful activities, *Early Years News*, 5, Autumn/Winter.

POST (2000) *Report on Early Years Learning*, Parliamentary Office of Science and Technology, Millbank, London.

Pugh, G. and De'Ath, E. (1989) *Working Towards Partnership in the Early Years*, National Children's Bureau, London.

Pugh, G. (2002) The consequences of inadequate investment in the early years, in J. Fisher (ed.) *The Foundations of Learning*, Open Universtity Press, Buckingham.

QCA/DfES (2000) *Curriculum Guidance for the Foundation Stage*, QCA/DfES, London.

QCA/DfES (2001) *Planning for Learning in the Foundation Stage*, DfES, London.

QCA/DfES (2003) *Foundation Stage Profile*, QCA/DfES, London.

Quick, S., Lambley, C., Newcombe, E. and Aubrey, C. (2002) *Implementing the Foundation Stage in Reception Classes*, DfES, London.

Race, P. and Smith, B. (1995) *500 Tips for Trainers*, Kogan Page, London.

RBK and C (1993) Priorities for early years co-ordinators, unpublished course report, Royal Borough of Kensington and Chelsea, London.

Richards, R. (1996) Learning through science in the early years, in G.M. Blenkin and A.V. Kelly (eds) *Early Childhood Education: A Developmental Curriculum*, Paul Chapman Publishing, London.

Riches, C. (1993) *Managing Change in Education*, E326, Open University Press, Milton Keynes.

Riley, D. (1983) *War in the Nursery*, Virago, London.

Roberts, R. (1995) *Self-Esteem and Successful Early Learning*, Hodder and Stoughton, London.

Rodd, J. (1994) *Leadership in Early Childhood*, Open University Press, Buckingham.

Rodd, J. (1998) *Leadership in Early Childhood*, 2nd edn, Open University Press, Buckingham.

Rodd, J. (2001) Can Young Children Learn to Learn? *Early Years Educator*, 3 (6), pp. 16–18.

Sammons, P., Sylva, K. Melhuish, E., Siraj-Blatchford, I., Taggart, B. and Elliot, K. (2003) *Measuring the Impact of Pre-school on Children's Social/Behavioural Development over the Pre-school Period*. EPPE Project Technical Paper 8b, Institute of Education, DfES, London.

Save the Children (1993) *Equality: A Basis for Good Practice*, Save the Children, London.

SCAA (1996) *Desirable Outcomes for Children's Learning*, DfEE/SCAA, London.

Schools Council (1984) *Guidelines for Internal Review and Development in Schools*, Longman, London.

Schweinhart, L. and Weikart, D. (1997) *Lasting Differences: The High/Scope Preschool Curriculum Comparison Study through Age 23*, High Scope Press, Ypsilanti, MI.

Schweinhart L.J., Weikart, D.P. and Larner, M.B. (1986) Consequences of three preschool curriculum models through age 15, *Early Childhood Quarterly*, 1 (1), pp. 15–45.

Sharp, C. (2002) School starting age: European policy and recent research, paper presented to the Local Government Association seminar 'When should children start school', November, London.

Sharp, C., Hutchison, D. and Whetton, C. (1994) How do season of birth and length of schooling affect children's attainment at Key Stage 1? *Educational Research*, 36 (2), pp. 107–21.

Sherman, A. (1996) *Rules, Routines and Regimentation: Young Children Reporting on their Schooling*, Educational Heretics Press, Nottingham.

Siraj-Blatchford, I. (1994) *The Early Years: Laying the Foundations for Racial Equality*, Trentham Books, Stoke-on-Trent.

Siraj-Blatchford, J. and MacLeod-Brudenell, I. (1999) *Supporting Science, Design and Technology in the Early Years*, Open University Press, Buckingham.

Siraj-Blatchford, I. and Clarke, P. (2000) *Supporting Identity, Diversity and Language in the Early Years*, Open University Press, Buckingham.

Siraj-Blatchford, I. and Siraj-Blatchford, J. (2003) *More than Computers*, Early Education, London.

Siraj-Blatchford, I., Sylva, K., Muttock, S. Gilden, R. and Bell, D. (2002) *Researching Effective Pedagogy in the Early Years*, DfES, London.

Siraj-Blatchford, I., Sylva, K., Taggart, B., Sammons, P., Melhuish, E. and Elliot, K. (2003) *Intensive Case Studies of Practice across the Foundation Stage*, DfES/Institute of Education, London.

Smith, A. and Langston, A. (1999) *Managing Staff in Early Years Settings*, Routledge, London.

Smith, P.K. (ed.) (1984) *Play in Animals and Humans*, Blackwell, Oxford.

Smith, T. (1980) *Parents and Preschool*, Grant McIntyre, London.

Stubbs, D.R. (1985) *Assertiveness at Work*, Gower Publishing, London.

Sure Start (2002) *Birth to Three Matters*, Sure Start Unit, DfES, London.

Sure Start (2003a) *Children's Centres – Developing Integrated Services for Young Children and their Families: Start Up Guidance Updated August 2003*, Sure Start Unit, DfES, London.

Sure Start (2003b) *Foundation Stage. Information Pack for Parents*, Sure Start Unit, DfES, London.

Sylva, K. (1994) The impact of early learning on children's later development, Appendix C in C. Ball *Start Right: The Importance of Early Learning*, RSA, London.

Sylva, K. (1997) The early years curriculum: evidence based proposals, paper given to SCAA, London.

Sylva, K. (2000) Early childhood education to ensure a 'fair start for all', in T. Cox *Combating Educational Disadvantage: Meeting the needs of Vulnerable Children*, Falmer Press, London.

Swann, R. and Gammage, P. (1993) 'Early Childhood Education … Where Are We Now?', in P. Gammage and J. Meighan (eds) *Early Childhood Education: Taking Stock*, Education Now Books, Nottingham.

Thomas, G. (1988) 'Hallo, Mrs Scatterbrain. Hallo, Mr Strong': assessing attitudes and behaviour in the nursery, in A. Cohen and L. Cohen (eds) *Early Education: The Pre-School Years*, Paul Chapman Publishing, London.

Thompson, N. (1996) *People Skills: A Guide to Effective Practice in the Human Services*, Macmillan, London.

Thomson, R. (2001) Breaking Point, *Nursery World*, 27 January, pp. 10–11.

Tizard, B. and Hughes, M. (1984) *Young Children Learning*, Fontana, London.

Tizard, B., Mortimore, J. and Burchell, B. (1981) *Involving Parents in Nursery and Infant Schools*, Grant McIntyre, London.

Tower Hamlets Early Years Service (2000) *Starting Points: Guidance for Assessment during the Foundation Stage*, Learning Design, London.

Tower Hamlets Early Years Service and Newham Early Years Unit (2000) *Planning for Progress 2*, Learning Design, London.

Toynbee, P. (2004) We can break the vice of the great unmentionable, *Guardian*, 5 January.

Trudell, P. (2002) Meeting the needs of disadvantaged children, in J. Fisher (ed.) *The Foundations of Learning*, Open University Press, Buckingham.

Vygotsky, L.S. (1932) *Thought and Language*, MIT Press, Cambridge, MA.

Vygotsky, L.S. (1978) *Mind in Society*, trans. and ed. by M. Cole, V. John-Steiner, S. Scribner and E. Souberman, Harvard University Press, Cambridge, MA.

Vygotsky, L.S. (1986) Thought and Language, MIT, Cambridge, MA. Revised and edited by A. Kozulin.

Wake, B. (1997) 'Retro-scope' – by way of an editorial, *Microscope*, Summer.

Watt, J. (1977) *Co-operation in Preschool Education*, SSRC, London.

Wells, G. (1986) *The Meaning Makers: Children Learning Language and Using Language to Learn*, Hodder and Stoughton, Sevenoaks.

Whalley, M. (1994) *Learning to be Strong*, Hodder and Stoughton, London.

Whalley, M. and the Pen Green Centre Team (1997) *Working with Parents*, Hodder and Stoughton, London.

Whalley, M. and the Pen Green Centre Team (2001) *Involving Parents in their Children's Learning*, Paul Chapman Publishing, London.

Whalley, M. (2004) *Management in Early Childhood Settings*, Paul Chapman Publishing, London.

Whitehead, M. (1996) *Developing Language and Literacy*, Hodder and Stoughton, London.

Whitehead, M. (1997) *Language and Literacy in the Early Years*, 2nd edn, Paul Chapman Publishing, London.

Whyte, J. (1983) *Beyond the Wendy House: Sex Role Stereotyping in Primary Schools*, Longman for Schools Council, York.

Wood, E. and Atfield, J. (1996) *Play, Learning and the Early Childhood Curriculum*, Paul Chapman Publishing, London.

Author Index

Abbott, L. 7
ABC Task Force 107
Adair, J. 58
Adams, S. 7, 85, 98, 114, 145, 148, 201, 223, 226, 256
Anderson, P. 100, 228, 231
Athey, C. 154, 163, 175
Attfield, J. 225, 226

Ball, C. 16, 79
Barrett, G. 81
Bate, M. 98
Bayley, R. 146
Bennett, N. 81
Berenstain, S. 82
Bertram, T. 4, 114, 233
Bilton, H. 134, 135, 147
Blenkin, G.M. 82, 109, 110, 131, 169
Brierley, J. 79
Briggs, R. 213
Brooker, L. 85, 99, 107
Browne, N. 85
Bruce, T. 16, 123, 126, 128, 130, 136, 145, 208, 221
Burchell, B. 101, 212

Carnegie Corporation 79
Carr, M. 7, 153
Chard, S. 108, 195, 196, 200
City of Salford EYDCP 153
Clark, A. 152
Clarke, P. 107, 243
Cleave, S. 98
Coles, M. 130
Community Playthings 134, 145
Cox, T. 243
Crawford, M. 56
CRE 231
Curtis, A. 125

Daines, C. 249, 255
Daines, J. 249, 255
Darlington, R. 109
David, T. 125, 129
De'Ath, E. 233
Derman-Sparks, L. 87, 107
DES 81
DfEE xiv, xv, 80
DfES xi, 17, 80, 84, 85, 118, 121, 236

Donaldson, M. 195
Dowling, M. 19, 83, 107, 235, 243
Drummond, M.J. 46, 152, 228
Dweck, C.S. 109, 195

Edgington, M. 83, 114, 121, 128, 134, 140, 145, 256
Education and Employment Committee 81, 140, 256
EEL 70
ESAC 140, 201
EYCG 16, 17, 160, 185, 195

Fabian, H. 14, 98, 107
Fawcett, M. 156, 157, 193
Featherstone, S. 145, 146
Fisher, J. 53, 146, 154

Gaine, B. 85
Gammage 165
Graham, B. 249
Grenier, J. 232
GTC 228, 230
Gura, P. 239

Harlen, W. 190
Hazareesingh, S. 100, 228, 231
Hill, E. 83
Hofkins, D. 257
Holdaway, D. 129
Holland, P. 85, 223, 226
Holt, J. 4, 123, 195
Hughes, M. 16, 85, 152, 163, 212
Hurst, V. 83, 126, 149, 152, 153, 154, 189, 226
Hutchin, V. 53, 153, 154, 155, 193

Industrial Society 15, 20
Ironbridge Gorge Museum 205
Islington Education 40

Johnston, J. 209
Jowett, S. 98

Katz, L. 108, 195, 196, 200
Kell, J. 81
Kelly, V. 82, 109
Kenway, P. 101
Kitson, N. 221

Kydd, L. 56

Lally, M. 104, 149, 153, 154, 185, 189, 228
Larner, M.B. 196
Lazar, I. 109
LEARN 134, 146, 153, 165, 169
Learning through Landscapes 140
Leggett, E. 109, 195
Lindon, J. 88, 90, 92, 126, 136, 146, 157, 159, 226, 231, 233, 243
Lloyd, E. 230
Lockett, A. 144
London Borough of Wandsworth 165

MacLeod-Brudenell, I. 235
MacNaughton, G. 36, 78
Maxime, J.E. 84
Meggitt, C. 159
Metz, M. 209
Milbank, J.E. 84
Miller, J. 116
Milner, D. 84
Montague-Smith, A. 209
Mortimore, J. 101, 212
Moss, P. 80, 152
Moyles, J. xii, 7, 85, 121, 126, 128, 148, 201, 226
Musgrove, A. 7, 148, 201, 226

Nabuco, E. 108
Nash, T. 212
National Commission on Education 79
NCRNE xiii, 235
Neugebauer, R. 25
Newham Early Years Unit 165, 169, 171, 194
NFER/SCDC 81
Nutbrown, C. 7, 175, 194

OFSTED xiv, 38
Osborn, A.E. 84
Ouvry, M. 134, 146

Pascal, C. 4, 114, 233
PAT (Professional Association of Teachers) 13
Pen Green Centre Team 16, 101, 107, 212, 243
Pen Green Family Centre 106, 114
Penn, H. 80, 230
Piachaud, D. 230
Play Safety Forum 95
Pompert, B. 218
POST 125, 163
Pugh, G. 100, 152, 228, 233

QCA/DfES xi, xiv, 1, 3, 5, 6, 14, 16, 37, 48, 50, 53, 69, 71, 81, 97, 101, 109, 123, 125, 126, 130, 132, 147, 151, 164, 195
Quick, S. 256

Race, P. 255
RBK&C 38
Richards, R. 209
Riches, C. 55, 56
Riley, D. 232
Roberts, R. 107
Rodd, J. 25, 36, 62, 70, 125
Ross, C. 85
Rouse, D. 152

Sammons, P. 84
Save the Children 86, 107
Schools Council 19
Schweinhart, L. 108, 196
Sharp, C. 108, 195
Sherman, A. 81, 108, 114
Simms, K. 100, 228, 231
Siraj-Blatchford, I. xii, xv, 2, 7, 81, 88, 95, 107, 125, 137, 149, 215, 217, 223, 226, 236, 243, 244
Siraj-Blatchford, J. 235, 236, 243
Smith, A. 36
Smith, B. 255
Smith, P.K. 126
Smith, T. 212
Stubbs, D.R. 25, 32
Sunderland, G. 159
Sure Start xv, 37, 40, 229
Sutherland, H. 230
Swann, R. 165
Sylva, K. 83, 108, 109, 121, 126

Thomas, G. 85
Thompson, N. 5, 255
Tizard, B. 16, 85, 101, 152, 163, 212
Tower Hamlets Early Years Service 153, 165, 169, 171, 194
Toynbee, P. 231
Trudell, P. 85, 230, 231, 243

van Keulen, A. 86
Vygotsky, L.S. 126, 129

Wake, B. 235
Wandsworth Borough Council 165, 193
Weikart, D. 108, 196
Wells, G. 16, 98, 152, 163
Whalley, M. 16, 78, 101, 107, 212, 243
Whitehead, M.R. 110, 126, 131, 169, 209
Whyte, J. 85
Wikeley, E. 212
Wood, E. 225, 226

Subject Index

abuse *see* child abuse
access to curriculum content 169–70
accidents 92, 94
accountability 67
action plan pro forma 60–1
active learning style 125
admissions
    gradual separation 103
    home visits 100, 102
    non-English speaking parents 84, 87
    policy on 84–8
    settling-in children 102–3, 170–2
    staggering 102
adult education 233
adult-initiated experiences 176–8, 179, 199,
    212–15
adults, training in work with 241
Advanced Skills Teachers *see* advisory
    team
advisory team
    encouraging development 247–9
    establishing principles 247–8
    identifying blocks to development
        248–9
    in-service courses 250–3
    in non-maintained settings 244
    organizing training 249–54
    relationships with other practitioners
        245–7
    resources provided by 254
    support networks for 255
age ranges 80, 113, 150
aggressive behaviour 94–5, 113–14, 222–3
alphabet recitation 209
analysis skills 4–5
animals 119–20
appraisal, staff 22–3
assembly 98, 138, 237
assertiveness
    encouraging children's 95, 113–14
    team members' 32–3
assessment
    of communication skills 187
    context of 189–90
    of creative development 189
    of emotional development 186
    Foundation Stage Profile 53, 148, 150, 190,
        191
    of language skills 187

    of literacy 187
    of mathematical development 187
    of personal development 186
    of physical development 186–7
    of progress 191, 192
    of science knowledge 188–9
    of social development 186
    of very young children 149–50
    see also record-keeping
attendance record 186
attitudes
    teacher's background and 228
    teacher's self-evaluation of 227–9
    towards learning 165, 186
auditory learning style 125
autonomy, children's 109, 197–9

bilingual children
    assessing 187
    communication with parents 230
    in curriculum planning 165
    emotional security of 103–5
    staff employed for 13
Birth to Three Matters 40
book area 132
boys
    aggressive play by 222–3
    learning style of 125
brain development 125
British Association for Early Childhood
    Education (Early Education) 31, 258
bullying 95

campaigner, teacher as 236–8
caretakers 13
change
    teachers as agents of 240–1
    see also managing change
characteristics *see* essential characteristics
child abuse 152, 233–5
child development
    curriculum appropriate to stage of
        123–4
    'education as development' view 82
    normal variations in 82–4
    teacher's knowledge of 7, 158–60, 197
child protection
    registers 233
    see also child abuse

child-initiated activity 178, 180–1, 217
    see also play
childcare see day-care
childrearing practices 231–2
Children's Centres xv, 80, 230–1, 258, 260
citizenship 121
class
    stereotyping 85, 230–1
    teachers' socio-economic background
        228
    see also social issues
classroom see environment
clay 132
cleaners 13
co-ordinator role
    birth to 5 practice 39–40
    case studies 71–7
    monitoring policy use 50–2
    raising status of teachers 241
    responsibilities of 37–9
    see also managing change; policy
        development
communication
    assessing child's skills 187
    teacher sharing feelings 120
    teacher's skills 3, 5–6
    within Foundation Stage team 19–21,
        29–30
composition, of family 231–2
computers, in the classroom 235–6
confidence 27, 30
conflict-handling 28, 30, 31–3
consolidation 127
construction
    developmental stage and 127
    materials for 133
counting see numeracy
creative development 128, 189
creative workshop area 133
creativity
    modelled by teacher 210
    teacher's 6–7
crisis management approach 18
current awareness 16
Curriculum Guidance for the Foundation Stage
    xiv, 16, 38, 165
curriculum planning
    access to curriculum content 169–70
    adult-initiated experiences 176–8, 179
    appropriate to developmental stage
        123–4
    child-initiated activity and 178, 180–1,
        217
    clarifying overall aims 164, 166–7
    deployment of adults 178, 180–1
    evaluating quality of curriculum 184–5
    implementing the plans 183–4

learning intentions 165, 168–70, 174,
    176, 178
and learning process 124–5
long-term 164–73
medium-term 173–5
need for flexibility 163, 182
observations for 176, 180–1
play in 126–8
purpose of 162–3
role of talk in 129–30
routines within 173
settling-in curriculum 170–2
short-term 175–82
special events 181–2
spontaneous happenings 172–3, 212–15
staffing rotas 173
timing within 170, 172–3
and whole-school policy 17

day-care
    context of nursery education in 80
    increasing need for 230, 232
degree level qualification 12
delegating responsibility 23, 29
demonstration of skills 215–16
development see child development;
    personal development; policy
    development
development plans 17
digital cameras 236
disadvantaged children 85, 230–1
discrimination
    class 85, 230–1
    race 84, 87
dispositions
    children's 196
    teacher's 197
dough 132

Early Education (the British Association for
    Early Childhood Education) 31, 258
Early Excellence Centres (EECs) xv, 11, 80,
    230–1
early years centres 79–80
Early Years Curriculum Guidelines from Birth
    to Five Year Olds 40
Early Years Development and Childcare
    Partnerships (EYDCPs) 80
'education as development' view 82
Effective Early Learning project 70
Effective Provision of Pre-school Education
    Project xiv–xv, 258
emotional development assessment 186
emotional security
    before admission 100, 102
    bilingual children 103–5
    information from parents 99–100

maintaining 105–7
need for 97–9
for parents 101–2
settling children into class 102–3,
170–2
empathy 3–4
enabling learning
acting as role model 208–11
adding equipment 202–3
demonstration of skills 215–16
displays 133, 203–4
extending interest 202–8
imparting knowledge 215–16
initiating activities 212–15
organizing outings 205–8
stimulating interest 202–8
sustaining interest 202–8
teaching strategies for 201–2
enthusiasm
in delivering training 66–7
teacher's 8
environment
book area 132
creative workshop area 133
graphics area 132–3
interactive displays 133, 203–4
organization of 133–4
outdoor 134–6
role-play areas 133
size of 131–2
storage 110–11, 117, 134
teacher's responsibility for 130
tidying up 111, 116–18
see also equipment
EPPE (Effective Provision of Pre-school
Education) project xiv–xv, 258
equality of opportunity 84–8
equipment
children's respect for 118–19
construction materials 133
malleable materials 132
mathematical 133
responsively adding to 202–3
safe use of 90
sand 132
scientific 133
water 132
see also environment; resources
essential characteristics
analysis skills 4–5
communication skills 3, 5–6
creativity 6–7
empathy 3–4
flexibility 4, 163, 182, 215
imagination 6–7
knowledge of child development 7,
158–60, 197

leadership skills 6
listening skills 5–6
optimism 8
playfulness 6, 200
principled beliefs 5, 17
record-keeping skills 7
reflection skills 4–5
sensitivity 200–1
spontaneity 4
warmth 3–4
see also leadership
evaluation
of curriculum quality 184–5
process of 68–70
purpose of 67–8
using policies in 52
see also record-keeping
experience, first-hand 125–8
experimentation, need for 126
exploration, child's 127
Extended Schools 230–1
external advisors see advisory team

family composition 231–2
feelings
sharing with children 120
teacher's 197
first-hand experience 125–8
flexibility 4, 163, 182, 215
focused observation 156–7, 181, 190
Forest School movement 141
forests, exploring 141–4
Foundation Stage, introduction of xiv, 1–3,
256–60
Foundation Stage co-ordinator see
co-ordinator role
Foundation Stage Profile 53, 148, 150, 190,
191

gender
brain development differences 125
learning styles and 125
role of women in society 232–3
sex stereotyping 85, 178, 210–11, 221–2,
232
teacher modelling anti-sexist behaviour
210–11
terminology used xvi
goals, for learning 196
government policy xiii–xv, 1–3, 79–81, 256,
260
group times 217

Hassan, Ben 40, 62
headteacher
help from 34
teacher's guidance to 238

health and safety
    accidents 92, 94
    aggression 94–5
    checking for hazards 89
    equipment use 90
    on outings 91–2
    parents' approach to 96
    risk-taking 95–6
    safety rules 90–1, 96
help *see* support networks
home visits 100, 102

imagination, teacher's 6–7
imaginative play 128, 219
imitation, encouraging 218–19
imparting knowledge 215–16
in-service courses 250–3
individuals
    children as unique 160–1
    team members as 22
influencing practice 240–1
informal noticing 154–5
INSET days 65
interactive displays 133, 203–4
Intercultural Education Project 104
Internet, children's access to 235–6
interpreters 230
interview
    questions 9–10
    selecting students 26

job descriptions 28

kinaesthetic learning style 125
knowledge
    of child development 7, 158–60, 197
    imparting 215–16
    playing with children to broaden 219

language *see* bilingual children;
    communication; talk
leadership
    achieving the task 15–20
    asking for help 34–5
    assessing skills of 15
    confidence and 27, 30
    conflict handling 28, 30, 31–3
    delegating 23, 29
    Motivator style of 25
    non-direct 12
    personal qualities for 6, 25–7
    positive aspects of 35
    respect for 31–3
    strengths 31
    support for 11–12
    support networks 30–1, 238, 239, 255
    team-building 20–3

unpopularity 28, 31
    weaknesses 31
learning
    autonomy of children and 109, 197–9
    goals for 196
    teachers learning how to learn 197
    see also enabling learning
learning intentions 165, 168–70, 174–5, 176,
    178
learning styles 125
legislation 237
listening skills 5–6
literacy
    alphabet recitation 209
    assessment of 187
    effect of strategy 195
    modelled by teacher 209
    role of talk in curriculum 129–30
local authority settings *see* advisory team
lunchtime supervisors 13

managing change
    case study 60–4
    different team types 54–6
    nature of change 56–9
    speed of 59–60
    see also training
mathematics
    assessing development 187
    equipment for 133
    see also numeracy
meetings 29–30
minibeast habitat 120
monitoring
    of curriculum quality 184–5
    Effective Early Learning project on 70
    process of 68–70
    purpose of 67–8
    using policies in 52
    see also record-keeping
Motivator style of leadership 25
movement, music and 133
music
    and movement 133
    played by teacher 210

National Campaign for Real Nursery
    Education (NCRNE) x, xiii, 31
National Vocational Qualifications 64
networks, support 30–1, 238, 239, 255
non-maintained settings *see* advisory team
non-specialist teachers, retraining 65,
    197
numeracy
    effect of strategy 105
    modelled by teacher 209
    see also mathematics

'nursery education' redefinition of x–xi, xiii–xv, 258
nursery nurses
    delegating to 23, 29
    health and safety knowledge of 89
    knowing individual 22
    as part of basic team 12–13
Nursery School Forum 258
nursery schools, closure of 257–8

observation
    focused observation 156–7, 181, 190
    informal noticing 154–5
    participant jottings 155–6
    of play 217–18
    of self-initiated activity 180–1
    for short-term planning 176
    as source of assessment 185
OFSTED inspection
    differing regimes 258
    of local authority settings 248
'one-stop shop' idea 80
open-ended questioning 215
opportunity see equality of opportunity
optimism, teacher's 8
organization
    of resources 131–4
    of space 131–2
    teacher's responsibilities for 130
    of time 137–41
out-of-class time 98, 138
outdoors
    environment 134–6
    importance of 139–44
    observing while 182
outings
    enabling learning through 205–8
    health and safety on 91–2
over-protection of children 95–6

parents
    adult education classes for 233
    approach to health and safety by 96
    communication with non-English speaking 230
    helping in class 177, 211
    information from 99–100, 152, 160–1
    making welcome 101–2
    as members of Foundation Stage team 14
    relationship with 3–4
    as role models 211–12
participant jottings 155–6
passive behaviour 113–14
personal development
    assessment of child's 186
    self-evaluation of attitudes 227–9

via community involvement 229–30
    see also training
personal qualities see essential characteristics
personality clashes 28, 34
pets 119–20
physical development 186–7
physical exercise 140
planning see curriculum planning
play
    imaginative 128, 219
    importance of 126–8
    observation of 217–18
    in reception classes 223
    sample policy for 47, 48–50
    teacher's ability to 6, 200
    see also playing with children
playing with children
    challenging stereotyped ideas 221–2
    challenging thinking during 219–21
    moving on repetitive play 222–3
    observation during 217–18
    role-play 218–19, 221
    to broaden children's knowledge 219
    to encourage imitation 218–19
    see also play
policy development
    on admissions 84–8
    common rationale of 47
    curriculum policy 164, 166–7
    differences of opinion 42–3
    purpose of 41–2, 44
    research for 43
    reviewing policies 52–3
    sample policy 47, 48–50
    structure of policy 45–50
    team involvement 42–4
    themes of 47
    use of policies 50–2
    see also government policy
politics
    Early Education 31, 258
    National Campaign for Real Nursery Education (NCRNE) x, xiii, 31
    teacher as campaigner 236–8
    see also government policy
pressure, resisting outside 5, 17
Primary Strategy 240
principles
    clarifying 16–17
    established by advisory team 247–8
    underpinning practice 5, 17
prioritizing 18–20

qualifications
    minimization of need for 81–2
    teacher's level of 12

see also training
questionnaire, team 19
questions
    for evaluation process 64
    for interview 9–10
    open-ended 215

race equality policy 86
racial stereotyping 84–5, 87, 221–2
ratio
    adult:child xiii–xiv, 115, 180
    advisory teacher:non-maintained
        setting 244
reading *see* literacy
realism, need for 18
reception class
    4-year olds in 80, 81, 237
    play in 223
    shared philosophy with 37–9
    transition to 98, 161
recognition of achievements 21
record-keeping
    attendance record 186
    children as unique individuals 160–1
    child's contribution to 152
    content of records 151
    contributors to records 151–2
    developmental approach to 147–8
    essential characteristic of teacher 7
    methods for 153–4
    observations for 154–7
    parents' contribution to 152, 160–1, 192
    process of 157–8
    purpose of 149–50
    see also assessment; curriculum planning
recruitment
    candidate's characteristics 8–10
    interview questions 9–10
reflection skills 4–5
registration 138–9
relationships
    advisory team with other practitioners
        245–7
    with children 199–201
    with parents 3–4, 14, 99–100, 152, 160–1,
        192
    within team 20–3
repetition 127
repetitive play 222–3
representation, in play 127
research, for policy development 43
resources
    encouraging sharing 110–11
    provided by advisory team 254
    for spontaneous happenings 173
    storage of 110–11, 117, 134
respect, gaining 31–3

responsibility
    child taking 116–19
    training for personal 239
    see also leadership
responsive displays 204
responsive teaching 196–201, 225
    see also playing with children
retraining non-specialist teachers 65, 197
risk-taking by children 95–6
role model
    advisory teacher as 244
    older children as 113
    parents as 211–12
    teacher as 208–11, 232–3
    team leader as 25
role-play
    areas for 133
    when playing with children 218–19, 221
rotas, staffing 173
routines 138
rules
    safety rules 90–1, 96
    staff ground rules 31–2

safety *see* health and safety
science
    assessment of knowledge in 188–9
    equipment for 133
    modelled by teacher 209–10
secretary, school 13
security *see* emotional security; health and
    safety
self-awareness, teacher's 228–9
settling children into class 102–3, 170–2
sex stereotyping 85, 178, 210–11, 221–2, 232
    see also gender
sharing 110–13
size
    of environment 131–2
    of team 58
skills
    vs. dispositions 196
    see also assessment; essential
        characteristics
social development
    adult-child interaction 114–16
    assertive behaviour 95, 113–14
    assessment of 186
    care for living creatures 119–20
    co-operation skills 121–3
    play and 128
    sharing 110–13
    taking responsibility 116–19
    teaching style and 108–10
    tidying up 111, 116–18
    turn-taking 110–13
social issues

child abuse 152, 233–5
childrearing practices 231–2
disadvantaged families 85, 230–1
discrimination 84, 85, 87, 230–1
family composition 231–2
personal development via community
    involvement 229–30
role of women in society 232–3
socio-economic status 85
software for children 235
special educational needs
    identified by nursery staff 85
    staff employed for 13
Specialist Teaching Assistant Qualification
    64–5
spontaneity
    in class 172–3, 212–15
    essential characteristic of teacher 4
staffing rotas 173
staggered admissions 102
starting nursery 98–9
status, teachers' 227, 241–2, 259
stereotyping
    challenging through playing with
        children 221–2
    class 85, 230–1
    racial 84–5, 87, 221–2
    sex 85, 178, 210–11, 221–2, 232
storage of resources 110–11, 117, 134
strengths, awareness of 31
student placements 13–14, 177
students, selecting 26
supervisors, lunchtime 13
support networks 30–1, 238, 239, 255
support staff 13
Sure Start 80, 230–1, 244

talk
    role of in curriculum 129–30
    see also literacy
tasks (of Foundation Stage team)
    break-down of 18–19
    clarifying principles 16–17
    defining 17
    main 15
    prioritizing 18–20
team
    additions to 13–14
    appraisal of members 22–3
    basic team members 12–13
    co-ordination within 20–1
    communication within 19–21, 29–30
    delegating within 23, 29
    involved in policy development 42–4
    knowing individuals in 22
    meetings 29–30
    other staff 13

parents as members of 14
    size of 58
    staff development 21–2
    team-building 20–3
    types of team 54–6
technology
    computers 235–6
    digital cameras 236
    Internet 235–6
    software 235
    television 235, 236
    use modelled by teacher 209–10
television
    effects on children 236
    increase in viewing 235
terminology xi, xiii–xiv, xvi, 81
tidying up 111, 116–18
time, organization of 137–41
time-management 30, 180
timing, within curriculum planning 170,
    172–3
training
    aims and objectives of 251
    child abuse detection 233–4
    delivering 65–7
    equality issues 86
    evaluation of 253
    following up 253–4
    group-work skills 241
    identifying training skills 251
    INSET days 65
    minimization of need for 81–2
    National Vocational Qualifications 64
    needs analysis 251
    nursery nurses' 12–13
    opportunities for 238–9
    organized by advisory team 249–54
    for personal responsibility 239
    planning 250–3
    programming 252
    retraining non-specialist teachers 65,
        197
    role in practice development 249–54
    for self-evaluation 229
    Specialist Teaching Assistant
        Qualification 64–5
    targeting group for 251
    trainer's self-evaluation 253
    venue 251
    working with adults 241
transition
    to Key Stage 1 257
    to reception class 98, 161
translators 230
turn-taking 110–13

unpopularity 28, 31

video equipment 236
visual learning style 125
voucher scheme 80

warmth 3–4
weaknesses, awareness of 31
welcome

children's daily 138–9
making parents feel 101–2
women
    role in society 232
    teachers still predominantly xvi
woodlands, exploring 141–4
writing *see* literacy